Participatory
Sportswriting

Participatory Sportswriting
An Anthology, 1870–1937

Zachary Michael Jack

McFarland & Company, Inc., Publishers
Jefferson, North Carolina, and London

LIBRARY OF CONGRESS CATALOGUING-IN-PUBLICATION DATA

Jack, Zachary Michael, 1973–
  Participatory sportswriting : an anthology, 1870–1937 / Zachary Michael Jack.
    p.   cm.
  Includes bibliographical references and index.

  ISBN 978-0-7864-3953-9
  softcover : 50# alkaline paper ∞

  1. Sports journalism — United States — Anecdotes.
  2. Sports — United States — Anecdotes. 3. Authors — United States — Anecdotes. 4. Sportswriters — United States — Anecdotes. I. Title.
  PN4784.S6J28   2009
  070.4'49796 — dc22   2008044461

British Library cataloguing data are available

©2009 Zachary Michael Jack. All rights reserved

No part of this book may be reproduced or transmitted in any form or by any means, electronic or mechanical, including photocopying or recording, or by any information storage and retrieval system, without permission in writing from the publisher.

On the cover: Bobby Jones (George Grantham Bain Collection, Library of Congress); antique typewriter ©2009 Shutterstock

Manufactured in the United States of America

McFarland & Company, Inc., Publishers
  Box 611, Jefferson, North Carolina 28640
  www.mcfarlandpub.com

ACKNOWLEDGMENTS

Thanks are due several key copyright holders and their representatives for the right to reprint this historical material.

Special thanks to Craig Tenney of Harold Ober and Associates for the rights to reprint "The Feel" by Paul Gallico from *Farewell to Sport*. Reprinted by permission of Harold Ober Associates Incorporated. Copyright, 1937, 1938 by Paul Gallico. Copyright renewed 1964, 1966 by Paul Gallico.

Sincere appreciation to Martin J. Elgison and the Jones family for the right to reprint a portion of Robert T. Jones's and O.B. Keeler's great chapter "The Biggest Year" from *Down the Fairway; The Golf Life and Play of Robert T. Jones, Jr.* (New York: Minton, Balch and Co., 1927). Used by permission of Jonesheirs, Inc.

Finally, heartfelt thanks to the content staff of the *Chicago Tribune* and Walter Wojtowicz for the privilege of reprinting "Gertrude Tells Own Story of How She Conquered Channel," 8/7/1926 by Gertrude Ederle. Copyrighted 8/7/1926, Chicago Tribune Company. All rights reserved. Used with permission.

Editor's Note

To bring readers the widest possible digest of historically influential participatory sportswriting, excerpts proved indispensable. Where, in many instances, an excerpt has been made from a single chapter or article, the word "From" precedes the title. For the convenience of scholars, a bibliography at the conclusion of this book identifies source volumes and lists specific page ranges of excerpted material, and other works referenced in the text. To preserve the dynamism of these athletic narratives, footnotes have been used only where necessary to indicate a run-in of separate chapters or sections, a run-in of non-contiguous sentences or paragraphs resulting in an excision of material, or where crucial contextual clarifications were needed.

Except as noted, readings have been arranged chronologically according to their first published copyright date as listed in the WorldCat database (WorldCat.org). In the event two or more readings were first published in the same year, the month of publication, where known, has been used to establish order. Where the month of publication was not readily ascertainable, readings within any given year were, in most instances, arranged alphabetically by last name of the author.

The language of these historic readings has been modified minimally. Where necessary, spelling has been modernized and typesetting clarified in accordance with modern usage.

TABLE OF CONTENTS

Acknowledgments   v
Editor's Note   vi
Preface: The Sporting "I" in a New Light   1
Introduction: "A Frolic of Immersion"— Participatory Sportswriting in the Gilded and Golden Ages   3

John Burroughs on Trout Fishing (1870)	17
Mark Twain on Surfing (1871)	21
Edward Whymper on Climbing the Matterhorn (1871)	23
Robert Louis Stevenson on Canoeing Across Europe (1878)	27
Charles Dickens on Climbing Mount Vesuvius (1879)	30
John Lyle King on Trout Fishing (1879)	34
Walt Whitman on "Wrestling" and Sailing (1881)	37
Theodore Roosevelt on Hunting the Antelope (1885)	40
James Naismith on Playing and Coaching Basketball (1941; events from 1891)	46
Winifred Louisa Leale on Target Shooting (1894)	55
Kate Martelli on Hunting the Tiger (1894)	57
Frances Elizabeth Willard on Bicycling (1895)	62
Joshua Slocum on Sailing Alone Around the World (1899)	67
Isabel Savory on Mountaineering in Kashmir (1900)	73
Frederick G. Aflalo on Hunting the Alligator (1907)	76
Jack London on Surfing (1908)	80
John Muir on Glaciering (1909)	88
John Neihardt on Paddling the Missouri River (1910)	102
Edward Lydell Fox on Ice-boating (1912)	107
Walter Camp on Coaching Football (1912)	110
Joseph Knowles on Trapping a Bear (1913)	112

Gertrude Buffington Phillips on Salmon Fishing	121
Wilma Anderson-Gilman on Pistol Shooting (1914)	125
Lewis R. Freeman on Swimming, Sprints, Canoe Races, Shotput, Cricket, Long- and High-Jumping, and Marathoning Versus the Fijians (1914)	127
Kathrene Gedney Pinkerton on Women's Canoeing (1914)	131
Hiram Connibear on Coaching College Crew (1914)	134
Horace Kephart on Spelunking (1914)	136
Malcolm Ross on Alpining (1914)	143
William Hanford Edwards on Officiating Football (1916)	149
Bernard Darwin on Golf (1919)	151
May H. Hosfield on Deep-sea Fishing for Barracuda (1919)	154
Zane Grey on Fishing for Bonefish (1919)	162
Ernest Hemingway on Rainbow Trout Fishing (1920)	167
Bill Tilden on the Psychology of Tennis (1921)	169
Lawrence S. Clark on "Autobumming" (1922)	173
Henry Ford on Auto Racing (1922)	178
Lewis R. Freeman on Playing Semipro Baseball in Montana (1922)	181
Fred H. Harris on Ski Jumping (1922)	183
Ernest Hemingway on Lugeing (1922)	188
Ring Lardner on Sport and Play (1922)	190
Albert Soiland on Transpacific Yacht Racing (1924)	194
Gertrude Ederle on Swimming the English Channel (1926)	200
Bobby Jones on Golfing the Majors (1927)	202
Amelia Earhart on Flying the Atlantic (1928)	205
Helen Wills on Wimbledon Tennis (1928)	211
Eddie Eagan on Boxing Against Jack Dempsey (1932)	219
Arnold Eric Sevareid on Canoeing from Minnesota to the Hudson Bay (1935)	223
Paul Gallico on Golfing with Bobby Jones, Catching Herb Pennock's Curveball, Auto Racing with Cliff Bergere at Indy and More (1937)	229
Bibliography	239
Index	243

Preface: The Sporting "I" in a New Light

by Zachary Michael Jack

One of my most prized possessions is a print by Golden Age sportsman-illustrator-artist John Henry "Hy" Hintermeister. I love it because it speaks volumes for all sports lovers, especially those charged with capturing the athletically transient, whether in word or image. The Hintermeister print, entitled "The Big Moment," shows a middle-aged man and a wide-eyed youth, presumably father and son, canoeing in a setting reminiscent of the American West. Salmon-colored bluffs and snow-covered peaks tower above a glassy, pine-lined river alive with reflected light. The Old Man paddles from the stern of the birchbark, his single oar dipped to suggest a glide. He sports a red and black flannel shirt, a rumpled fisherman's cap, and dung-brown suspenders. His kindly, clean-shaven face looks benign, world-wise. In the bow, his hatless companion, the very image of youthful, coiffed exuberance, holds a tensioned rod in one hand, a net in the other, as, bug-eyed and overeager, he leans perilously over the edge to haul in his prize catch.

For me, Hintermeister exquisitely captures the ebb and flow of a sporting life—the desperate, almost frenetic bliss that attends the proverbial bite and, at the opposite end, the sprawling moments of beatific inaction, symbolized by the old man's wry gaze, wherein one is content to witness. The picture, resplendent in its salmon pink, red rock, and sky blue, also floats this truism: the golden moments of a sporting day, life, or age flare but briefly.

It is this capital-"I" *Ineffable* that I aim to bottle in this first-of-its-kind collection of first-person, participatory sportswriting from the Gilded and Golden Ages that boasted the likes of Robert Louis Stevenson, Theodore Roosevelt, Walt Whitman, Frances Elizabeth Willard, John Muir, Jack London, Ernest Hemingway, Ring Lardner, Bill Tilden, Bobby Jones, Helen Mills, Paul Gallico, and many more who prowled America's sporting grounds with something approaching absolute zeal, breaking precedent and setting records that, in many cases, would never be matched. Theirs was an amateur age that wonderfully intermixed ego with egolessness. From roughly 1870 to 1930 sporting selves grew brash enough to attempt any sport, and, at the same time, stayed sufficiently cool to document the wild ride. Thus, the nearly 50 best-of readings in this historical digest celebrate those Gilded and Golden Age sportsmen and women for whom the athletic experience was not enough, for whom capturing the ineffable in writing proved part and parcel to the sporting performance.

As a former newspaper sports editor, I witnessed the fleeting, golden moments of athletes at their apogee, their absolute zenith. From the stands, notebook in hand, I watched young men and women who, for the most part, would never again play sanctioned, competitive sports after high school or college, but who, for a moment at least, achieved their full potential. At times, their small "big moments" proved so incendiary, burned so passionately and cleanly, I almost had to look away. My job in those days was to record such feats in the still-golden light with which those moments — days, months, or years later — would return as dreams to the very athletes who performed them. Such visions as would light a sometimes difficult path through humdrum adulthoods.

As its many devotees know, sportswriting is an act predicated on the ultimate impossibility of apprehending the ephemeral. And yet I could not, and cannot, think of anything I would rather do than seek out such moments as they occur, like staying up all night for a glimpse of a meteor. I firmly believe that had I not myself been an athlete, a participant in many of the grand and frustrating games I covered, I would not have been in position to catch the blazing comet's tail of the athletic act.

The athlete and the sportswriter, then, commingle in our personal and national sporting history. Sometimes, when the stars align, their two orbits overlap to form the writer-athlete or the athlete-writer — the crux of this collection. When it happens, this seldom seen joining of exuberant sportsman and dutiful recorder burns white-hot.

In this light, then, I offer *Participatory Sportswriting: An Anthology, 1870–1937.*

Zachary Michael Jack
Fall 2008

Introduction: "A Frolic of Immersion"—Participatory Sportswriting in the Gilded and Golden Ages

by Zachary Michael Jack

> It is all very well, sitting here in cool shade of the beach, but you are a man, one of the kingly species, and what that Kanaka can do, you can do yourself. Go to. Strip off your clothes that are a nuisance in this mellow clime. Get in and wrestle with the sea; wing your heels with the skill and power that reside in you; bit the sea's breakers, master them, and ride upon their backs as a king should.
> —Jack London, *The Cruise of the Snark*

In many ways, the Gilded and Golden Ages of Sport, broadly defined in this first-of-its-kind compendium of historic participatory sportswriting, echo our own sports-loving, sports-abundant days. Nearly one hundred years out from the apex of the Golden Age in the 1910s and 1920s, our own sports era deeply echoes earlier halcyon times when sportsmen and sportswomen constituted, as sports journalist Grantland Rice put it, "a flame that lit up the sporting skies and covered the world."

Our new sporty millennium, after all, features much-ballyhooed, much-loathed home run king Barry Bonds just as the Golden Age featured the famous and infamous exploits of Babe Ruth and Shoeless Joe Jackson. Today we celebrate the record-breaking triumphs of Tiger Woods just as Golden Agers followed Bobby Jones's precedent-making 1930 Grand Slam. Likewise, while the Gilded and Golden Ages both begot and nurtured a true renaissance of middle-class, amateur participation in sport, especially hunting and fishing, hiking and climbing, skiing and water sport, so our own time births next-generation recreations in the form of extreme sports. Thus, one notes an uncanny symmetry of thought when, for example, one considers Robert Louis Stevenson's conclusions upon canoeing across Belgium and France in 1878 ("The slug of a fellow, who is never ill nor well, has a quiet time of it in life, and dies all the easier.... I am sure I would rather be a bargee than occupy any position under heaven that required attendance at an office") alongside journalist Eddy L. Harris's sentiments in 1988 before canoeing the length of the Mississippi River ("I've never minded looking stupid and I have no fear of failure. I decided to canoe down the Mississippi River ... to find out what I was made of.") Golden Ager Paul Gallico, the gold standard among participatory sports journalists, put it best in his manifesto "The Feel," wherein he argues that touch is "an important adjunct to seeing." Gallico continues, "The average person says: 'Here, let me see that,' and holds out his hand. He doesn't mean 'see,' because he is already seeing it. What he means is that he wants to get it into his hands and feel it so as to become better acquainted."

In our age, as in the Gilded and Golden Age featured in this collection, feeling—*doing*—proves requisite to believing.

"No right way is easy in this rough world. We must risk our lives to save them."
— John Muir, *Stickeen*

Writing in 1910, British sports chronicler Ralph Henry Nevill captured the distinctive flavor of the Golden Age in his book *Sporting Days and Sporting Ways*, wherein he defines a golden age as belonging to the athletic expeditionary and man of leisure all at once, in sum a "man of pleasure who was then a recognized type, much toleration being extended to the most unconventional ways and doings." Readers in both Golden Ages, ours and Nevill's, relish the diamond-in-the-rough participatory account — a "frolic of immersion" as sportsman John Lyle King put it at the dawn of the Gilded Age in 1871.

Careful review of the sportswriting produced in a Golden Age, however near or distant, literal or figurative, reveals a symbiotic flourishing of sport and literature, and, implicit in both, the celebration of *authorship*. The conflation of sports and letters dates back at least to Xenophon's fourth century B.C. treatises *The Sportsman* and *On Horsemanship*. In both, Xenophon, at once a student of Socrates and, apropos to this volume, a skilled horseman, blended the literary and sporting arts in experiential narratives. He considered the knowledge born of athletic practice unattainable by mere study and nothing short of divine. "To the gods themselves is due the discovery," Xenophon writes in *The Sportsman*, tracing the god-breathed lineage of sporting genius from Theseus, via Odysseus, through to Achilles, among other legendary Greeks.

Golden Ages, too, whether Xenophon's or our own, characteristically delight in amateurism. Here again, our contemporary sports world echoes eerily with the original Golden Age as defined by Grantland Rice and his contemporaries. In the midst of a Golden Age, the pace and pursuit of sporting milestones quicken; age-old records fall with alarming frequency; precedent flies out the window. In the Gilded and Golden Ages of the late nineteenth and early twentieth centuries, sportsmen and women vied for a share of the record books as well as deep gains in self-knowledge. Sailor-adventurer Joshua Slocum, for example, set out to solo circumnavigate the globe in his good ship *Spray* in 1895; Boston illustrator Joseph Knowles left his comfortable home in 1913 to become the first modern man, he claimed, to survive the Maine woods for two months living alone as a "primitive"; Amelia Earhart took to the air in 1928 aboard *The Friendship* to become the first woman to fly across the Atlantic; in the early 1930s — at the close of the conventional Golden Age of Sport — two mere high school students, Eric Sevareid and Walter Port, undertook the canoe trip of a lifetime in which they became the first on record to paddle the roughly 2250 miles between the Minnesota River and Canada's Hudson Bay. Something there is in a Golden Age that calls the sportsman and woman to high adventure, as *The Minneapolis Star* editor George H. Adams attests in his introduction to Sevareid's *Canoeing with the Cree*. Adams, whose belief in the boys and their mission convinced him to publish their serial accounts, writes, "They demonstrated ... that the spirit of personal adventure is not yet dead, that opportunities for adventurous living have not yet disappeared. It refreshes me to think that, and it must be doubly refreshing and encouraging to the young boys and girls of America, who sense that the days of frontier living, with their adventures, are gone." Adams was a good-spirited cheerleader to be sure, but he was also a savvy businessman who knew a good story when he heard one. And Adams had company in his move towards expanded sports coverage, as Harford Powel writes in 1932 in his introduction to the anthology he helped edit with Grantland Rice, *The Omnibus of Sport*. Powel observes, "The newspapers, in these days, give us a real opportunity. Their editors know that we are becoming, for the first time in history, a sport-loving nation."

In the Gilded and Golden Age of Sport, as in our own era, sportswriters enjoyed reputations as popular as well as literary celebrities. In our own time, literary sportswriters Frank Deford, Rick Reilly, and John Feinstein, to name a few, have gone multi-media, their stars crossing genres and demographics in much the same way that Ring Lardner and Paul Gallico, to name two whose work graces these pages, achieved popular acclaim in the Jazz Age. Twentieth century history shows that as the stock of athletes goes, so goes the stock of the sports journalists who cover them. In other words, the torrent of sportive firsts produced by a Golden Age can't help but follow the laws of supply and demand — the more stunning the athletic feats, the more superlatives for which we must reach to put those feats into words. In a sports-rich, exuberant age like Gallico's, a writer-athlete could be forgiven moments of ecstatic word drunkenness on the page, such as this effusive gem from Gallico's *Farewell to Sport*: "It [the 1920s] was a wonderful, chaotic universe of clashing colors, temperaments, and emotions, of brave deeds performed sometimes against odds seemingly insuperable, mixed with mean and shameful acts of pure skullduggery, cheapness, snide tricks, filth, and greed, moments of sheer, sweet courage and magnificence when the flame of the human spirit and the will to triumph burned so brightly that it choked your throat and blinded your eyes to be watching it."

In such an awe-inspiring epoch, the weekend athlete or sideline journalist finds himself in a precarious, though stimulating, position. As the on-field exploits of his favorite gladiators grow increasingly unreachable — borderline divine — he is compelled to consider his own mortality against his heroes' seeming immortality. His own incredulity, or inadequacy, is, in other words, piqued. If he is both thoughtful and bold, he takes to the field in the quintessential self-metric — an emboldened even foolhardy attempt to reproduce the results achieved by the pros. "After all," as Golden Age outdoorsman extraordinaire Horace Kephart wrote, "it is not the magnitude of results, but the uncertainty about them, that makes a game worth playing."

Sometimes, after his self-assigned "field day," the participant sportsman-writer discovers himself still sufficiently awe-inspired that he can't help but indulge in the "gee-whiz" school of sportswriting epitomized by Golden Age sports journalist Grantland Rice. Even as hardboiled a character as Gallico could admit to being charmed into "hero worship" and "gee-whiz" sentiment by the sweet, stellar accomplishments of the gentlemanly Bobby Jones. Exploring the sports reporter's characteristic vacillation, scholar Charles Fountain writes in *Sportswriter: The Life and Times of Grantland Rice*, "As a society of fans, we invest our emotion in sport, and emotion leads us to irrational extremes — blind love and hero-worship when things are going well; bitterness, anger and affixing responsibility for deep and genuine hurt when things go poorly. The Gee Whiz! writer is the optimist, anticipating heroics and triumph, yet somehow able to be both heartbroken *and* exhilarated in defeat." By contrast, Fountain continues, "the Aw Nuts! writer is the skeptic who writes with a how-can-you-let-these-guys-break-your-heart-they're-scarcely-worth-the-bother sort of defiance."

In the face of such a stark dichotomy, *Paricipatory Sportswriting* offers a vital if not overlooked middle road, a sportswriting Tao, neither naive nor dismissive by virtue of the rare participatory perspective brought to bear. Participatory practice enabled, for example, the world-wise, world-weary Paul Gallico's earnest worship of Jones precisely because he teed it up with him. As a consequence, any adulation the sportswriter might direct toward "The Immortal Bobby" was both informed and honestly earned. Immersion sports reporting, then, remains as crucial to our golden age as to the historic Gilded and Golden Age that first gave rise to its popularity. Experiential journalism of the kind highlighted here guards against the angst and augury borne of idle or armchair speculation. Even Ah Nuts! sports journalist Ring Lardner preaches the benefits of doing in his essay "Sport and Play," wherein he writes, "Hero-worship is the national disease that does most to keep the grandstands full and the playgrounds empty." As a cure Lardner advocated — what else — a healthful mix, metaphorically speaking, of real quarterbacking and armchair quarterbacking.

Our own golden age of participatory sportswriting comes coupled with the dangerous allures of Social Darwinism, just as it did in the days of Gallico and Lardner. Survival of the fittest compels the twenty-first-century viewer as much as it did the Golden Age readers of yesterday. In recent years, for example, 23 million viewers have tuned in weekly broadcasts of the television show *Survivor*, and yet, as historians and old sports saws know, there is nothing new under the sun. Way back in 1913 Golden Age sportsman Joseph Knowles trekked into the New England back country to live alone for two months in his own version of what he might have called "Survivor Maine." In the days before television, his accounts were published serially in the *Boston Post* and syndicated nationwide, enticing readers to newsstands each week to follow the hand-to-mouth sporting adventure.

A new generation of American television programs such as *Animal Planet* and *Man Versus Wild* now celebrate exactly the kind of visceral, real-life sporting encounters savored by strenuous life adherent Theodore Roosevelt in his hunting and rough riding sagas of the Gilded Age. The daring feats displayed in the late Steve Irwin's phenomenally popular TV series *The Crocodile Hunter* were preceded by the thrill-seeking sportsmen of the Golden Age, especially Frederick G. Aflalo and his alligator-baiting slogs through the Florida Everglades in the early 1900s. Popular entertainments in our new millennium, such as the television series *The Amazing Race*, broadcast only the latest, adrenaline-laced version of the gentler, cross country rallies and rambles of the Golden Age, known variously as "Fording" or "Autobumming" across America's unpaved interior. So integral a part of the nascent consumer automobile industry was car racing that Henry Ford himself, as detailed in his autobiography *My Life and Work*, took the wheel to race his Model B. Likewise, so moving was writer Lawrence S. Clark's 1922 "Fording" of more than 2000 miles across ten midwestern states, it caused him to gush, "Autobumming, fliveristing, motor caravanning, call it what you will. It's the greatest sport on earth."

More poignantly, we have the Gilded and Golden Age, roughly inclusive of 1870 to 1935, to thank for the explosion of sporting opportunities for women celebrated in the contemporary anthology *Whatever It Takes: Women on Women's Sport*, among others. In their thought-provoking introduction, editors Joli Sandoz and Joby Winans trace the first American collegiate female ballplayer to Vassar College in 1866, less than five short years from the beginning of the time period included in the wide-angle view offered by *Participatory Sportswriting*. In their opening remarks, Sandoz and Winans wonder aloud, "What did the first woman ever to step onto a basketball court think back in 1892?" And yet their excellent anthology, including only a few brief snippets from accounts prior to 1925, fails to answer their own, historically-pressing question. And though the editors wisely dedicate their collection to "women's personal nonfiction writings focused on their participation in a particular competitive sport," the few Golden Age excerpts included are fragmentary and mostly discursive — pieces that reflect, opine, or explain women in sport but thwart the female athlete from speaking for herself in the first-person and fresh from the playing field.

Participatory Sportswriting, the first collection of its kind devoted exclusively to first-hand accounts from the Gilded and Golden Age, attempts to answer the questions others have only posed. What was it like to hunt a wild tiger in India during the Raj? Kate Martelli's sporty travelogue "Tigers I Have Shot" answers the question in the moment rather than decades removed from staring into the eye of the tiger. What was it like for women's sports pioneer Isabel Savory to plummet down icy alpine chasms while mountain climbing in Kashmir? Herein, Savory satisfies reader curiosity completely and sans intermediary. Finally, what was it like for celebrated suffragist and educational pioneer Frances Elizabeth Willard to ride a bike for sport back in 1895? The answer comes, as it should, in the author's own words: "I began to feel that myself plus the bicycle equaled myself plus the world, upon whose spinning wheel we must all learn to ride, or fall into the sluiceways of oblivions and despair."

Participatory Sportswriting includes an unprecedented number of readings from women athletes of the Gilded Age, as it was the Gilded Age, overlapping with and emerging on the other side of the Victorian era, that birthed modern women's athletics. In Karen Kenney's important study, "The Realm of Sports and the Athletic Woman, 1850–1900," she cites 1870, the beginning of the period covered in this book, as the launch point of modern women's sport. By the 1890s, Kenney writes, "the girl who went fishing, climbed trees, and jumped fences was no longer inevitably looked upon as a tomboy or regarded with severe disappointment." In fact, her analysis confirms what the readings in *Participatory Sportswriting* seek to *show* rather than to tell: the gains in confidence, fitness, and leadership made possible by expanded opportunities in women's sports.

Identifying the important role of physical fitness curricula in land-grant colleges and universities, Kenney goes on to cite at least seven baseball clubs in existence at Vassar College as early as the 1870s and football, tennis, golf, and hunting clubs that followed thereafter. In short, the 1870s marked the beginning of a broader golden age of women's sport worldwide that would reach an apogee with Gertrude Ederle's historic swim of the English Channel in 1926 — during which she bested the previous men's time by over two hours — and Helen Wills's incredible run through championship tennis in the 1920s.

> "A man little dreams what he can accomplish until he is put to the test."
> — Joseph Knowles, *Alone in the Wilderness*

The first quarter of the twentieth century, Charles Fountain writes, amounted to an exuberant melting pot — a right place/right time for young sports journalists and aficionados. In his study *Sportswriter: The Life and Times of Grantland Rice*, Fountain argues that three momentous events of modern American journalism coalesced just as Grantland Rice arrived in New York in 1911. The loss of the *Titanic* in 1912, the gunning down of McKinley, the San Francisco Earthquake — all these, Fountain claims, heralded an age of dramatic action, the epoch of the "great story" made up of "riveting events" that "render a newspaper not a luxury but a lifeline."

Covering such unforgettable events, in the midst of the yellow and tabloid journalism movements of William Randolph Hurst and Joseph Pulitzer, seemed to simultaneously call for both reckless abandonment and caution. On one hand, a story such as the San Francisco Earthquake did not need embellishment or sensationalist coverage — it was pure, unadulterated tragedy. On the other hand, the yellow press thrived on histrionics, making the larger than life loom still larger. Sportswriters were, of course, fully ensconced in the debate concerning accuracy and objectivity. And as the Freudian psychology of the era posited universal bias, certainly sportswriters were as biased as any other reporter, perhaps more so, as they were often also fans or boosters or bettors. In the era of the Black Sox scandal, which profoundly disillusioned generations of sportswriters from Ring Lardner to James T. Farrell, the journalist had to work especially hard to keep his objectivity, and his head up.

The advent of participatory journalism as popularized by Paul Gallico at the New York *Daily News* brought the objectivity question to a head. In a Golden Age of bona fide sports heroes and goats, was a sportswriter who stepped onto the field or into the woods to document his own first-person, athletic experience an antidote to muckraking and rumor mongering or further proof of yellow journalism's self-serving methodologies? Was the sportswriter who laced up his or her sneakers in search of journalistic verity "researching" the athletic act or merely lionizing himself or herself, enacting the excesses of a Gilded Age. If journalism was evolving into a discipline not necessarily of objectivity but, as Bill Kovach and Tom Rosenthiel claim in *The Elements of Journalism*, a "discipline of verification," how could participatory sportswriters and sports journalists verify their claims if they were utterly alone in their sports quests, if they were accompanied only by friends and family members, or if they were recollecting an event through the filter of a faulty memory? If no less an accomplished writer than Jack London could, under the guise of sport journalism, racially bait African American heavyweight champion Jack Johnson while importuning white contender Jim Jeffries with hyperbole such as "The White Man must be rescued," could London's first-person nonfiction account of surfing, "A Royal Sport," be trusted?

A still more intriguing case of journalistic integrity, or lack thereof, born of participatory sports in the Golden Age of athletic myth and mythmakers, is Joseph Knowles, whose historically controversial work is reprinted in this collection. In a dramatic if not knuckle-headed participation, Knowles left civilization for a two-month experiment in Jack London-styled primitivism in the Maine woods. Covering the event, the *Boston Post* reported that Knowles took no equipment and no clothes into his sixty-day survival trial in the rugged border region. But when Knowles triumphantly returned to civilization two months later wearing the skin of the bear he claimed to have killed, the *Post's* rival, the Boston *American*, cried foul, according to historian Roderick Nash, arguing that Knowles's expedition had been a hoax. Though Knowles vehemently denied any wrongdoing or slight of hand, Nash points out this so-called "primitive man" was never able to repeat his experiment, though he made plans to do so with a "female companion." In any case, Knowles came out the winner, as the public wanted to believe in his daring exploits and did, voting with their feet as well as their dollar. Nash documents crowds of up to 20,000 listening to Knowles speak in Boston Common and lists sales of Knowles's now sadly forgotten book, *Alone in the Wilderness*, at over 300,000.

Questions of authenticity confront the journalism of the Golden Age as much as they do our own journalism scandal-plagued days. While later participatory journalists would develop their own self-checks (multiple witnesses in the case of Paul Gallico's sparring with Jack Dempsey, for instance, or the use of video recording technology decades later by Gallico heir apparent George Plimpton), assessment of the daring, sometimes unbelievable narratives of the Gilded and Golden Age requires alternate criteria. One potential barometer for assessing the veracity of such uncanny accounts of athletic prowess is what poet John Keats called "Negative Capability," namely a quality evident "when man is capable of being in uncertainties, Mysteries, doubts without any irritable reaching after fact & reason." Certainly, the circumspection Knowles evinces in his first chapter ("To be sure," he writes, "doing a thing for the first time has its usual and mysterious side; but it is not necessarily wonderful.") suggests he possessed an ambivalent mindset if not a fully-fledged sense of negative capability. Jack London, too, in his novice effort to "surf-ride," as he called it, openly expressed his dependence on his more experienced mates ("And I realized that if it hadn't been for [them], I'd have been disemboweled.") A less truthful writer, one assumes, would have feigned hero-

Even Amelia Earhart, whose contributions to the historic, transatlantic flight of *The Friendship* are said to have been exaggerated, writes modestly, even comically, of her tagalong, backseat status: "Me, I am holding down a pile of flying suits."

Ultimately, *Participatory Sportswriting* seeks the faithful recording of an era as told by the sporting men and women who lived it on the field of play. Instances of self-deprecation outnumber episodes of self-aggrandizement. As a rule, contributors exhibit a conspicuous degree of modesty about what are, by most standards, intrepid acts. This characteristic humility, known in literary studies as a "topoi of modesty," should give us cause to believe, as Kovach and Rosenthiel insist, that journalists of today and yesterday should be "humble about their own skills." In this sense, Golden Age greats known for their swagger — Jack London, Zane Grey, and Ernest Hemingway, in particular — emerge here in a new, sympathetic light. A case in point is London, whose race admonition morphs into race admiration as he watches the consummate skill of the dark-skinned Kanakas surfing Waikiki in "The Royal Sport." Of one particular "brown Mercury" London stands in awe, writing, "He is a Kanaka — and more, he is a man, a member of the kingly species that has mastered matter ... and lorded it over creation."

Thus, ultimately, participatory writer-athletes self-referee their own actions, conscience, and reportorial ethics. Their quest for sportsmanlike integrity therefore exists on the highest possible plain, in much the same way that conventional wisdom holds that self-policed sports (golf, to name an oft-cited example) remain the most honorable. The first-person, participatory sportswriter's discipline of verification is essentially, by extension, the testing of his or her mental and physical mettle in the most extreme, unforgiving crucible. As always, the first-person sportswriter who attempts a sport in order to write it more faithfully and fairly is not *guaranteed* greater adulation or self-awareness, but the popularity of such accounts across the generations — from Jack London to Paul Gallico to George Plimpton — suggests the practice offers its own considerable physical, mental, and spiritual rewards.

> "I admire it when it stands firmly upon its legs, and I love it when it wobbles. But when it gains power with increasing odds, grows big with obstacles, I worship it."
> — John Neihardt, *The River and I*

While it took the popular successes of Paul Gallico and George Plimpton to earn this special breed of hands-on journalism a handle — "participatory journalism" — first-person and eyewitness sportswriting prospered long before it was named. In the nineteenth century, sportswriting, such as it was, existed as a bastard, jointly and disparately claimed by soldiers, literary writers, explorers, naturalists, and outdoorsmen and women. Up and through the end of the Victorian era in 1901, such topical, professional, and stylistic eclecticism remained the norm. To succeed in sport, to adventure sportingly, one did not have to be a professional sports star or trained journalist but could, instead, be an Average Jane or Joe fully stoked by burning passions for athletic adventure. O. B. Keeler, for instance, who served as golfer Bobby Jones's confidant, cowriter, and friend, makes his amateurism the crux of *The Autobiography of an Average Golfer*, writing, "The lowly duffer as a rule is far too modest to break out in type and let fly in the general direction of the golfing public a narrative of his own humble *Odyssey*. So far as I know, the short and simple annals of the poor golfer are yet to be exposed in print."

Indeed, in crucial ways, the amateur sportswriter, if they were also an amateur sports participant, enjoyed an advantage in the insight department, a fact well noted by Gallico. Gallico penned his essay "The Feel" as a kind of manifesto for participatory sportswriting, declaring, "I do not insist that a curiosity and capacity for feeling sports is necessary to be a successful writer, but it is fairly obvious that a man who has been tapped on the chin with five fingers wrapped up in a leather boxing glove and propelled by the arm of an expert knows more about that particular sensation than one who has not, always provided he has the gift of expressing himself." For the record, Gallico, who was knocked cold by Jack Dempsey for the express purpose of learning the sensation, practiced what he preached.

If such an intellectually acrobatic act as writing could be undertaken and sometimes succeeded at with little or no formal training, then surely, goes the logic of the "I" sportsman, sport could and should be attempted and written about by the amateur. In fact, where the Golden Age of Sport, as this volume defines it, overlaps with the late Victorian era, amateurism was celebrated as encouraging character, modesty, and purity. In his monograph *The Victorians and Sport*, historian Mike Huggins documents the Victorians' almost schizophrenic attitude towards games and gaming, a mixed legacy that lasted well into the Golden Age, waxing and waning according to the latest act of sportive glory or treachery. Huggins fingers the debate between the middle class and lower working classes, between amateurism and professionalism respectively, as a "primarily fault line in Victorian society." On one side, the literary strain of sportswriting, predisposed to imbue athletics with symbolic virtue, habitually favored the amateur over the professional. As an example, Huggins cites Sir Arthur Conan Doyle's claim that sports were not about winning and losing but about rendering men "fit for the serious duties of life." On the other side, Huggins demonstrates how the high bar implicit in the amateur ideal created false hopes in fans, hopes which gave way to profound disillusionment after professional sports gambling scandals of the 1910s. Huggins likewise attends to yet another aspect of the darker side of overzealous amateurism: what he terms the "snobbishness, hypocrisy, and double standards" of exclusionary amateur societies who did their best to put sport out of reach of the masses.

Despite its less than monolithic beneficence, amateurism ruled the Gilded and Golden Age. Even sportswriters of the era such as Grantland Rice, inclined to see as much value in professional as in amateur sports, defined sport at its best by harkening back to the days of the amateur. In labeling the years 1919–1939 as a true "Golden Age of Competition" Rice's honor roll, in his introduction to Allison Danzig and Peter Brandwein's *Sport's Golden Age: A Close-up of the Fabulous Twenties* makes his criteria plain. What made Bobby Jones, Babe Ruth, Jack Dempsey and the other giants of the Golden Age so great, Rice insists, is "character, class, and crowd appeal"— in short, that which the gentlemanly or gentlewomanly amateur might already hold in spades. Interestingly, Rice implies, though fails to mention, athletic acumen in his equation.

Participatory Sportswriting celebrates both the athletic act and the ability to record that act. In doing so, it favors, almost exclusively, the first-person participatory accounts of amateur athletes whose narratives consider the figurative as well as the literal import of the game. In doing so, this book enacts R. Scott Kretchmar's contention in his essay "Distancing: An Essay on the Abstract Thinking in Sports Performances"—namely that "there is nothing inherently incompatible between spontaneous, 'thought-less' play and distancing." In other words, the athlete can both engage in and narrate his experience, concretely and abstractly. This compound sports vision, once achieved, yields unusually robust metaphors, metaphors peculiar to the amateur participant, as when Frances Elizabeth Willard writes this of her inside-out understanding of her bike, Gladys: "Gradually, item by item, I learned the location of every screw and spring, spoke and tire, and every beam and bearing that went to make up Gladys. This was not the lesson of a day, but of many days and weeks, and it had to be learned before we could get on well together. To my mind the infelicities of which we can see so much in life grow out of lack of time and patience thus to study and adjust the natures.... Indeed, I found a whole philosophy of life in the wooing and the winning of my bicycle."

The difficult but productive tension of participatory sportswriting has, dating back to the Golden Age, become a kind of holy grail of popular sports coverage perhaps because it makes the spectator privy to previously inaccessible thoughts, emotions, and sensations as experienced by the increasingly rarified athlete in the stadium. In this sense, *Participatory Sportswriting* assumes that the writer-athlete is fully sentient while athletically engaged, and that his or her first-person reportage constitutes the most rare, most elusive, and most potentially instructive literature in sport.

> "After all, it is not the magnitude of results, but the uncertainty about them, that makes a game worth playing."
> — Horace Kephart, "Adventures in a Cavern"

This book plays grateful host to extraordinary sports pioneers — trailblazers who were emphatically and energetically non-specialists as well as Renaissance men and women. Among the contributors to this historic volume of nonfiction sportswriting are sports-devoted literary luminaries — Charles Dickens, Robert Louis Stevenson, Walt Whitman, Frances Elizabeth Willard, Ernest Hemingway, John Neihardt, Jack London, Zane Grey, Ring Lardner, and Paul Gallico; outdoorsmen — John Burroughs and John Muir, most famously;— pilots, sailors, and military men — Amelia Earhart, Albert Soiland, and Joshua Slocum, respectively; politicians and businessmen — Teddy Roosevelt and Henry Ford in particular — and a host of white collar professionals (illustrators, lawyers, doctors, deans, and more) moonlighting as sporty thrill seekers, not to mention the era's greatest amateur athletes (Bobby Jones, Helen Wills, Bill Tilden, Gertrude Ederle, and more). All of them were writers.

In the chronologically-organized pages that follow, all sportive pastimes are given equal opportunity. However, to remain historically accurate, outdoor sports such as hunting, fishing, and canoeing make up a generous percentage of the narratives, as many of the conventional American team sports (baseball, football, basketball, and the like) were yet in their infancy in the Gilded Age. Another key factor in the tilt towards the outdoor or "field" sports is the simple fact, supported by scholarship, that women's participation before 1870 and even into the 1880s and 1890s was largely limited to hunting, shooting, yachting, and riding. Huggins and others have pointed out that a large percentage of Victorian men feared that sport would "unsex" women and would make them unduly masculine, a view resisted ardently by Frances Elizabeth Willard among others. *Participatory Sportswriting* purposefully follows the dynamic growth of sport during the sixty-year period from 1870 to 1930, expanding, as it reaches the twentieth century, to include a number of narratives of unconventional sports such as caving and ice-boating, team sports such as baseball and football, and "new sports" such as auto racing and airplane derbying made possible by the internal combustion engine.

Not included in this collection are accounts from exclusively professional athletes, those whose reminiscences typically lack the requisite writer's craft and journalist's methodology. Also intentionally absent are strictly paint-by-numbers, how-to manuals, which constituted the bulk of sports publishing during the era. To wit, while a brief excerpt from golfing amateur Bobby Jones appears herein, instructional golfing treatises from early Golden Age professionals such as Harry Vardon do not. The raison d'être of this anthology, after all, is narrativity not discursivity or pedantry. While there is nothing inherently wrong with the ubiquitous how-to sports literature, it does tend to exacerbate amateurs' sense of inadequacy, making them susceptible to the latest cure-all tip, or Band-Aid fix. On the contrary, *Participatory Sportswrit-*

ing endeavors to empower, embolden, and appropriately honor the sporting amateur brave enough to put pen to paper and pedal to the metal.

One particular selection meriting further explanation vis à vis the all-amateur prescription is the short piece from tennis great Helen Wills, an athlete Grantland Rice ranks among the best of the Golden Age, regardless of gender. Because Wills writes her account of Wimbledon as an observer sidelined by an appendectomy in 1926 and because she did not turn pro until 1927, Wills has been heartily welcomed into this volume along with others who long resisted the call to turn pro — Bill Tilden and Bobby Jones, to name two. In fact, Wills's compound vision, first as competitor and later as a self-styled locker room "reporter," fulfills the spirit of this collection beautifully.

Throughout, first-person accounts have been privileged, as much to honor the originality and audacity of the unabashed "I" as to ensure the hoped for level of intimacy. In particular, the Golden Age sportswoman's use of "I" stands as an emblem of social justice via redemptive authorship. To wit: in mounting her bicycle, Frances Elizabeth Willard takes a *real* step, a real pedal, towards gender equity; likewise, Amelia Earhart demands equality in launching herself across the Atlantic in *The Friendship*. In service to such momentous athletic and historical events as these, only the real thing — the firsthand nonfiction — will do. Mere fiction would surely strike readers as disingenuous. In a very few cases, and consistent with the sometimes awkward narrative gymnastics of the era, writers have opted to avoid the "I" by using more convoluted constructions such as "The Man," "The Reporter," or "The Writer." In any case, their authorial immediacy impresses, regardless of the pronoun employed.

Beyond the injunction that contributors be amateurs writing defacto first-person, nonfiction accounts, the pages of this collection were open to anyone engaging in sport directly and experientially — whether as player, coach, or referee — and writing about it verily. In particular, the collection gives space to athletic "conversion narratives" in which such literary scribblers such as Charles Dickens and Mark Twain abandon the comforts of their desk-bound fictions for "real world" sporting nonfictions. Moreover, *Participatory Sportswriting*, emphasizing authors writing true accounts of their athletic experiences, suggests a symbiotic relationship between athletic practice and athletic writing. Who but the vigorous Walt Whitman, for instance, would think to describe his restorative wrestling regimen as an "invisible physician" and "silent delicious medicine." Who but John Burroughs could advise readers that trout fishing the Delaware River was "better, though bitterer, than the writers have described." Certainly, there is something about the participation-focused sporting life that works its magic on the way we see, think, and write, making our writing tougher and, at the same time, more *feeling* than we thought possible.

In the final analysis, *Participatory Sportswriting* concerns sports adventure — hearing its call, engaging in it, writing about it, no matter how risky or unlikely the undertaking. It's about women and men finding the courage to compete rather than retreat. It celebrates a time in American history, the Gilded and Golden Age of Sport, as well as a time in one's personal sporting life, whether that time is a middle-aged crises or a youthful adventure, that finds us re-envisioning ourselves and our world by *doing*, by breaking through.

In describing in *The Sportsman* how the huntsman must cope with inclement weather, the ancient Greek Xenophon captures the call to adventure perfectly: "Then is the time for the sportsman to take the haye nets and set off with a comrade up to the hills, and leave the cultivated lands behind."

John Burroughs on Trout Fishing (1870)

Wildly popular during his day and the author of more than thirty books, John Burroughs grew up in New York's Catskills and early on engaged in mountain climbing, fishing, and hiking. A literary sportsman as well as a literary naturalist, the long-lived Burroughs was a close friend of several of the Gilded and Golden Age's greatest sportsmen, including Walt Whitman, John Muir, Theodore Roosevelt, and Henry Ford. In his work, Burroughs consistently argues for realism in favor of sentimentalism among sportsmen-naturalists. His participatory books included Pepaction: A Summer Voyage *describing the author's sport-minded float down the Pepaction branch of the Delaware River. The essay excerpted here originally ran in the October 1870 issue of the* The Atlantic Monthly. *It describes fishing the headwaters of the Delaware River in New York, one of a few tracts left in the state, Burroughs claimed, "where one can get a glimpse of genuine backwoods life, and as fresh an article in the way of camping out as can be had anywhere." Though Burroughs is commonly mistaken as a preservationist in the mold of John Muir, his brand of conservationism, allowing for the hunting of bear and deer, for example, was much closer to Teddy Roosevelt's.*

From "Speckled Trout"

While my companions were cutting wood and making other preparations for the night, it fell to my lot, as the most successful angler, to provide the trout for supper and breakfast. How shall I describe that wild, beautiful stream, with features so like those of all other mountain streams? And yet, as I saw it in the deep twilight of those woods on that June afternoon, with its steady, even flow, and its tranquil, many-voiced murmur, it made an impression upon my mind distinct and peculiar, fraught in an eminent degree with the charm of seclusion and remoteness. The solitude was perfect; and I felt that strangeness and insignificance which the civilized man must always feel when opposing himself to such a vast scene of silence and wildness. The trout were quite black, like all wood trout, and took the bait eagerly. I followed the stream till the deepening shadows warned me to turn back. As I neared camp, the fire shone far through the trees, dispelling the gathering gloom, but blinding my eyes to all obstacles at my feet. I was seriously disturbed on arriving to find that one of my companions had cut an ugly gash in his shin with the axe, while felling a tree. As we did not carry a fifth wheel, it was not just the time or place to have any of our members crippled, and I had bodings of evil. But, thanks to the healing virtues of the balsam, which must have adhered to the blade of the axe, and double thanks to the court-plaster with which Orville had supplied himself before leaving home, the wounded leg, by being favored that night and the next day, gave us little trouble.

That night we had our first fair and square camping out — that is, sleeping on the ground with no shelter over us but the trees — and it was in many respects the pleasantest night we spent in the woods. The weather was perfect and the place was perfect, and for the first time we were exempt from the midges and smoke; and then we appreciated the clean new page we had to work on. Nothing is so acceptable to the camper-out as a pure article in the way of woods and waters. Any admixture of human relics mars the spirit of the scene. Yet I am willing to confess that, before we were through those woods, the marks of an axe in a tree was a welcome sight. On resuming our march next day we followed the right bank of the Beaverkill, in order to strike a stream which flowed in from the north, and which was the outlet of Balsam Lake, the objective point of that day's march. The distance to the lake from our camp could not have been over six or seven miles; yet traveling as we did, without path or guide, climbing up banks, plunging into ravines, making detours around swampy places, and forcing our way through woods choked up with much fallen and decayed timber, it seemed at least twice that distance, and the mid-afternoon sun was shining when we emerged into what is called the "Quaker Clearing," ground that I had been over nine years before, and that lies about two miles south of the lake. From this point we had a well-worn path that led us up a sharp rise of ground, then through level woods till we saw the bright gleam of the water through the trees.

I am always struck on approaching these little mountain lakes with the extensive preparation that is made for them in the conformation of the ground. I am thinking of a depression, or natural basin in the side of the mountain or on its top, the brink of which I shall reach after a little steep climbing; but instead of that, after I have accomplished the ascent, I find a broad sweep of level or gently undulating woodland that brings me after a half-hour or so to the lake, which lies in this vast lap like a drop of water in the palm of a man's hand.

Balsam Lake was oval shaped, scarcely more than half a mile long and a quarter of a mile wide, but presented a charming picture, with a group of dark gray hemlocks filling the valley about its head, and the mountains rising above and beyond. We found a cowhouse in good repair, also a dugout and paddle and several floats of logs. In the dugout I was soon creeping along the shady side of the lake, where the trout were incessantly jumping for a species of black fly, that, sheltered from the slight breeze, were dancing in swarms just above the surface of the water. The gnats were there in swarms also, and did their best toward balancing the accounts by preying upon me while I preyed upon the trout, which preyed upon the flies. But by dint of keeping my hands, face, and neck constantly wet, I am convinced that the balance of blood was on my side. The trout jumped most within a foot or two of shore, where the water was only a few inches deep. The shallowness of the water perhaps accounted for the inability of the fish to do more than lift their heads above the surface. They came up mouth wide open, and dropped back again in the most impotent manner. Where there is any depth of water, a trout will jump several feet into the air; and where there is a solid, unbroken sheet or column, they will scale falls and dams fifteen feet high.

We had the very cream and flower of our trout-fishing at this lake. For the first time we could use the fly to advantage; and then the contrast between laborious tramping along shore, and sitting in one end of a dugout and casting your line right and left with no fear of entanglement in brush or branch, while you was gently propelled along, was of the most pleasing character.

There were two varieties of trout in the lake—what it seems proper to call silver trout and golden trout; the former were the slimmer and seemed to keep apart from the latter. Starting from the outlet and working round on the eastern side toward the head, we invariably caught these first. They glanced in the sun like bars of silver. Their sides and bellies were indeed as white as new silver. As we neared the head, and especially as we came near a space occupied by some kind of watergrass that grew in the deeper part of the lake, the other variety would begin to take the hook, their bellies a bright gold color, which became a deep orange on their fins; and as we returned to the place of departure with the bottom of the boat strewn with these bright forms intermingled, it was a sight not soon to be forgotten. It pleased my eye so, that I would fain linger over them, arranging them in rows and studying the various hues and tints. They were of nearly a uniform size, rarely one over ten or under eight inches in length, and it seemed as if the hues of all the precious metals and stones were reflected from their sides. The flesh was deep salmon color; that of brook trout is generally much lighter. Some hunters and fishers from the valley of the Mill Brook, whom we met here, told us the trout were much larger in the lake, though far less numerous than they used to be. This, I think, is generally the case; brook trout do not grow large till they become scarce. It is only in streams that have been long and much fished that I have caught them as much as sixteen inches in length.

The liveliest sport I had on Balsam Lake was during a heavy thundershower. How the trout can distinguish the fly when it rains so hard that the surface of the water seems an inch or two deep with bubbles is more than I can tell; yet I know they did, and that very readily. As the rain began to come down pretty briskly, Aaron headed the boat for camp. My fly was dragging, and as we were shooting over the water grass which waved to and fro beneath the surface, two flame-finned beauties darted from the green depths and were instantly hooked. On this hint we backed water, took up a position with head to the wind, and for nearly an hour, amid the pouring rain and rattling thunder, the sport went on. I had on two flies, and usually both were snapped at the moment they touched the water. But the sport did not degenerate into wanton slaughter, for many were missed and many merely slapped the hook with their tails; and when we were a few short of a hundred, the blue sky shone out, and, drenched to the skin, we rowed leisurely back to camp.

The "porcupigs" were numerous about the lake, and not at all shy. One night the heat became so intolerable in our oven-shaped cowhouse, that I was obliged to withdraw from under its cover and lie down a little to one side. Just at daybreak as I lay rolled in my blanket, something awoke me. Lifting up my head, there was a porcupine with his forepaws on my hips. He was apparently as much surprised as I was; and to my inquiry as to what he at that moment might be looking for, he did not pause to reply, but hitting me a slap with his tail which left three or four quills in my blanket, he scampered off down the hill into the brush.

Being an observer of the birds, of course every curious incident connected with them fell under my notice. Hence as we stood about our campfire one afternoon, looking out over the lake, I was the only one to see a little commotion in the water, half hidden by the near branches, as of some tiny feathered swimmer struggling to reach the shore. Rushing to its rescue in the canoe, I found a yellow-rumped warbler, quite exhausted, clinging to a twig that hung down into the water; I brought the drenched and helpless thing to camp, and, putting it into a basket, hung it up to dry. An hour or two afterward I heard it fluttering in its prison, and cautiously lifting the lid to get a better glimpse of the lucky captive, it darted out and was gone in a twinkling. How came it in the water? That was my wonder, and I can only guess that it was a young bird that had never before flown over a pond of water, and, seeing the clouds and blue sky so perfect down there, thought it was a vast opening or gateway into another summer land, perhaps a short cut to the tropics, and so got itself into trouble. How my eye was delighted also with the redbird that alighted for a moment on a dry branch above the lake, just where a ray of light from the setting sun fell full upon it. A mere crimson point, and yet how it offset that dark somber background!

I have thus run over some of the features of an ordinary trouting excursion to the woods. People, inexperienced people, sitting in their rooms and thinking of these things, of all the poets have sung and romancers written, are apt to get sadly taken in when they attempt to realize their dreams. They expect to enter a sylvan paradise of trout, cool retreats, laughing brooks, picturesque views, balsamic couches, etc., instead of which they find hunger, rain, smoke, toil, gnats, mosquitoes, dirt, broken rest, vulgar guides, and salt pork; and they are very apt not to see where the fun comes in. But he who goes in a right spirit will not he disappointed, and will find the taste of this kind of life better, though bitterer, than the writers have described.

Mark Twain on Surfing (1871)

Overlooked as a travel, sports, and adventure nonfictionist, Mark Twain traveled well and widely, often engaging in sports en route, a process he called "vagabondizing" in his prefatory note to Roughing It. *An early gonzo journalist, Twain's sports and travel "journalism" amounts to a mixture of sketch, reportage, polemic, and lampoon. The call to adventure that resulted in* Roughing It *proved to be his brother's appointment as a territorial secretary of Nevada during the Civil War, which gave Twain a good excuse to head West and take up a freewheeling brand of participatory journalism. In the passage below, the always game Samuel Clemens tries his hand at surfing or "surf-bathing." Twain sent his dispatches from the Sandwich Islands for publication in the Sacramento* Union, *where they were eagerly read.*

FROM "A RIDE IN A CANOE" AND "SURF-BATHING"

At noon, we hired a Kanaka to take us down to the ancient ruins at Honaunan in his canoe—price two dollars—reasonable enough, for a sea voyage of eight miles, counting both ways.

The native canoe is an irresponsible looking contrivance. I cannot think of anything to liken it to but a boy's sled runner hollowed out, and that does not quite convey the correct idea. It is about fifteen feet long, high and pointed at both ends, is a foot and a half or two feet deep, and so narrow that if you wedged a fat man into it you might not get him out again. It sits on top of the water like a duck, but it has an outrigger and does not upset easily, if you keep still. This outrigger is formed of two long bent sticks like plow handles, which project from one side, and to their outer ends is bound a curved beam composed of an extremely light wood, which skims along the surface of the water and thus saves you from an upset on that side, while the outrigger's weight is not so easily lifted as to make an upset on the other side a thing to be greatly feared. Still, until one gets used to sitting perched upon this knife blade, he is apt to reason within himself that it would be more comfortable if there were just an outrigger or so on the other side also.

I had the bow seat, and Billings sat amidships and faced the Kanaka, who occupied the stern of the craft and did the paddling. With the first stroke the trim shell of a thing shot out from the shore like an arrow. There was not much to see. While we were on the shallow water of the reef, it was pastime to look down into the limpid depths at the large bunches of branching coral — the unique shrubbery of the sea. We lost that, though, when we got out into the dead blue water of the deep. But we had the picture of the surf, then, dashing angrily against the crag-bound shore and sending a foaming spray high into the air. There was interest in this beetling border, too, for it was honeycombed with quaint caves and arches and tunnels, and had a rude semblance of the dilapidated architecture of ruined keeps and castles rising out of the restless sea. When this novelty ceased to be a novelty, we turned our eyes shoreward and gazed at the long mountain with its rich green forests stretching up into the curtaining clouds, and at the specks of houses in the rearward distance and the diminished schooner riding sleepily at anchor. And when these grew tiresome we dashed boldly into the midst of a school of huge, beastly porpoises engaged at their eternal game of arching over a wave and disappearing, and then doing it over again and keeping it up — always circling over, in that way, like so many well-submerged wheels. But the porpoises wheeled themselves away, and then we were thrown upon our own resources. It did not take many minutes to discover that the sun was blazing like a bonfire, and that the weather was of a melting temperature. It had a drowsing effect, too.

In one place we came upon a large company of naked natives, of both sexes and all ages, amusing themselves with the national pastime of surf-bathing. Each heathen would paddle three or four hundred yards out to sea, (taking a short board with him), then face the shore and wait for a particularly prodigious billow to come along; at the right moment he would fling his board upon its foamy crest and himself upon the board, and here he would come whizzing by like a bombshell! It did not seem that a lightning express train could shoot along at a more hair-lifting speed. I tried surf-bathing once, subsequently, but made a failure of it. I got the board placed right, and at the right moment, too; but missed the connection myself. The board struck the shore in three-quarters of a second, without any cargo, and I struck the bottom about the same time, with a couple of barrels of water in me. None but natives ever master the art of surf-bathing thoroughly.

Edward Whymper on Climbing the Matterhorn (1871)

Like American artist-sportsman Joseph Knowles, Edward Whymper came to participatory and adventure sportswriting by way of his first career: illustrating. In nearly every way, the man regarded as the most famous British mountaineer of his era embodied the swashbuckling, dauntless Victorian. Obsessed with the idea of being the first to ascend the Matterhorn, Whymper raced the Italians to the top in 1865, bringing together a motley expeditionary crew. The ad-hoc group consisted of competing alpinists (Michael Croz, Charles Hudson, and Lord Francis Douglas), two second-choice local guides (Peter Taugwalder the elder and his son, Peter), and the less than skillful Douglas Hadow in an if-you-can't-beat-'em-join-'em collaborative push for the summit. Though Whymper's unlikely assemblage conquered the mountain via its less traveled eastern face, the climb ended in tragedy, as Croz, Hudson, Douglas, and Hadow fell to their death when the rope that tied them to the other men inexplicably gave way. Because of the competitive nature of the climb, a post-mortem investigation into whether the rope had been cut ensued, though theories of sabotage were never substantiated.

Ever the survivor, Whymper would go on to make pioneering scientific expeditions into the interior of Greenland in the late 1860s and to the top of several Ecuadoran peaks in 1880, ascents which would yield a medal from the Royal Geographical Society for his study of altitude sickness and a book, Travels amongst the Great Andes of the Equator *(1892)*. The author exhaustively documented nearly all of his sporting adventures both in writing and in pictures, including the illustrations for his most famous book, Scrambles Among the Alps, *(1871)*. The mountaineer's most famous engraving, the frontispiece for the 1871 volume from which this passage appears, depicts the mysterious "fog-bow" described in the following, harrowing account.

From "The Ascent of the Matterhorn" and "Descent of the Matterhorn"

The last doubt vanished! The Matterhorn was ours! Nothing but 200 feet of easy snow remained to be surmounted!

You must now carry your thoughts back to the seven Italians who started from Breil on the 11th of July. Four days had passed since their departure, and we were tormented with anxiety lest they should arrive on the top before us. All the way up we had talked of them, and many false alarms of "men on the summit" had been raised. The higher we rose, the more intense became the excitement. What if we should be beaten at the last moment? The slope eased off, at length we could be detached, and Croz and I, dashing away, ran a neck-and-neck race, which ended in a dead heat. At 1:40 P.M. the world was at our feet, and the Matterhorn was conquered. Hurrah! Not a footstep could be seen.

It was not yet certain that we had not been beaten. The summit of the Matterhorn was formed of a rudely level ridge, about 350 feet long, and the Italians might have been at its further extremity. I hastened to the southern end, scanning the snow right and left eagerly. Hurrah! Again, it was untrodden. Where were the men? I peered over the cliff, half doubting, half expectant. I saw them immediately — mere dots on the ridge, at an immense distance below. Up went my arms and my hat. "Croz! Croz! Come here!"

"Where are they, Monsieur?"

"There, don't you see them, down there?"

"Ah! the *coquins*, they are low down."

"Croz, we must make those fellows hear us."

We yelled until we were hoarse. The Italians seemed to regard us — we could not be certain. "Croz, we *must* make them hear us; they *shall* hear us!" I seized a block of rock and hurled it down, and called upon my companion, in the name of friendship, to do the same. We drove our sticks in, and prized away the crags, and soon a torrent of stones poured down the cliffs. There was no mistake about it this time. The Italians turned and fled.

Still, I would that the leader of that party could have stood with us at that moment, for our victorious shouts conveyed to him the disappointment of the ambition of a lifetime. He was the man, of all those who attempted the ascent of the Matterhorn, who most deserved to be the first upon its summit. He was the first to doubt its inaccessibility, and he was the only man who persisted in believing that its ascent would be accomplished. It was the aim of his life to make the ascent form the side of Italy, for the honor of his native valley. For a time he had the game in his hands: he played it as he thought best; but he made a false move, and he lost it. Times have changed with [Jean Antoine] Carrel. His supremacy is questioned in the Val Tournanche; new men have arisen; and he is not longer recognized as *the* chasseur above all others: but so long as he remains the man that he is today, it will not be easy to find his superior.

The others had arrived, so we went back to the northern end of the ridge. Croz now took the tent pole, and planted it in the highest snow. "Yes," we said, "there is the flagstaff, but where is the flag?"

"Here it is," he answered, pulling off his blouse and fixing it to the stick. It made a poor flag, and there was no wind to float it out, yet it was seen all around. They saw it at Zermatt — at the Riffel — in the Val Tournanche. At Breil, the watchers cried, "Victory is ours!" They raised 'bravos' for Carrel, and 'vivas' for Italy, but hastened to put themselves *en fête*. On the morrow they were undeceived. All was changed; the explorers returned sad — cast down — disheartened — confounded — gloomy.

"It is true," said the men. "We saw them ourselves — they hurled stones at us! The old traditions *are* true — there are spirits on the top of the Matterhorn!"

We returned to the southern end of the ridge to build a cairn, and then paid homage to the view. The day was one of those superlatively calm and clear ones which usually precede bad weather. The atmosphere was perfectly still, and free from all clouds or vapors. Mountains fifty — nay a hundred — miles off, looked sharp and near. All their details — ridge and crag, snow and glacier — stood out with faultless definition. Pleasant thoughts of happy days in bygone years came up unbidden, as we recognized the old, familiar forms. All were revealed — not one of the principal peaks of the Alps was hidden. I seem them clearly now — the great inner circles of giants, backed by the ranges, chains, and *massifs*. First came the Dent Blanche, hoary and grand; the Gabelhorn and pointed Rothhorn; and then the peerless Weisshorn: the towering Mischabelhörner, flanked by the Allaleinhorn, Strahlhorn, and Rimpfischorn; then Monte Rosa — with its many Spitzes — the Lyskamm and the Breithorn. Behind were the Bernese Oberland, governed by the Finsteraarhorn; the Simplon and St. Gothard groups; the Disgrazia and the Orteler. Towards the south we looked down to Chivasso on the plain of the Piedmont, and far beyond. The Viso — one hundred miles away — seemed close upon us; the Maritime Alps — one hundred and thirty miles distant — were free from haze. Then came my first love — the Pelvoux; the Ecrins and the Meije; the clusters of the Graians; and lastly, in the west, gorgous in the full sunlight, rose the monarch of all — Mont Blanc. Ten thousand feet beneath us were the green fields of Zermatt, dotted with chalets, from which blue smoke rose lazily. Eight thousand feet below, on the other side, were the pastures of the Breil. There were forests black and gloomy, and meadows bright and lively; bounding waterfalls and tranquil lakes; fertile lands and savage wastes; sunny plains and frigid *plateaux*. There were the most rugged forms, and the most graceful outlines — bold, perpendicular cliffs, and gentle, undulating slopes; rocky mountains and snowy mountains, somber and solemn, of glittering and white, with walls — turrets — pinnacles — pyramids — domes — cones — and spires! There was every combination that the world can give, and every contrast that the heart could desire.

We remained on the summit for one hour — "one crowded hour of glorious life." It passed away too quickly, and we began to prepare for the descent.

A few minutes later, a sharp-eyed lad ran into the Monte Rose hotel, to Seiler, saying that he had seen an avalanche fall from the summit of the Matterhorn on to the Matterhorngletcher.* The boy was reproved for telling idle stories; he was right, nevertheless, and this was what he saw.

Michael Croz had laid aside his axe, and in order to give Mr. Hadow greater security, was absolutely taking hold of his legs, and putting his feet, one by one, into their proper positions. As far as I know, no one was actually descending. I cannot speak with certainty, because the two leading men were partially hidden from my sight by an intervening mass of rock, but it is my belief, from the movements of their shoulders, that Croz, having done as I have said, was in the act of turning round to go down a step or two himself; at this moment Mr. Hadow slipped, fell against him, and knocked him over. I heard one startled exclamation from Croz, then saw him and Mr. Harlow flying downwards; in another moment Hudson was dragged from his steps, and Lord F. Douglas immediately after him. All this was the work of a moment. Immediately we heard Croz's exclamation, old Peter and I planted ourselves as firmly as the rocks would permit: the rope was taut between us, and the jerk came on us both as on one man. We held; but the rope broke midway between Taugwalder and Lord Francis Douglas. For a few seconds we saw our unfortunate companions sliding downwards on their backs, and spreading out their hands, endeavoring to save themselves. They passed from our sight uninjured, disappeared one by one, and fell form precipice to precipice on to the Matterhorngletscher below, a distance of nearly 4000 feet in height. From the moment the rope broke it was impossible to help them.

So perished our comrades! For the space of half-an-hour we remained on the spot without moving a single step. The two men, paralyzed by terror, cried like infants, and trembled in such a manner as to threaten us with the fate of the others. Old Peter rent the air with exclamations of "Chamounix! Oh, what will Chamounix say?" He meant who would believe that Croz could fall? The young man did nothing but scream or sob, "We are lost! We are lost! Fixed between the two, I could neither move up nor down. I begged young Peter to descend, but he dared not. Unless he did, we could not advance. Old Peter became alive to the danger, and swelled the cry. "We are lost! We are lost!" The father's fear was natural — he trembled for his own son; the young man's fear was cowardly — he thought of self alone. At last old Peter summoned up courage and changed his position to a rock to which he could fix the rope; the young man then descended, and we all stood together. Immediately we did so, I asked for the rope which had given way, and found, to my surprise — indeed, to my horror — that it was the weakest of the three

---

*The running-in of a portion of a separate, contiguous chapter, "Descent of the Matterhorn" is here indicated by the insertion of a line space preceding the run–in material. The sentence here noted represents the first sentence of the third full paragraph of the run–in chapter. Please note that Whymper's voluminous, tangential footnotes as they appeared in the original volume have been omitted.

ropes. It was not brought, and should not have been employed, for the purpose for which it was used. It was old rope, and, compared with others, was feeble. It was intended as a reserve, in case we had to leave much rope behind, attached to rocks. I saw at once that a serious question was involved, and made him give me the end. It had broken in midair, and it did not appear to have sustained previous injury.

For more than two hours afterwards I thought almost every moment that the next would be my last; for the Taugwalders, utterly unnerved, were not only incapable of giving assistance, but were in such a state that a slip might have been expected from them at any moment. After a time, we were able to do that which should have been done at first, and fixed rope to firm rocks, in addition to being tied together. These ropes were cut from time to time, and were left behind. Even with their assurance the men were afraid to proceed, and several times old Peter turned with ashy face and faltering limbs, and said, with terrible emphasis, "I cannot!"

About 6 P.M., we arrived at the snow upon the ridge descending towards Zermatt, and all peril was over. We frequently looked, but in vain, for traces of our unfortunate companions; we bent over the ridge and cried to them, but no sound returned. Convinced at last that they were neither within sight nor hearing, we ceased from our useless efforts; and, too cast down for speech, silently gathered up our things, and little effects of those who were lost, preparatory to continuing the descent. When, lo a mighty arch appeared, rising above the Lyskamm, high into the sky. Pale, colorless, and noiseless, but perfectly sharp and defined, except where it was lost in the clouds, this unearthly apparition seemed like a vision from another world, and, almost appalled, we watched with amazement the gradual development of two vast crosses, one on either side. If the Taugwalders had not been the first to perceive it, I should have doubted my senses. They thought it had some connection with the accident, and I, after a while, that it might bear some relation to ourselves. But our movements had no effect upon it. The spectral forms remained motionless. It was a fearful and wonderful sight, unique in my experience, and impressive beyond description, coming at such a moment.

Robert Louis Stevenson on Canoeing Across Europe (1878)

Considered a pioneering work of participatory outdoor sports literature, An Inland Voyage details twenty-six-year-old Robert Louis Stevenson's jour-

ney down the Oise River from Belgium to France with his friend Sir Walter Grindlay Simpson. In the passage below, both Stevenson and his canoe share the sobriquet "Arethusa," while "Cigarette" refers both to Simpson and to Simpson's vessel. Their so-called "canoes," rigged with sails, more closely resembled kayaks approximating the "Rob Roy" style popularized by Scottish sportsman John MacGregor in his book A Thousand Miles in the Rob Roy Canoe (1866).

An admitted novice at sail, the Scotsman Stevenson had much to prove both to himself and to his no-nonsense father as he hoisted the sail in Antwerp, Belgium just a year after earning, per his father's wishes, a law degree from Edinburgh University and passing the bar in Scotland. In his poetry collection Underwoods (1887), Stevenson defends his growing interest in travel and literature to his father, a lighthouse engineer, writing, "Say not of me that weakly I declined/The labours of my sires, and fled the sea/The towers we founded and the lamps we lit,/To play at home with paper like a child." Herein, Stevenson — as with so many young participatory journalists to follow — sets out to test his mettle, writing, "We usually find ourselves a great deal braver and better than we thought." Less than five years after completing his inland journey, Stevenson would draw on his worldwide travels by land and by sea to publish his classic work Treasure Island (1883)

From "Antwerp to Boom" and "On the Willebroek Canal"

We made a great stir in Antwerp Docks. A stevedore and a lot of dock porters took up the two canoes, and ran with them for the slip. A crowd of children followed cheering. The *Cigarette* went off in a splash and a bubble of small breaking water. Next moment the *Arethusa* was after her. A steamer was coming down, men on the paddle box shouted hoarse warnings, the stevedore and his porters were bawling from the quay. But in a stroke or two the canoes were away out in the middle of the *Scheldt*, and all steamers, and stevedores, and other 'long-shore vanities were left behind.

The sun shone brightly; the tide was making four jolly miles an hour; the wind blew steadily, with occasional squalls. For my part, I had never been in a canoe under sail in my life; and my first experiment out in the middle of this big river was not made without some trepidation. What would happen when the wind first caught my little canvas? I suppose it was almost as trying a venture into the regions of the unknown as to publish a first book, or to marry. But my doubts were not of long duration; and in five minutes you will not be surprised to learn that I had tied my sheet.

I own I was a little struck by this circumstance myself; of course, in company with the rest of my fellow men, I had always tied the sheet in a sailing boat, but in so little and crank a concern as a canoe, and with these charging squalls, I was not prepared to find myself follow the same principle, and it inspired me with some contemptuous views of our regard for life. It is certainly easier to smoke with the sheet fastened, but I had never before weighed a comfortable pipe of tobacco against an obvious risk, and gravely elected for the comfortable pipe. It is a commonplace that we cannot answer for ourselves before we have been tried. But it is not so common a reflection, and surely more consoling, that we usually find ourselves a great deal braver and better than we thought. I believe this is everyone's experience, but an apprehension that they may belie themselves in the future prevents mankind from trumpeting this cheerful sentiment abroad. I wish sincerely, for it would have saved me much trouble, there had been some one to put me in a good heart about life when I was younger; to tell me how dangers are most portentous on a distant sight; and how the good in a man's spirit will not suffer itself to be overlaid, and rarely or never deserts him in the hour of need. But we are all for tootling on the sentimental flute in literature, and not a man among us will go to the head of the march to sound the heady drums.

The canal was busy enough.* Every now and then we met or overtook a long string of boats, with great green tillers; high sterns with a window on either side of the rudder, and perhaps a jug or a flowerpot in one of the windows; a dinghy following behind; a woman busied about the day's dinner, and a handful of children. These barges were all tied one behind the other with tow ropes, to the number of twenty-five or thirty; and the line was headed and kept in motion by a steamer of strange construction. It had neither paddlewheel nor screw; but by some gear not rightly comprehensible to the unmechanical mind, it fetched up over its bow a small bright chain which lay along the bottom of the canal, and paying it out again over the stern, dragged itself forward, link by link, with its whole retinue of loaded skows. Until one had found out the key to the enigma, there was something solemn and uncomfortable in the progress of one of these trains, as it moved gently along the water with nothing to mark its advance but an eddy alongside dying away into the wake.

Of all the creatures of commercial enterprise, a canal barge is by far the most delightful to consider. It may spread its sails, and then you see it sailing high above the treetops and the windmill, sailing on the aqueduct, sailing through the green corn lands: the most picturesque of things amphibious. Or the horse plods along at a foot pace as if there were no such thing as business in the world, and the man dreaming at the tiller sees the same spire on

---

The running-in of a portion of a separate, contiguous chapter, "On the Willebroek Canal" is here indicated by the insertion of a line space preceding the run-in material. The sentence here noted represents the first sentence of the second paragraph of the run-in chapter.

the horizon all day long. It is a mystery how things ever get to their destination at this rate, and to see the barges waiting their turn at a lock affords a fine lesson of how easily the world may be taken. There should be many contented spirits on board, for such a life is both to travel and to stay at home.

The chimney smokes for dinner as you go along; the banks of the canal slowly unroll their scenery to contemplative eyes; the barge floats by great forests and through great cities with their public buildings and their lamps at night; and for the bargee, in his floating home, "traveling abed," it is merely as if he were listening to another man's story or turning the leaves of a picture book in which he had no concern. He may take his afternoon walk in some foreign country on the banks of the canal, and then come home to dinner at his own fireside.

There is not enough exercise in such a life for any high measure of health, but a high measure of health is only necessary for unhealthy people. The slug of a fellow, who is never ill nor well, has a quiet time of it in life, and dies all the easier.

I am sure I would rather be a bargee than occupy any position under heaven that required attendance at an office. There are few callings, I should say, where a man gives up less of his liberty in return for regular meals. The bargee is on shipboard—he is master in his own ship—he can land whenever he will—he can never be kept beating off a lee shore a whole frosty night when the sheets are as hard as iron; and so far as I can make out, time stands as nearly still with him as is compatible with the return of bedtime or the dinner hour. It is not easy to see why a bargee should ever die.

Charles Dickens on Climbing Mount Vesuvius (1879)

>Charles Dickens, whose first-person, investigative journalism often shed light on the condition of the poor, the imprisoned, and the downtrodden, here relays a firsthand account of his hair-raising ascent of Mount Vesuvius. Dickens, his wife Kate, her sister Georgina, and the Dickenses' five children left London by coach in July of 1844 destined for Italy, with Frenchman John Roche as their guide.
>
>In the letter below, written to his friend and attorney Thomas Mitton and collected in The Letters of Charles Dickens, the legendary man of letters registers incredulity at the tragedy and injury resulting from what he had intended as a mere leisure excursion. The image the author conjures is wholly tragicomic—the two women in his life, Kate and Georgina, carried up the

side of the mountain in a Cleopatra-styled litter, the women themselves becoming "indecent" when the servants' grips became so tight they unintentionally ripped the clothing literally off the ladies' backs. Lost in Dickens's seemingly amused recounting is the disappearance of one of the expedition "grunts," who plummets down the mountainside and is not heard from again.

In his minor work Pictures From Italy *(1846), Dickens the travel journalist delivers a more restrained, less personable rendering of the foolhardy climb that the great author here self-deprecatingly describes as made by men "resolved (like jackasses) to climb that hill to the brink, and look down into the crater itself." Dickens's letter is included as one of the earliest representations of Gilded Age participatory sportswriting by virtue of its publication date, 1879. His accounts in both* Pictures *and* Letters *remain two of the most celebrated and enduring volcano encounter narratives, earning special mention in the recent monograph* Volcanoes in Human History *(2002). Compelled by the dramatic geometry of the steep volcanic cone he traversed, Dickens's original letter included small hand-drawn angles illustrating the shapes and slopes to his readers — effects here approximated with standard typographical symbols, bolded and surrounded by quotes for proper emphasis.*

From "The Letters of Charles Dickens"

Saturday, February 22nd — Yesterday evening, at four o'clock, we began (a small party of six) the ascent of Mount Vesuvius, with six saddle horses, an armed guard, and twenty-two guides.* The latter rendered necessary by the severity of the weather, which is greater than has been known for twenty years, and has covered the precipitous part of the mountain with deep snow, the surface of which is glazed with one smooth sheet of ice from the top of the cone to the bottom. By starting at that hour I intended to get the sunset about halfway up, and night at the top, where the fire is raging. It was an inexpressibly lovely night without a cloud; and when the day was quite gone, the moon (within a few hours of the full) came proudly up, showing the sea, and the Bay of Naples, and the whole country, in such majesty as no words can express. We rode to the beginning of the snow and then dismounted. Catherine and Georgina were put into two litters, just chairs with poles, like those in use in England on the fifth of November; and a fat Englishman, who was of the party, was hoisted into a third, borne by eight men. I was accom-

---

*Dickens penned the letter to Mitton in two parts and sent them under single cover addressed "My Dear Mitton" and dated "February 17, 1845," explaining the phrase "since I left off as above" in the sentence here noted. In the February 17 portion of the letter, omitted here, Dickens complains — about being "beset by visitors," about Naples, and about the weather — though he looks forward to the ascent of Vesuvius, Herculaneum, and Pompeii. Part two of the letter, dated February 22, appears in its entirety minus the closing, "Ever Faithfully," and the final paragraph, which reads, "Address as usual. All letters are forwarded. The children well and happy. Best regards."

modated with a tough stick, and we began to plough our way up. The ascent was steep at this line "/"— very nearly perpendicular. We were all tumbling at every step; and looking up and seeing the people in advance tumbling at every step; and looking up and seeing the people in advance tumbling over one's very head, and looking down and seeing hundreds of feet of smooth ice below, was, I must confess, anything but agreeable. However, I knew there was little chance of another clear night before I leave this, and gave the word to get up, somehow or other. So on we went, winding a little now and then, or we should not have got on at all. By prodigious exertions we passed the region of snow, and came into that that of fire — desolate and awful, you may well suppose. It was like working one's way through a dry waterfall, with every mass of stone burnt and charred into enormous cinders, and smoke and sulfur bursting out of every chink and crevice, so that it was difficult to breathe. High before us, bursting out of a hill at the top of the mountain shaped like this "^," the fire was pouring out, reddening the night with flames, blackening it with smoke, and spotting it with red-hot stones and cinders that fell down again in showers. At every step everybody fell, now into a hot chink, now into a bed of ashes, now over a mass of cindered iron; and the confusion in the darkness (for the smoke obscured the moon in this part), and the quarreling and shouting and roaring of the guides, and the waiting every now and then for somebody who was not to be found, and was supposed to have stumbled into some pit or other, made such a scene of it as I can give you no idea of. My ladies were now on foot, of course; but we dragged them on as well as we could (they were thorough game, and didn't make the least complaint), until we got to the foot of that topmost hill I have drawn so beautifully. Here we all stopped, but the head guide, an English gentleman of the name of Le Gros — who has been here many years and has been up the mountain a hundred times — and your humble servant, resolved (like jackasses) to climb that hill to the brink, and look down into the crater itself. You may form some notion of what is going on inside it, when I tell you that it is a hundred feet higher than it was six weeks ago. The sensation of struggling up it, choked with fire and smoke, and feeling at every step as if the crust of ground between one's feet and the gulf of fire would crumble in and swallow one up (which is the real danger), I shall remember for some time, I think. But we did it. We looked down into the flaming bowels of the mountain, and came back again, alight in half a dozen places, and burnt from head to foot. You never saw such devils. And *I* never saw anything so awful and terrible.

    Roche had been tearing his hair like a madman, and crying that we should all three be killed, which made the rest of the party very comfortable, as you may suppose. But we had some wine in a basket, and all swallowed a little of that and a great deal of sulfur before we began to descend. The usual way, after the fiery part is past — you will understand that to be all the flat top of the mountain, in the center of which, again, rises the little hill I have drawn — is to slide down the ashes, which, slipping from under you, make a gradually increasing ledge under your feet, and prevent your going too fast. But when we came to this steep place last night, we found nothing there but one smooth solid sheet of ice. The only way to get down was for the guides to make a chain, holding each other's hands, and beat a narrow track in it into the snow below with their sticks. My two unfortunate ladies were taken out of their litters again, with half a dozen men hanging on to each, to prevent their falling forward, and we began to descend this way. It was like a tremendous dream. It was impossible to stand, and the only way to prevent oneself from going sheer down the precipice, every time one fell, was to drive one's stick into one of the holes that guides had made, and hold on to that. Nobody could pick one up, or stop one, or render one of the least assistance. Now, conceive my horror, when, this Mr. Le Gros I have mentioned, being on one side of Georgina and I on the other, suddenly staggers away from the narrow path on the smooth ice, gives us a jerk, lets go, and plunges headforemost down the smooth ice into the black night, five hundred feet below! Almost at the same instant, a man far behind, carrying a light basket on his head with some of our spare cloaks in it, misses his footing and rolls down in another place, and after him, rolling over and over like a black bundle, goes a boy, shrieking as nobody but an Italian can shriek, until the breath is tumbled out of him.

The Englishman is in bed today, terribly bruised but without any broken bones. He was insensible at first and a mere heap of rags; but we got him before the fire, in a little hermitage there is halfway down, and he so far recovered as to be able to make some supper, which was waiting for us there. They boy was brought in with his head tied up in a bloody cloth, about half an hour after the rest of us were assembled. And the man who had the basket was not found when he left the mountain at midnight. What became of the cloaks (mine was among them) I know as little. My ladies' clothes were so torn off their backs that they would not have been decent, if there could have been any thought of such things at such a time. And when we got down to the guides' house, we found a French surgeon (one of another party who had been up before us) lying on a bed in a stable, which God knows what horrible breakage about him, but suffering acutely and looking like death. A pretty unusual trip for a pleasure expedition, I think!

I am rather stiff today but am quite unhurt, except a slight scrape on my right hand. My clothes are burnt to pieces. My ladies are the wonder of Naples, and everybody is open-mouthed.

John Lyle King on Trout Fishing (1879)

A true amateur sportsman, lawyer John Lyle King's lyrical account of leaving industrial Chicago to canoe, fish, and hunt along the Menominee, Michigami, and Brulé Rivers in Michigan's Upper Peninsula appeared in installments in the Chicago Sunday Times *and* Chicago Sunday Tribune. *Derivative of Thoreau and Burroughs, King makes a greater effort towards journalistic accuracy than the aforementioned. The adapted passage below, from* Trout Fishing on the Brulé River, *describes King's whitewater experience, intimating the peace and fellowship possible in a sporting journey among friends.*

From "Prefatory and Personal" and "Chapter VII"

The exhaustion that comes of the inordinate and exacting frets and activities of business, the languor and inertia of summer fervors, the ennui and satiety that follow the dissipations of social life, may find in the great wilderness retreats a grateful reprieve and a speedy reparation. When the haunts of game in the woods and the lairs of fish in the streams incite the passion for sport to couple itself with the quest and yearning for rest and vitalization, the wayfarer's pathway in the wilderness becomes a pilgrimage through abounding scenes of diversion and into a realm of fascination. The restraints and stress of civilization and the city, for the time, are exchanged for exhilarating freedom and simplicity of nature. The respited sportsman, with only the rod or gun as the scepter of his commanding will throughout the rude domain, gratifies himself and luxuriates alike in the footsteps of the advance and in the repose of the halt. He realizes in a fullness of meaning gained from happy experience, that, indeed, "there is a pleasure in the pathless woods."

The wilderness of Northwest are free, vast franchises of gunning and fishing. The many rivers which vein these immense tracts with running waters, and the numberless lakes in recesses of the woods, are inexhaustible commons of piscary, of whose affluent stores whosoever will, may, without let, partake. For an excursion, and on a vacation furlough, to one of these streams noted for trout, three of the Chicago lawyers in August joined in a party. These were James L. High, author of the works on "Injunctions," "Extraordinary Legal Remedies," etc., Josiah H. Bissell, compiler of "Bissell's Reports," and the writer, together with Lorenzo Pratt, a Chicago capitalist.

The party sought recreation and mental rest. Other members of the bar had journeyed some of those regions, in their vacation freedom, on a tour of rest, sport and pleasure. They had found and reported a full and rare fruition of enjoyment, in their wanderings to and on the Brulé River. A like expedition, with identical purposes, following the path of Cook, Campbell, Judge Blodgett and others, promises equal and similar delight and good. It was a journey and sojourn in open air, made up of canoeing, tenting, portaging and roughing generally, with the incidents of shooting and fishing.

The outfit and supplies were provided in Chicago, and sent by the Chicago & Northwestern railway to Section Eighteen, a station of that road eighteen miles beyond Marinette, Wisconsin. The other accessories — a team for the land route and the guides — were engaged in advance at Marinette, and met the party at Section Eighteen. The canoes were to be procured at Badwater, on the Menominee, where the water travel began.

The guides were Indians. One of them was George Kaquotash, a full-blooded Menominee, muscular, lithe, active — a veteran of the woods and of the Brulé. The other was Mitchell Thebault, mostly Menominee, with a French infusion of blood and name, with his complexion paled to a hue a little lighter than the usual Indian copper tint. Though with the manners and habits, in some degree, of civilized life, they were essentially, in nature and native dialect, Indians. In another August a second excursion to the Brulé river was made by the same Chicago party, excepting that Mr. Franklin Denison, also a Chicago lawyer, took the place of Mr. Bissell.

We had by this time familiarized ourselves with the peculiarities and caprices of the birchbark, and felt at home and at ease in it, so that it was no longer a precarious or ticklish navigation to us.* We knew now how to shift positions, how to stretch out or to stand erect, and had mastered the niceties of balancing ourselves and the canoe. For its ease, grace, lightness, quickness and docility of motion, the birchbark canoe is peerless and superb among watercraft; and the Menominee we expected to find precisely the stream of canoe navigation, in its most favorable conditions.

The Twin Falls are three miles apart. While the Indians were transferring the canoes and their burden around the upper falls, we scrambled to the foot, and High ventured a cast of a brilliant red fly in the whirl, though it was quite improbable that a pike or a bass would be enticed by such a flaring gawd. Nevertheless, though all chances were against him, he whipped the water with the fly just the same, thinking if he did not win, he would at least deserve success. He saved his fly and restored the fictitious insect to the company of its fellow entomological gewgaws, in his fly-book, in its perfect integrity, for future use.

In the eddy of the lower fall, I thought the water looked as if it should

---

The running-in of a portion of a separate, noncontiguous chapter, "Chapter VII" is here indicated by the insertion of a line space preceding the run-in material. The sentence here noted represents the first sentence of the run-in chapter.

be a lair of fish, and that a pickerel might be captured by one not too fastidious to try a killing bait. I rigged my tackle, and experimented with a scrap of pork on the hook, but the swine's flesh decoyed no perch, bass or pickerel that I could grapple with hook of steel. Not even one of the abounding pitiful chubs was hungry enough to offer it a nibble. I was not long in satisfying myself that fishing in that pool was not my vocation. After pushing out and getting fairly under way, George saw a couple of deer grazing water herbage afar off. It was only a momentary vision. They vanished.

Soon again we had another sensation of deer — a splendid buck feeding in the bushes. The boys slyly stole the canoes thereaway. Pratt's ardor was enkindled; he shouldered arms, and held at the ready; the buck lifted his spreading antlers, and then dropped his nose to the grass again. George was stealthily paddling the canoe, with a fair show of stealing unawares, within shooting range. We were expecting great things of Pratt, but owing, probably, to a fluster of buck fever, he pulled an ill-timed trigger, and though the deer was not harmed, the water was badly torn up about midway between the buck's pasturing place and ourselves. The deer bounded and ricocheted into the forest, where the woodbine twines. Pratt admitted that his premature firing was a mistake, worse even than would be that of shooting at a pigeon and killing a crow; but as the deer was just going to spring, he had to spring the trigger then, or lose the shot.

The next event, further down, was a frolic of immersion. We had turned ashore to lunch, and after dealing full justice to the spread, Bissell and Pratt were impetuously seized with a mania for a swim in the Menominee. The performance was marvelously brisk and brief. They plunged in the crystal tide with a slapdash precipitance, but the reduction of their temperature from the frigid inclemency of the stream was so instantaneous and the effect was so glacial that with "chattering teeth and bristling hair upright," they rebounded, and plunged out, with surprising agility, Bissell rather in the lead.

Two miles further on, was the head of the portage around Big Quiniseck Falls. It was the scene of a surprise party. At about the same moment Wirt Dexter's party and our own reached the spot. With him, were Jesse Spaulding, of Chicago, and a Mr. Smith, a Bostonian lawyer, en route to the Brulé. Their suite and outfit were complete. They had four Indians of the Chippewa order of redmen, but they were lean, stunted-looking weaklings and manikins aside of our brawny and robust aborigines; also, a weazened, shriveled little mulatto cook, who seemed a scullion apart, with no affinity for his fellows of the retinue, who, in their turn, seemed to look tomahawks at the kitchen satellite, and as if they would like to strip his scalp in the first convenient bushes. The cargo was immense. Tents, cots, hair mattresses, stools, cases, barrels, kegs, crockery, valises, gun-cases, as if for a whole season's campaign. Pratt thought their equipage for roughing it was hardly complete without a piano and brussels carpet. But he is rather peculiar and high-toned, and we did not accord with him in that hypotheses. The couple of hours spent there, while both retinues were making portages of the loads, were a delightful episode in our forest adventure. Our converse was mainly on matters of the woods. Dexter has been a forest-ranging Michigander, as apt in handling a trout rod or rifle in his vacations, as he is in practice with the mysteries of Coke and Chitty in term time. There is not much about game of his native state, that which swims, goes on foot or sweeps on the wing, with which he is not familiar. His reminiscences of hunting and fishing, flavored as they were with the fragrance of Partagas, greatly entertained us.

This portage was a little more than two miles in length. It was over a rolling, hillocky surface, and though the path was not so barricaded with trunks of trees to be climbed over as most of the carries, it was yet tedious and wearisome. But at the foot of the declivity, where the trail ends, a large rock towers thirty feet above the water at its base. From this peak of rock, a splendid view burst upon the sight, in an outlook of magnificent scenery. Off, at the right, the river avalanches down a steep incline, and pitches tumultuously far, and rolls into waves, with clouds of spray, "showering wide sleet of diamond drift and pearly hail." The water spreads and rounds out into a circular bay or basin of nearly a half-mile diameter, and this is partially girded round with cliffs wooded with heaviest pageantry of forest pines and cedars, except at the further side, where the river contracts and glides away in a smooth flow or stretch between level shores and the richest of verdure.

The scene, resplendent in the setting sun, was enchanting and worthy of some master to commemorate. It was the spontaneous resolve of all the party that the tent should be pitched on the rock, in view of scenery so picturesque and striking; and there, from the summit of the rock, and in the last rays of the sun fading and in the twilight glimmering on, we quietly enjoyed the situation with wonder and delight. We were among the splendors of primeval nature.

Walt Whitman on "Wrestling" and Sailing (1881)

The three short passages that follow, grouped for thematic purposes under the editorial umbrella "Three Athletic Selections from Specimen Days*," demonstrate Walt Whitman's zeal for unmitigated sportive pleasure. The first and second readings detail Whitman's restorative wrestling regimen while con-*

valescing at the Safford Farm at Timber Creek. In the third passage, Whitman recounts an uplifting, head-clearing sail on Manhattan Bay.

Whitman praised the athlete as the epitome of American vigor. The quintessential American vagabond was himself a sportsman who turned to exercise, specifically wrestling, to recuperate from a stroke. In Sportsmen and Gamesmen, sport historian John Dizikes writes, "One of Walt Whitman's most cherished images was that of a future in which America would be populated by a race of 'freedom's athletes,' individuals whose lives would be marked by a quality of 'brave delight.'" In "Song of Myself," from Leaves of Grass, Whitman expresses a similar idea in his own inimitable free verse: "I am the teacher of athletes,/He that by me spreads a wider breast than my own proves the width of my own."

"THREE ATHLETIC SELECTIONS FROM *SPECIMEN DAYS*"

"Spring Overtures, Recreations"

February 20. A solitary and pleasant sundown hour at the pond, exercising arms, chest, my whole body, by a tough oak sapling thick as my wrist, twelve feet high — pulling and pushing, inspiring the good air. After I wrestle with the tree awhile, I can feel its young sap and virtue welling up out of the ground and tingling through me from crown to toe, like health's wine. Then for addition and variety I launch forth in my vocalism; shout declamatory pieces, sentiments, sorrow, anger, etc., from the stock poets or plays — or inflate my lungs and sing the wild tunes and refrains I heard of the blacks down south, or patriotic songs I learned in the army. I make the echoes ring, I tell you! As the twilight fell, in a pause of these ebullitions, an owl somewhere the other side of the creek sounded "too-oo-oo-oo-oo," soft and pensive (and I fancied a little sarcastic) repeated four or five times. Either to applaud the negro songs — or perhaps an ironical comment on the sorrow, anger, or style of the stock poets.

"The Oaks and I"

September 5, 1877. I write this, 11 A.M., sheltered under a dense oak by the bank, where I have taken refuge from a sudden rain. I came down here, (we had sulky drizzles all the morning, but an hour ago a lull,) for the before-mentioned daily and simple exercise I am fond of— to pull on that young hickory sapling out there — to sway and yield to its tough-limber upright stem — haply to get into my old sinews some of its elastic fiber and clear sap. I stand on the turf and take these health-pulls moderately and at intervals for nearly an hour, inhaling great draughts of fresh air. Wandering by the creek, I have three or four naturally favorable spots where I rest — besides a chair I lug with me and use for more deliberate occasions. At other spots convenient I have selected, besides the hickory just named, strong and limber boughs of beech or holly, in easy-reaching distance, for my natural gymnasia, for arms, chest, trunk muscles. I can soon feel the sap and sinew rising through me, like mercury to heat. I hold on boughs or slender trees caressingly there in the sun and shade, wrestle with their innocent stalwartness — and *know* the virtue thereof passes from them into me. (Or maybe we interchange — maybe the trees are more aware of it all than I ever thought.)

But now pleasantly imprisoned here under the big oak — the rain dripping, and the sky covered with leaden clouds — nothing but the pond on one side, and the other a spread of grass, spotted with the milky blossoms of the wild carrot — the sound of an axe wielded at some distant woodpile — yet in this dull scene, (as most folks would call it), why am I so (almost) happy here and alone? Why would any intrusion, even from people I like, spoil the charm? But am I alone? Doubtless there comes a time — perhaps it has come to me — when one feels through his whole being, and pronouncedly the emotional part, that identity between himself subjectively and Nature objectively which Schelling and Fichte are so fond of pressing. How it is I know not, but I often realize a presence here — in clear moods I am certain of it, and neither chemistry nor reasoning nor esthetics will give the least explanation. All the past two summers it has been strengthening and nourishing my sick body and soul, as never before. Thanks, invisible physician, for thy silent delicious medicine, thy day and night, thy waters and thy airs, the banks, the grass, the trees, and even the weeds!

"Manhattan from the Bay"

June 25. Returned to New York last night. Out today on the waters for a sail in the wide bay, southeast of Staten island — a rough, tossing ride, and a free sight — the long stretch of Sandy Hook, the highlands of Navesink, and the many vessels outward and inward bound. We came up through the midst of all, in the full sun. I especially enjoyed the last hour or two. A moderate seabreeze had set in; yet over the city, and the waters adjacent, was a thin haze, concealing nothing, only adding to the beauty. From my point of view, as I write amid the soft breeze, with a sea temperature, surely nothing on earth of its kind can go beyond this show. To the left the North River with its far vista — nearer, three or four warships, anchored peacefully — the Jersey side, the banks of Weehawken, the Palisades, and the gradually receding blue, lost in the distance — to the right the East River — the mast-hemmed shores — the grand obelisk-like towers of the bridge, one on either side, in haze, yet plainly defined, giant brothers twain, throwing free graceful interlinking loops high across the tumbled tumultuous current below — (the tide is just changing to its ebb) — the broad water-spread everywhere crowded — no, not crowded, but thick as stars in the sky — with all sorts and sizes of sail and steam vessels, plying ferry-boats, arriving and departing coasters, great ocean Dons, iron-black, modern, magnificent in size and power, filled with their incalculable value of human life and precious merchandise — with here and there, above all, those daring, careening things of grace and wonder, those white and shaded swift-darting fish-birds, (I wonder if shore or sea elsewhere can outvie them,) ever with their slanting spars, and fierce, pure, hawk-like beauty and motion — first-class New York sloop or schooner yachts, sailing, this fine day, the free sea in a good wind. And rising out of the midst, tall-topped, ship-hemmed, modern, American, yet strangely oriental, V-shaped Manhattan, with its compact mass, its spires, its cloud-touching edifices grouped at the center — the green of the trees, and all the white, brown and gray of the architecture well blended, as I see it, under a miracle of limpid sky, delicious light of heaven above, and June haze on the surface below.

Theodore Roosevelt on Hunting the Antelope (1885)

Theodore Roosevelt's conservationist beliefs were rooted in international experiences as a hunter. Adept as a horseman, a "rough rider," Roosevelt pursued every imaginable kind of game in a life lived as an avid huntsman, yet he remained particularly enamored of the antelope, an obsession that resulted in his voluminous monograph The Deer Family. *In the excerpt below from* Hunting Trips on the Prairie and in the Mountains, *a young Roosevelt describes his first hunt for the antelope in the Badlands, where Roosevelt had established a ranch. The future President believed not just in hunting and conservation but, like Whitman, in a deeper connection between athleticism and free people. In* The Strenuous Life; Essays and Addresses *(1900), Roosevelt wrote, "I preach to you, then, my countrymen, that our country calls not for the life of ease but for the life of strenuous endeavor. The twentieth century looms before us big with the fate of many nations. If we stand idly by, if we seek merely swollen, slothful ease and ignoble peace, if we shrink from the hard contests where men must win at hazard of their lives and at the risk of all they hold dear, then the bolder and stronger peoples will pass us by, and will win for themselves the domination of the world."*

"A Trip on the Prairie"

I never but once took a trip of any length with antelope hunting for its chief object. This was one June, when all the men were away on the roundup.

As is usual during the busy half of the ranchman's year, the spring and summer, when men have no time to hunt and game is out of condition, we had been living on salt pork, beans, potatoes, and bread; and I had hardly had a rifle in my hand for months; so, finding I had a few days to spare, I thought I should take a short trip on the prairie, in the beautiful June weather, and get a little sport and a little fresh meat out of the bands of pronghorn bucks, which I was sure to encounter. Intending to be gone but a couple of days, it was not necessary to take many articles. Behind my saddle I carried a blanket for bedding, and an oilskin coat to ward off the wet; a large metal cup with the handle riveted, not soldered, on, so that water could be boiled in it; a little tea and salt, and some biscuits; and a small waterproof bag containing my half dozen personal necessaries — not forgetting a book. The whole formed a small, light pack, very little encumbrance to stout old Manitou. In June, fair weather can generally be counted on in the dry plains country.

    I started in the very earliest morning, when the intense brilliancy of the stars had just begun to pale before the first streak of dawn. By the time I left the river bottom and struck off up the valley of a winding creek, which led through the Badlands, the eastern sky was growing rosy; and soon the buttes and cliffs were lit up by the level rays of the cloudless summer sun. The air was fresh and sweet, and odorous with the sweet scents of the springtime that was but barely passed; the dew lay heavy, in glittering drops, on the leaves and the blades of grass, whose vivid green, at this season, for a short time brightens the desolate and sterile-looking wastes of the lonely western plains. The rosebushes were all in bloom, and their pink blossoms clustered in every point and bend of the stream; and the sweet, sad songs of the hermit thrushes rose from the thickets, while the meadowlarks perched boldly in sight as they uttered their louder and more cheerful music. The roundup had passed by our ranch, and all the cattle with our brands, the Maltese cross and cut dewlap, or the elk horn and triangle, had been turned loose; they had not yet worked away from the river, and I rode by long strings of them, walking in single file off to the hills, or standing in groups to look at me as I passed.

    Leaving the creek I struck off among a region of scoria buttes, the ground rising into rounded hills through whose grassy covering the red volcanic rock showed in places, while boulder-like fragments of it were scattered all through the valleys between. There were a few clumps of bushes here and there, and near one of them were two magpies, who lit on an old buffalo skull, bleached white by sun and snow. Magpies are birds that catch the eye at once from their bold black and white plumage and long tails; and they are very saucy and at the same time very cunning and shy. In spring we do not often see them; but in the late fall and winter they will come close round the huts and outbuildings on the lookout for any thing to eat. If a deer is hung up and they can get at it they will pick it to pieces with their sharp bills; and their carnivorous tastes and their habit of coming round hunters' camps after the game that is left out, call to mind their kinsman, the whiskey jack or moose bird of the northern forests.

After passing the last line of low, rounded scoria buttes, the horse stepped out on the border of the great, seemingly endless stretches of rolling or nearly level prairie, over which I had planned to travel and hunt for the next two or three days. At intervals of ten or a dozen miles this prairie was crossed by dry creeks, with, in places in their beds, pools or springs of water, and alongside a spindling growth of trees and bushes; and my intention was to hunt across these creeks, and camp by some waterhole in one of them at night.

I rode over the land in a general southerly course, bending to the right or left according to the nature of the ground and the likelihood of finding game. Most of the time the horse kept on a steady single-foot, but this was varied by a sharp lope every now and then, to ease the muscles of both steed and rider. The sun was well up, and its beams beat fiercely down on our heads from out of the cloudless sky; for at this season, though the nights and the early morning and late evening are cool and pleasant, the hours around noon are very hot. My glass was slung alongside the saddle, and from every one of the scattered hillocks the country was scanned carefully far and near; and the greatest caution was used in riding up over any divide, to be sure that no game on the opposite side was scared by the sudden appearance of my horse or myself.

Nowhere, not even at sea, does a man feel more lonely than when riding over the far-reaching, seemingly never-ending plains; and, after a man has lived a little while on or near them, their very vastness and loneliness and their melancholy monotony have a strong fascination for him. The landscape seems always the same, and after the traveler has plodded on for miles and miles he gets to feel as if the distance was indeed boundless. As far as the eye can see there is no break; either the prairie stretches out into perfectly level flats, or else there are gentle, rolling slopes, whose crests mark the divides between the drainage systems of the different creeks; and when one of these is ascended, immediately another precisely like it takes its place in the distance, and so roll succeeds roll in a succession as interminable as that of the waves of the ocean. Nowhere else does one seem so far off from all mankind; the plains stretch out in death-like and measureless expanse, and as he journeys over them they will for many miles be lacking in all signs of life. Although he can see so far, yet all objects on the outermost verge of the horizon, even though within the ken of his vision, look unreal and strange; for there is no shade to take away from the bright glare, and at a little distance things seem to shimmer and dance in the hot rays of the sun. The ground is scorched to a dull brown, and against its monotonous expanse any objects stand out with a prominence that makes it difficult to judge of the distance at which they are. A mile off one can see, through the strange shimmering haze, the shadowy white outlines of something which looms vaguely up till it looks as large as the canvas-top of a prairie wagon; but as the horseman comes nearer it shrinks and dwindles and takes clearer form, until at last it changes into the ghastly staring skull of some mighty buffalo, long dead and gone to join the rest of his vanished race.

When the grassy prairies are left and the traveler enters a region of alkali desert and sagebrush, the look of the country becomes even more grim and forbidding. In places the alkali forms a white frost on the ground that glances in the sunlight like the surface of a frozen lake; the dusty little sagebrush, stunted and dried up, sprawls over the parched ground, from which it can hardly extract the small amount of nourishment necessary for even its weazened life; the spiny cactus alone seems to be really in its true home. Yet even in such places antelope will be found, as alert and as abounding with vivacious life as elsewhere. Owing to the magnifying and distorting power of the clear, dry plains air, every object, no matter what its shape or color or apparent distance, needs the closest examination. A magpie sitting on a white skull, or a couple of ravens, will look, a quarter of a mile off, like some curious beast; and time and again a raw hunter will try to stalk a lump of clay or a burnt stick; and after being once or twice disappointed, he is apt to rush to the other extreme, and conclude too hastily that a given object is not an antelope, when it very possibly is.

During the morning I came in sight of several small bands or pairs of antelope. Most of them saw me as soon as or before I saw them, and after watching me with intense curiosity as long as I was in sight and at a distance, made off at once as soon as I went into a hollow or appeared to be approaching too near. Twice, in scanning the country narrowly with the glasses, from behind a sheltering divide, bands of pronghorn were seen that had not discovered me. In each case the horse was at once left to graze, while I started off after the game, nearly a mile distant. For the first half mile I could walk upright or go along half stooping; then, as the distance grew closer, I had to crawl on all fours and keep behind any little broken bank, or take advantage of a small, dry watercourse; and toward the end work my way flat on my face, wriggling like a serpent, using every stunted sagebrush or patch of cactus as a cover, bare-headed under the blazing sun. In each case, after nearly an hour's irksome, thirsty work, the stalk failed. One band simply ran off without a second's warning, alarmed at some awkward movement on my part, and without giving a chance for a shot. In the other instance, while still at very long and uncertain range, I heard the sharp barking alarm-note of one of the pronghorn; the whole band instantly raising their heads and gazing intently at their would-be destroyer. They were a very long way off; but, seeing it was hopeless to try to get nearer, I rested my rifle over a little mound of earth and fired. The dust came up in a puff to one side of the nearest antelope; the whole band took a few jumps and turned again; the second shot struck at their feet, and they went off like so many racehorses, being missed again as they ran. I sat up by a sagebrush thinking they would of course not come back, when to my surprise I saw them wheel round with the precision of a cavalry squadron, all in line and fronting me, the white and brown markings on their heads and throats showing like the facings on soldiers' uniforms; and then back they came charging up till again within long range, when they wheeled their line as if on a pivot and once more made off, this time for good, not heeding an ineffectual fusillade from the Winchester. Antelope often go through a series of regular evolutions, like so many trained horsemen, wheeling, turning, halting, and running as if under command; and their coming back to again run the (as it proved very harmless) gauntlet of my fire was due either to curiosity or to one of those panicky freaks which occasionally seize those ordinarily wary animals, and cause them to run into danger easily avoided by creatures commonly much more readily approached than they are. I had fired half a dozen shots without effect; but while no one ever gets over his feeling of self-indignation at missing an easy shot at close quarters, any one who hunts antelope and is not of a disposition so timid as never to take chances, soon learns that he has to expect to expend a good deal of powder and lead before bagging his game.

By midday we reached a dry creek and followed up its course for a mile or so, till a small spot of green in the side of a bank showed the presence of water, a little pool of which lay underneath. The ground was so rotten that it was with difficulty I could get Manitou down where he could drink; but at last both of us satisfied our thirst, and he was turned loose to graze, with his saddle off, so as to cool his back, and I, after eating a biscuit, lay on my face on the ground — there was no shade of any sort near — and dozed until a couple of hours' rest and feed had put the horse in good trim for the afternoon ride. When it came to crossing over the dry creek on whose bank we had rested, we almost went down in a quicksand, and it was only by frantic struggles and flounderings that we managed to get over.

On account of these quicksands and mud holes, crossing the creeks on the prairie is often very disagreeable work. Even when apparently perfectly dry the bottom may have merely a thin crust of hard mud and underneath a fathomless bed of slime. If the grass appears wet and with here and there a few tussocks of taller blades in it, it is well to avoid it. Often a man may have to go along a creek nearly a mile before he can find a safe crossing, or else run the risk of seeing his horse mired hard and fast. When a horse is once in a mud hole, it will perhaps so exhaust itself by its first desperate and fruitless struggle that it is almost impossible to get it out. Its bridle and saddle have to be taken off; if another horse is along the lariat is drawn from the pommel of the latter's saddle to the neck of the one that is in, and it is hauled out by main force. Otherwise a man may have to work half a day, fixing the horse's legs in the right position and then taking it by the forelock and endeavoring to get it to make a plunge; each plunge bringing it perhaps a few inches nearer the firm ground. Quicksands are even more dangerous than these mud holes, as, if at all deep, a creature that cannot get out immediately is sure to be speedily engulfed. Many parts of the Little Missouri are impassable on account of these quicksands. Always in crossing unknown ground that looks dangerous it is best to feel your way very cautiously along, and, if possible, to find out some cattle trail or even game trail which can be followed.

For some time after leaving the creek nothing was seen; until, on coming over the crest of the next great divide, I came in sight of a band of six or eight pronghorn about a quarter of a mile off to my right hand. There was a slight breeze from the southeast, which blew diagonally across my path towards the antelopes. The latter, after staring at me a minute, as I rode slowly on, suddenly started at full speed to run directly up wind, and therefore in a direction that would cut the line of my course less than half a mile ahead of where I was. Knowing that when antelope begin running in a straight line they are very hard to turn, and seeing that they would have to run a longer distance than my horse would to intercept them, I clapped spurs into Manitou, and the game old fellow, a very fleet runner, stretched himself down to the ground and seemed to go almost as fast as the quarry. As I had expected, the latter, when they saw me running, merely straightened themselves out and went on, possibly even faster than before, without changing the line of their flight, keeping right upwind. Both horse and antelope fairly flew over the ground, their courses being at an angle that would certainly bring them together. Two of the antelope led, by some fifty yards or so, the others, who were all bunched together. Nearer and nearer we came, Manitou, in spite of carrying myself and the pack behind the saddle, gamely holding his own, while the antelope, with outstretched necks, went at an even, regular gait that offered a strong contrast to the springing bounds with which a deer runs. At last the two leading animals crossed the line of my flight ahead of me; when I pulled short up, leaped from Manitou's back, and blazed into the band as they went by not forty yards off, aiming well ahead of a fine buck who was on the side nearest me. An antelope's gait is so even that it offers a good running mark; and as the smoke blew off I saw the buck roll over like a rabbit, with both shoulders broken. I then emptied the Winchester at the rest of the band, breaking one hind leg of a young buck. Hastily cutting the throat of, and opening, the dead buck, I again mounted and started off after the wounded one. But, though only on three legs, it went astonishingly fast, having had a good start; and after following it over a mile, I gave up the pursuit, though I had gained a good deal; for the heat was very great, and I did not deem it well to tire the horse at the beginning of the trip. Returning to the carcass, I cut off the hams and strung them beside the saddle; an antelope is so spare that there is very little more meat on the body.

This trick of running in a straight line is another of the antelope's peculiar characteristics which frequently lead it into danger. Although with so much sharper eyes than a deer, antelope are in many ways far stupider animals, more like sheep, and they especially resemble the latter in their habit of following a leader, and in their foolish obstinacy in keeping to a course they have once adopted. If a horseman starts to head off a deer, the latter will always turn long before he has come within range, but quite often an antelope will merely increase his speed and try to pass ahead of his foe. Almost always, however, one if alone will keep out of gunshot, owing to the speed at which he goes, but if there are several in a band which is well strung out, the leader only cares for his own safety and passes well ahead himself. The others follow like sheep, without turning in the least from the line the first followed, and thus may pass within close range. If the leader bounds into the air, those following will often go through exactly the same motions; and if he turns, the others are very apt to each in succession run up and turn in the same place, unless the whole band are maneuvering together, like a squadron of cavalry under orders, as has already been spoken of.

After securing the buck's hams and head (the latter for the sake of the horns, which were unusually long and fine), I pushed rapidly on without stopping to hunt, to reach some large creek which should contain both wood and water, for even in summer a fire adds greatly to the comfort and coziness of a night camp. When the sun had nearly set we went over a divide and came in sight of a creek fulfilling the required conditions. It wound its way through a valley of rich bottom land, cottonwood trees of no great height or size growing in thick groves along its banks, while its bed contained many deep pools of water, some of it fresh and good. I rode into a great bend, with a grove of trees on its right and containing excellent feed. Manitou was loosed, with the lariat round his neck, to feed where he wished until I went to bed, when he was to be taken to a place where the grass was thick and succulent, and tethered out for the night.

James Naismith on Playing and Coaching Basketball (1891)

Though published by the YMCA in 1941, Canadian-born Dr. James Naismith's belated remembrance of the creation of the game of basketball is here presented not by its chronological publication date but by the time period, the early 1890s, that it documents. Like Walter Camp and Hiram Connibear, Naismith's inclusion in this collection comes by virtue of his role as an athlete (Naismith was a gymnastics, lacrosse, and rugby stand-out at McGill University) and, moreover, as a participant-coach, the man credited with inventing and popularizing basketball from his physical education teaching post at the YMCA International Training School in Springfield, Massachusetts. Unlike Hiram Connibear, whose sport, college crew, gradually declined in prominence, Naismith lived to see his game prosper unbelievably and immediately—Naismith hung up his peach baskets in 1891, and, by 1900, there were already several colleges and universities fielding teams for intercollegiate competition.

Naismith's contributions to the Golden Age of Sport transcended basketball, as he would leave the YMCA to obtain a medical degree and a physical education professorship and chaplaincy at the University of Kansas, where he would coach the university team for ten years. To his credit, Naismith never sought financial compensation for the game he is said to have invented nor quite understood why the game came to be taken so seriously. According to Naismith's Kansas State Historical Society profile, he reportedly once commented to his student and future successor, the legendary Kansas coach Forrest "Phog" Allen, "Basketball is just a game to play. It doesn't need a coach." The historic chapter that follows recounts Naismith's struggles to inculcate exactly that joyful spirit in his young charges at the YMCA. Naismith is credited with many firsts during the Golden Age of Sport, including the first to introduce the helmet to American football and the first to coach a five-man basketball team. He also lived to see his game become an Olympic sport in 1936.

"The Origin of Basketball"

Two weeks had almost passed since I had taken over the troublesome class. The time was almost gone; in a day or two I would have to report to the faculty the success or failure of my attempts. So far they had all been failures, and it seemed to me that I had exhausted my resources. The prospect before me was, to say the least, discouraging. How I hated the thought of going back to the group and admitting that, after all my theories, I, too, had failed to hold the interest of the class. It was worse than losing a game. All the stubbornness of my Scotch ancestry was aroused, all my pride of achievement urged me on; I would not go back and admit that I had failed.

The day before my two weeks ended I met the class. I will always remember that meeting. I had nothing new to try and no idea of what I was going to do. The class period passed with little order, and at the end of the hour the boys left the gym. I can still see that group of fellows filing out the door. As that last pair of grey pants vanished into the locker room, I saw the end of all my ambitions and hopes.

With weary footsteps I mounted the flight of narrow stairs that led to my office directly over the locker room. I slumped down in my chair, my head in my hands and my elbows on the desk. I was a thoroughly disheartened and discouraged young instructor. Below me, I could hear the boys in the locker room having a good time; they were giving expression to the very spirit that I had tried so hard to evoke. I had been a student the year before, and I could picture the group in that locker room. A towel would snap and some fellow would jerk erect and try to locate the guilty individual. Some of it was rough play, but it was all in fun, and each of them entered into it with that spirit. There would be talking and jesting, and I could even imagine the things that the group would be saying about my efforts. I was sure that the fellows did not dislike me, but I was just as sure that they felt that I had given them nothing better than the other instructors.

As I listened to the noise in the room below, my discouragement left me. I looked back over my attempts to see, if possible, the cause of my failures. I passed in review the gymnastic games that I had tried, and I saw that they were impossible. They were really children's games; the object that was to be obtained changed with each play, and no man could be interested in this type of game. It was necessary to have some permanent objective that would keep the minds of the participants active and interested.

As I thought of the other games that I had tried, I realized that the normal individual is strongly influenced by tradition. If he is interested in a game, any attempt to modify that game sets up an antagonism in his mind. I realized that any attempt to change the known games would necessarily result in failure. It was evident that a new principle was necessary; but how to evolve this principle was beyond my ken.

As I sat there at my desk, I began to study games from the philosophical side. I had been taking one game at a time and had failed to find what I was looking for. This time I would take games as a whole and study them.

My first generalization was that all team games used a ball of some kind; therefore, any new game must have a ball. Two kinds of balls were used at that time, one large and the other small. I noted that all games that used a small ball had some intermediate equipment with which to handle it. Cricket and baseball had bats, lacrosse and hockey had sticks, tennis and squash had rackets. In each of these games, the use of the intermediate equipment made the game more difficult to learn. The Americans were at sea with a lacrosse stick, and the Canadians could not use a baseball bat.

The game that we sought would be played by many; therefore, it must be easy to learn. Another objection to a small ball was that it could be easily hidden. It would be difficult for a group to play a game in which the ball was in sight only part of the time.

I then considered a large ball that could be easily handled and which almost anyone could catch and throw with very little practice. I decided that the ball should be large and light, one that could be easily handled and yet could not be concealed. There were two balls of this kind then in use, one the spheroid of rugby and the other the round ball of soccer. It was not until later that I decided which one of these two I would select.

The type of a ball being settled, I turned next to the point of interest of various games. I concluded that the most interesting game at that time was American rugby. I asked myself why this game could not be used as an indoor sport. The answer to this was easy. It was because tackling was necessary in rugby. But why was tackling necessary? Again the answer was easy. It was because the men were allowed to run with the ball, and it was necessary to stop them. With these facts in mind, I sat erect at my desk and said aloud: "If he can't run with the ball, we don't have to tackle; and if we don't have to tackle, the roughness will be eliminated."

I can still recall how I snapped my fingers and shouted, "I've got it!"

This time I felt that I really had a new principle for a game, one that would not violate any tradition. On looking back, it was hard to see why I was so elated. I had as yet nothing but a single idea, but I was sure that the rest would work out correctly.

Starting with the idea that the player in possession of the ball could not run with it, the next step was to see just what he could do with it. There was little choice in this respect. It would be necessary for him to throw it or bat it with his hand. In my mind, I began to play a game and to visualize the movements of the players. Suppose that a player was running, and a teammate threw the ball to him. Realizing that it would be impossible for him to stop immediately, I made this exception: when a man was running and received the ball, he must make an honest effort to stop or else pass the ball immediately. This was the second step of the game.

In my mind I was still sticking to the traditions of the older games, especially football. In that game, the ball could be thrown in any direction except forward. In this new game, however, the player with the ball could not advance, and I saw no reason why he should not be allowed to throw or bat it in any direction. So far, I had a game that played with a large light ball; the players could not run with the ball, but must pass it or bat it with the hands; and the pass could be made in any direction.

As I mentally played the game, I remembered that I had seen two players in a soccer game, both after the ball. One player attempted to head the ball just as the other player kicked at it. The result was a badly gashed head for the first man. I then turned this incident to the new game. I could imagine one player attempting to strike the ball with his fist, and, intentionally or otherwise, coming in contact with another player's face. I then decided that the fist must not be used in striking the ball.

The game now had progressed only to the point where it was "keep away" and my experience with gymnastic games convinced me that it would not hold the interest of the players. The next step was to devise some objective for the players. In all existing games there was some kind of a goal, and I felt that this was essential. I thought of the different games, in the hope that I might be able to use one of their goals. Football had a goal line, over which the ball must be carried, and goalposts, over which the ball might be kicked. Soccer, lacrosse, and hockey had goals into which the ball might be driven. Tennis and badminton had marks on the court inside which the ball must be kept. Thinking of all these, I mentally placed a goal like the one used in lacrosse at each end of the floor.

A lacrosse goal is simply a space six feet high and eight feet wide. The players attempt to throw the ball into this space; the harder the ball is thrown, the more chance to make a goal. I was sure that this play would lead to roughness, and I did not want that. I thought of limiting the sweep of the arms or of having the ball delivered from in front of the person, but I knew that many would resent my limiting the power of the player.

By what line of association it occurred to me I do not know, but I was back in Bennie's Corners, Ontario, playing Duck on the Rock. I could remember distinctly the large rock back of the blacksmith shop, about as high as our knees and as large around as a wash tub. Each of us would get a "duck," a stone about as large as our two doubled fists. About twenty feet from the large rock we would draw a base line, and then in various manners we would choose one of the group to be guard, or "it."

To start the game, the guard placed his duck on the rock, and we behind the base line attempted to knock it off by throwing our ducks. More often than not, when we threw our ducks we missed, and if we went to retrieve them, the guard tagged us; then one of us had to change places with him. If, however, someone knocked the guard's "duck" off the rock, he had to replace it before he could tag anyone.

It came distinctly to my mind that some of the boys threw their ducks as hard as they could; when they missed, the ducks were far from the base. When they went to retrieve them, they had farther to run and had more chance of being tagged. On the other hand, if the duck was tossed in an arc, it did not go so far. If the guard's duck was hit, it fell on the far side of the rock, whereas the one that was thrown bounced nearer the base and was easily caught up before the guard replaced his. When the duck was thrown in an arc, accuracy was more effective than force.

With this game in mind, I thought that if the goal were horizontal instead of vertical, the players would be compelled to throw the ball in an arc; and force, which made for roughness, would be of no value.

A horizontal goal, then, was what I was looking for, and I pictured it in my mind. I would place a box at either end of the floor, and each time the ball entered the box it would count as a goal. There was one thing, however, that I had overlooked. If nine men formed a defense around the goal, it would be impossible for the ball to enter it; but if I placed the goal above the players' heads, this type of defense would be useless. The only chance that the guards would have would be to go out and get the ball before the opponents had an opportunity to throw for goal.

I had a team game with equipment and an objective. My problem now was how to start it. Again I reviewed the games with which I was familiar. I found that the intent of starting any game was to give each side an equal chance to obtain the ball. I thought of water polo, where the teams were lined up at the ends of the pool and at a signal the ball was thrown into the center. There was always a mad scramble to gain possession of the ball, and it took only an instant for me to reject this plan. I could see nine men at each end of the gym, all making a rush for the ball as it was thrown into the center of the floor; and I winced as I thought of the results of that collision.

I then turned to the game of English rugby. When the ball went out of bounds on the sideline, it was taken by the umpire and thrown in between two lines of forward players. This was somewhat like polo, but the players had no chance to run at each other. As I thought of this method of starting the game, I remembered one incident that happened to me. In a game with Queen's College, the ball was thrown between the two lines of players. I took one step and went high in the air. I got the ball all right, but as I came down I landed on a shoulder that was shoved into my midriff. I decided that this method would not do. I did feel, though, that if the roughness could be eliminated, that tossing up the ball between two teams was the fairest way of starting a game. I reasoned that if I picked only one player from each team and threw the ball up between them, there would be little chance for roughness. I realize now how seriously I underestimated the ingenuity of the American boy.

When I had decided how I would start the game, I felt that I would have little trouble. I knew that there would be questions to be met; but I had the fundamental principles of a game, and I was more than willing to try to meet these problems. I continued with my day's work, and it was late in the evening before I again had a chance to think of my new scheme. I believe that I am the first person who ever played basketball; and although I used the bed for a court, I certainly played a hard game that night.

The following morning I went into my office, thinking of the new game. I had not yet decided what ball I should use. Side by side on the floor lay two balls, one a football and the other a soccer ball.

I noticed the lines of the football and realized that it was shaped so that it might be carried in the arms. There was to be no carrying of the ball in this new game, so I walked over, picked up the soccer ball, and started in search of a goal.

As I walked down the hall, I met Mr. Stebbins, the superintendent of buildings. I asked him if he had two boxes about eighteen inches square. Stebbins thought a minute, and then said: "No, I haven't any boxes, but I'll tell you what I do have. I have two old peach baskets down in the store room, if they will do you any good."

I told him to bring them up, and a few minutes later he appeared with the two baskets tucked under his arm. They were round and somewhat larger at the top than at the bottom. I found a hammer and some nails and tacked the baskets to the lower rail of the balcony, one at either end of the gym.

I was almost ready to try the new game, but I felt that I needed a set of rules, in order that the men would have some guide. I went to my office, pulled out a scratch pad, and set to work. The rules were so clear in my mind that in less than an hour I took my copy to Miss Lyons, our stenographer, who typed the following set of thirteen rules.

The ball to be an ordinary *Association* football.

1. The ball may be thrown in any direction with one or both hands.
2. The ball may be batted in any direction with one or both hands (never with the fist).
3. A player cannot run with the ball. The player must throw it from the spot on which he catches it; allowance to be made for a man who catches the ball when running at a good speed.
4. The ball must be held in or between the hands; the arms or body must not be used for holding it.
5. No shouldering, holding, pushing, tripping, or striking, in any way the person of an opponent shall be allowed; the first infringement of this rule by any person shall count as a foul, the second shall disqualify him until the next goal is made, or, if there was evident intent to injure the person, for the whole of the game, no substitute allowed.
6. A foul is striking at the ball with the fist, violation of Rules 3, 4, and such as described in Rule 5.
7. If either side makes three consecutive fouls, it shall count a goal for the opponents. (Consecutive means without the opponents in the meantime making a foul.)
8. A goal shall be made when the ball is thrown or batted from the grounds into the basket and stays there, providing those defending the goal do not touch or disturb the goal. If the ball rests on the edge and the opponent moves the basket, it shall count as a goal.
9. When the ball goes out of bounds, it shall be thrown into the field and played by the person first touching it. In case of a dispute, the umpire shall throw it straight into the field. The thrower-in is allowed five seconds. If he holds it longer it shall go to the opponent. If any side persists in delaying the game, the umpire shall call a foul on them.

10. The umpire shall be judge of the men and shall note the fouls and notify the referee when three consecutive fouls have been made. He shall have power to disqualify men according to Rule 5.
11. The referee shall be judge of the ball and shall decide when the ball is in play, in bounds, to which side it belongs, and shall keep the time. He shall decide when a goal has been made, and keep account of the goals, with any other duties that are usually performed by a referee.
12. The time shall be two fifteen-minute halves, with five minutes rest between.
13. The side making the most goals in that time shall be declared the winners. In case of a draw, the game may, by agreement of the captains, be continued until another goal is made.

When Miss Lyons finished typing the rules, it was almost class time, and I was anxious to get down to the gym. I took the rules and made my way down the stairs. Just inside the door there was a bulletin board for notices. With thumb tacks I fastened the rules to this board and then walked across the gym. I was sure in my own mind that the game was good, but it needed a real test. I felt that its success or failure depended largely on the way that the class received it.

The first member of the class to arrive was Frank Mahan. He was a southerner from North Carolina, had played tackle on the football team, and was the ringleader of the group. He saw me standing with a ball in my hand and perhaps surmised that another experiment was to be tried. He looked up at the basket on one end of the gallery, and then his eyes turned to me. He gazed at me for an instant, and then looked toward the other end of the gym. Perhaps I was nervous, because his exclamation sounded like a death knell as he said, "Huh! Another new game!"

When the class arrived, I called the roll and told them that I had another game, which I felt sure would be good. I promised them that if this was a failure, I would not try any more experiments. I then read the rules from the bulletin board and proceeded to organize the game.

There were eighteen men in the class; I selected two captains and had them choose sides. When the teams were chosen, I placed the men on the floor. There were three forwards, three centers, and three backs on each team. I chose two of the center men to jump, then threw the ball between them. It was the start of the first basketball game and the finish of the trouble with that class.

As was to be expected, they made a great many fouls at first; and as a foul was penalized by putting the offender on the sidelines until the next goal was made, sometimes half of a team would be in the penalty area. It was simply a case of no one knowing just what to do. There was no teamwork, but each man did his best. The forwards tried to make goals and the backs tried to keep the opponents from making them. The team was large, and the floor was small. Any man on the field was close enough to the basket to throw for goal, and most of them were anxious to score. We tried, however, to develop team work by having the guards pass the ball to the forwards.

The game was a success from the time that the first ball was tossed up. The players were interested and seemed to enjoy the game. Word soon got around that they were having fun in Naismith's gym class, and only a few days after the first game we began to have a gallery. The class met at eleven-thirty in the morning, and the game was in full swing by twelve o'clock. Some teachers from the Buckingham Grade School were passing the gym one day, and hearing the noise, decided to investigate. They could enter the gallery through a door that led to the street. Each day after that, they stopped to watch the game, sometimes becoming so interested that they would not have time to get their lunch. These teachers came to me one day and asked me why girls could not play that game. I told them that I saw no reason why they should not, and this group organized the first girls' basketball team.

It is little wonder that the crowd enjoyed the game. If we could see it today as it was played then, we would laugh too. The players were all mature men; most of them had mustaches, and one or two had full beards. Their pants were long, and their shirts had short sleeves. Sometimes when a player received the ball, he would poise with it over his head to make sure that he would make the goal. About the time that he was ready to throw, someone would reach up from behind and take the ball out of his hands. This occurred frequently and was a never-ending source of amusement. No matter how often a player lost the ball in this manner, he would always look around with a surprised expression that would plainly say, "Who did that?" His embarrassment only added to the laughter of the crowd. It was shortly after the first game that Frank Mahan came to me before class hour and said, "You remember the rules that were put on the bulletin board?"

"Yes, I do," I answered.

"They disappeared," he said.

"I know it," I replied. "Well, I took them." Frank said. "I knew that this game would be a success, and I took them as a souvenir, but I think now that you should have them."

Mahan told me that the rules were in his trunk and that he would bring them down later. That afternoon he entered my office and handed me the two typewritten sheets. I still have them, and they are one of my prized possessions. At the Christmas vacation a number of the students went home and some of them started the game in their local YMCA's. There were no printed rules at that time, and each student played the game as he remembered it. It was not until January, 1892, that the school paper, called the *Triangle*, first printed the rules under the heading, "A New Game."

One day after the students returned from their vacation, the same Frank Mahan came to me and asked me what I was going to call the game. I told him that I had not thought of the matter but was interested only in getting it started. Frank insisted that it must have a name and suggested the name of Naismith ball. I laughed and told him that I thought that name would kill any game. Frank then said, "Why not call it basketball?"

"We have a basket and a ball, and it seems to me that would be a good name for it," I replied.

It was in this way that basketball was named. When the first game had ended, I felt that I could now go to Doctor Gulick and tell him that I had accomplished the two seemingly impossible tasks that he had assigned to me: namely, to interest the class in physical exercise and to invent a new game.

Winifred Louisa Leale on Target Shooting (1894)

>*Winifred Louisa Leale's unexpected success — she had only picked up her first rifle four years earlier — in an open competition in Bisley, England, outside London, in 1891, won her unimagined press, an aftermath she describes in the short excerpt below in addition to giving a few hands-on pointers on handling a Martini-Henry rifle. Culled from Violet Greville's 1894 anthology* Ladies in the Field: Sketches in Sport, *the article suggests the importance of Bisley, which remains the national center for rifle shooting in the United Kingdom and yearly hosts sport shooting competitions. The U.K's National Rifle Association is also headquartered there.*

"Rifle Shooting"

At the Bisley Meeting of 1891, I took part in some of the competitions open to all comers. The measure of success which I achieved has gained a publicity for which I was scarcely prepared, and has brought around me a group of correspondents who have plied me with questions as to my experience in rifle shooting, and the rise and progress of my devotion to an accomplishment so unusual for ladies, and even deemed by many to be somewhat out of their reach.

I purpose, therefore, to put a few notes together, in which I shall endeavor to answer some of the questions proposed to me, and to relate such passages of my experience as may serve to encourage those of my own sex who may have some ambition in this direction.

It was a little more than four years ago when I first handled a Martini-Henry rifle. I was looking on at the shooting one afternoon at the Guernsey Wimbledon, and wondered if it was a very difficult thing to hit the target, which appeared to me to be such a mere speck when seen from so great a distance. I had, some time before this, fired a few shots with a piece at an impromptu target, but rifle shooting looked to me far more real and interesting. At length I succeeded in persuading my father to allow me to try my hand at a shot with a rifle.

I remember that there was some discussion, at that time, about the recoil, but as I was so very ignorant of the management and powers of the rifle, I did not give this really serious question the necessary attention. I believe that had I heard, at this early stage, as much about recoil as I have since, I should probably have been afraid to shoot with a Martini.

A certain militiaman, who is now one of our best shots, related to me a curious incident which happened to him when be first fired with a service rifle. He was shooting in the prone position, and, after pulling the trigger, he heard a great noise, and immediately there was a good deal of smoke about; but the rifle had disappeared. On looking round, however, he saw his rifle behind him! He had been resting the under part of the butt lightly on his shoulders, and holding the rifle loosely; thus the force of the recoil had actually driven it past him over his shoulder.

I have heard of many other cases of the recoil becoming dangerous; but I believe it is from fear of being "kicked" that recruits fail to hold their rifles properly while pulling the trigger.

In my own case, certainly, "ignorance was bliss"; for, in firing my first shot, I was enabled to give my whole attention to keeping the rifle steady, and placing it firmly against my shoulder for that purpose alone undisturbed by any fear of recoil. And I believe that this absence of fear is the chief reason why I have been able to use a Martini-Henry rifle without suffering from the recoil.

Thinking from the experience of my first shot that shooting was easy, I was anxious to go on with it. Many experienced shots volunteered information which was very helpful; but I soon discovered that I was wrong in thinking that rifle shooting was merely a matter of seeing the bull's eye over the sights. The first difficulty was that of keeping the rifle steady. I had to learn exactly how to hold it and for this I had to study position.

I had fired my first shot in the kneeling position. I did not then know of any other, except the standing and lying down. The former I could not manage, as the rifle was too heavy to hold up without any support for the arms; and the lying down position seemed to me, then, to require a great deal of practice. This conjecture has been well justified by my subsequent experience. I have never since fired from the kneeling position, as a much better one was recommended to me, namely, the sitting position. In this way I can have a rest for both arms, which is an advantage over the other method in which it is only possible to rest one.

Having chosen a position, I found that it needed a great deal of studying. It was then that I discovered another great difficulty, i.e., that of pulling the trigger without disturbing the aim. I received some advice on this subject which at first sounded rather curious. I was told to squeeze the trigger "like I would a lemon" and to let it go off without my knowing. This accomplishment requires a great deal of practice, but is well worth the trouble of learning; for I am confident that it is the great secret of good shooting.

During my first few months of shooting, I only used to think of taking a correct aim at the bull's eye, and trying to keep still while pulling the trigger. I was so absorbed in this effort, that it did not occur to me for some time that there was much more than this dexterity to be gained in order to be sure of making a good score. There remained the great question of finding the bull's eye.

This, of course, involves the scientific part of rifle shooting ; and although, at first, I was alarmed at the difficulty of the subject, I soon saw that the shooting would become tame and monotonous without it.

The range where I was in the habit of practicing (and still do practice) is near the sea. The targets have the sea for a background, and, as is often the case near the sea, we have a great deal of wind. It was quite easy to understand that the wind would affect the course of the bullet; but it did not turn out to be so easy as it appeared, to calculate in feet and inches how much allowance should be made for this source of disturbance. Fortunately "young shots" are not expected to be able to find out this for themselves by the long and painful discipline of repeated failure; and it is always easy for them to obtain advice from persons on the range who have had more experience than themselves. I was very fortunate in that way myself and feel very grateful for the good instruction I have received from several "crack shots."

Kate Martelli on Hunting the Tiger (1894)

Kate Martelli, wife to Colonel Martelli who was then serving as a colonial superintendent in central India, strives for journalistic reportage in this fascinating first-person sport narrative. Careful not to exaggerate her story or upstage her husband, Martelli's story is rich in subtext vis à vis British imperialism, Victorian gender norms, and then-prevailing attitudes about wildlife. Reminiscent in many ways of George Orwell's famous short story "Shooting an Elephant," Martelli's piece, culled from Violet Greville's 1894 anthology Ladies in the Field: Sketches in Sport, *is notable for its sober, clear-eyed, unapologetic witness.*

"Tigers I Have Shot"

My personal experiences of tiger shooting in India have been neither on a large scale nor of a very heroic and exciting nature; yet, such as they are, I gladly place them upon record for the sake of those who may not have had the good fortune to see sport of this particular kind. Tiger shooting, however, has been so well and so often described that I cannot hope to be able to tell anything of a novel character about it.

It has been my good fortune to "assist" (in the French sense of the word) at the death of five tigers. And here I should premise that, according to the laws of Indian sport, a tiger is considered the trophy of the gun that first hits it, whether that shot prove fatal or not. As will be seen presently, I succeeded in killing the third of the five, but it was my husband's tiger and not mine, as my first shot missed it. I did not *kill* the first and second of the five, but they were my tigers because I was the first to hit them. In the case of the fourth tiger I was the first to hit, and with a second shot I killed it ; but the tiger was mine by virtue of the first shot, not the second. This is a not unfair rule, because the first shot often proves fatal, even though for a time the tiger manages to get away, and if some rule of the kind were not in existence, and the tiger were supposed to belong to the gun that appeared to administer the *coup de grâce*, there would be a great deal of indiscriminate firing, which would result, to say the least of it, in the skin being hopelessly ruined.

But to come to my story. In January 1887, my husband, Colonel Martelli, who was at the time Political Agent and Superintendent of the Estates of Rewa, Central India (the Maharajah being a minor), was making his annual tour, and we were in camp at Govindghur, about fourteen miles from the capital. There were with us my sister, the agency surgeon and the usual tribe of camp followers.

After we had been in camp about a week, a shikari brought us news that there was unquestionably a tiger not many miles away. To discover more exactly where he was, buffaloes were tied as bait to trees in four or five places, at a radius of three or four miles from the camp, and we waited in much excitement for further intelligence. As apparel of a very noticeable or attractive character is obviously unsuited to a tiger hunt, I gave my native tailor overnight some plain cotton material, and he presented it to me in the morning, dyed green and made up into a serviceable dress. He had also covered my Terai sunhat with the same material. Early in the morning word came into camp that we were to be on the alert, and, about 10:00 A.M., news reached us that the tiger had been seen.

We started off immediately, my husband and I on one elephant, and the doctor and my sister on another. Seated behind us in the howdah was a shikari, carrying our guns. My weapon was a 450 double express rifle, by Alex Henry.

We had had Chota Hazrie, so took a lunch-breakfast with us. Passing on our way what we thought would be a charming spot for our *déjeuner*, we left our servant Francis there with our hamper. Imagine our disgust when, upon reaching this spot, hungry and expectant, on our return, we found that Francis had disappeared, and with him all traces of the hoped-for meal. It turned out afterwards that some bears had come unexpectedly upon the scene, and Francis had, not altogether unnaturally, sought refuge in flight.

Ignorant of the fate of our breakfast, however, we pushed on, and about two miles from camp met the head shikari — Mothi Singh by name. Acting under his instructions, we dismounted and followed him through the jungle. We pushed along what professed to be a path, but of which all I can say in its favor is that it was slightly better than the jungle of grass and underwood through which it passed, more than once indeed boughs and branches had to be cut down to make it possible for my sister and myself to get along.

We at length reached a rock, fifteen or twenty feet in height, on the summit of which Mothi Singh placed us, and past which the tiger would be driven. I was to have first shot. The beaters, three hundred or four hundred in number, now began their work, shouting, beating drums and tom-toms, blowing bugles, firing blank cartridges, and steadily pressing forward in our direction. We, of course, maintained the most profound silence, and watched with the deepest interest for the appearance of the tiger. As we waited, all sorts of creatures, scared by the beaters, passed us — pag and deer, peafowl and jungle fowl, the majestic sambhur, and the pretty nilghai, not to mention foxes and jackals, went by within shot, but for today, at any rate, they were safe. At last came the tiger. He advanced like an enormous cat, now crouching upon the ground, now crawling forward, now turning round to try and discover the meaning of the unwanted noise behind him. When he was about eighty yards from us, I fired and hit him on the shoulder; then the others fired, and the tiger bolted. At this moment Hera Sahib, the commander-in-chief of the Rewa army, and who had been directing "the beat," came up on an elephant, and, as he had brought with him a spare elephant, my husband mounted the latter, and they went off together in search of the tiger, leaving us upon the rock.

Two hours later they came upon the wounded tiger hiding in the jungle. The moment he saw that he was discovered, he charged Hera Sahib's elephant, and the latter, being a young animal, bolted. The tiger then turned and charged the elephant my husband was riding, which stood his ground. The tiger, charged underneath the elephant, but fortunately my husband got a snap-shot at him and rolled him over. He crept into the jungle again, however, but was now past serious resistance, and although he made a brave attempt to reach his enemies, he was easily dispatched. He measured over nine feet in length.

My husband's tour over, we returned to our headquarters at Rewa, and a very few days later, in the dusk of the evening, news came that another tiger had been seen in the same neighborhood as that in which we shot the first. My husband and I started off at three the next morning in a dog-cart; our horse was only half broken in, and I was driving. About eleven and a half miles from Govindghar our steed deposited us in a ditch, and we were compelled to walk the rest of the way there. At Govindghar elephants were in waiting for us, and we made our way in much the same fashion as on the previous occasion to the rock of which I have already told. The beat, too, was precisely similar to the former one. Presently the tiger appeared. I was so struck by his magnificent appearance, that, although I was to have first shot, I waited so long that eventually my husband and I fired together. The tiger facing us, I fired again, and then, in his rage, he charged straight at the rock on which we were standing. As he came on I fired a third time, and hit him between the shoulders. He disappeared somewhere at the base of the rock, and, although he was out of sight; we could hear him growling with pain. We did not dare, of course, to come down from our rock, as we had no idea where he was, or to what extent he was crippled, but, after waiting about half-an-hour Hera Sahib came up on an elephant and killed him. It turned out that the tiger had crept under another rock at the base of that on which we were standing, and was too badly wounded to come out and face his foes. This tiger was a much handsomer, and a larger one than the first.

Not long after the above, my husband was appointed Political Agent, Eastern States, Rajputana, which consists of Bhurtpore, Dholepore, and Karowlie. Each state has its own Rajah. I did no more tiger shooting until the early part of the year 1891.

In February then we went to Karowlie, and on our arrival there we were met by the Maharajah, who at once informed us that news had just arrived that a tiger was in the neighborhood, and courteously asked us to accompany him in pursuit of it. We gladly accepted this invitation, and were told to hold ourselves in readiness, as a gun would be fired from the palace as soon as definite information arrived, and it would then be necessary to start at once.

The gun was fired at about noon and off we went, the Maharajah and his retinue, and our two selves. We were conducted through very thick jungle to the Maharajah's shooting-box, about nine miles distant. We were able to ride only a portion of the way, part of the remainder I was carried in a *Tonjon* (sedan chair), and for the rest of the journey I had to walk and struggle through the dense jungle as best I could. The box we found to consist of a small stone tower, built on the edge of a ravine. We were posted upon the top of the tower, and the tiger was to be driven up the ravine and within shot of our rifles.

The Maharajah is a very keen sportsman and a capital shot, but with great politeness he insisted upon my firing first. Alas, when the moment arrived — and the tiger — the jungle was so thick that I could hardly see the animal, and, I regret to say, I missed him altogether. My husband fired and wounded the tiger severely; I then fired again and killed him.

News was brought to us not to leave our post as there was another tiger in the jungle. The Maharajah had been much put out at my missing my first shot and so losing the tiger, but insisted courteously on my having an opportunity of retrieving my disaster; of course I was only too glad to avail myself of his kindness.

A few minutes later the second tiger appeared, and, getting a better view of him than of his predecessor, I succeeded in hitting him in the chest. The Maharajah then fired and put a second bullet into him; I fired and gave him his *coup de grâce*.

Within a week news was brought to Karowlie that another tiger had made his appearance, this time about ten miles away, and in quite another direction. The whole country in this neighborhood was cut up by ravines, and when we arrived at the place indicated to us, we found that there was no rock which we could turn into a citadel, no handy tree from whose branches we might fire upon the foe, and of course no shooting-box; and, as in addition, it was quite impossible to bring the elephants along, we had to take our stand on foot and hope for the best. Should the wounded tiger charge us, we should have to make sure of stopping him before he could reach us. With us, on this occasion, were three young officers, who had never been present at a tiger hunt, and who probably had never seen a tiger out of the Zoological Gardens. Accordingly, they were allowed to draw for choice of places and for first shot. They naturally selected the coign of vantage, and between them slew the tiger. I did not even see him till he was dead. They went off immediately, in a great state of elation ; but the Maharajah told me that there was a panther in the jungle. Presently the animal came in sight with a tremendous rush, and I fired, wounding him severely; but although we traced him for some miles we saw no more of him and he got away.

This is all I have to tell. If from the description I have given, anyone should be inclined to say that the tiger does not appear to have much chance of escape, the answer is that it is not intended that he should have any. Tigers are shot in India, not as game is in England for hunting, to give amusement to men, horses and dogs, not as in pheasant or partridge shooting, with a remote reference to the demands of the table, but to save the lives of the natives and their cattle. If you don't kill the tiger, he will kill you. But although the odds are on the shikari and against the tiger, whether you fire from the back of an elephant, from the top of a rock, or in the branch of a tree, there is always room, unfortunately, for a misadventure, and consequently tiger shooting will always be a useful school for endurance, judgment and self-reliance.

Frances Elizabeth Willard on Bicycling (1895)

Overlooked as a pioneering work of participatory sportswriting, Frances Elizabeth Willard's inimitable A Wheel Within a Wheel *remains a fascinating and historically revealing read. Willard, dean of women at the Woman's College of Northwestern in Evanston, Illinois, president of the Women's Christian Temperance Union (WCTU), and a prolific author, joins the turn-of-the-century bicycling craze in the reading that follows. Willard's participation stands out from other accounts written by bike-enthused males, as she takes three months from a busy life to learn to ride a bike she personifies as "Gladys," that "Harbinger of Health and Happiness," as she puts it in her dedication. To her then-incredulous readers, Willard explains, "I did it from pure natural love of adventure—a love long hampered and impeded, like a brook that runs underground, but in this enterprise bubbling up again." The medical benefits of the bicycle, documented several years after* A Wheel Within a Wheel *in Dr. Neesen's Book on Wheeling: Hints & Advice to Men and Women from the Physician's Standpoint are also alluded to in Benjamin Ward Richardson's introduction to* A Wheel Within a Wheel, *wherein he writes of Willard: "The truths about cycling are well told from one who knows practically what she is about; the pains she has exhibited in learning to ride with pleasure, safety, and usefulness, are extremely interesting."*

"The Process" and "Conclusion"

Courtiers wittily say that horseback riding is the only thing in which a prince is apt to excel, for the reason that the horse never flatters and would as soon throw him as if he were a groom. Therefore it is only by actually mastering the art of riding that a prince can hold his place with the noblest of the four-footed animals.

Happily there is now another locomotive contrivance which is no flatterer, and which peasant and prince must master, if they do this at all, by the democratic route of honest hard work. Well will it be for rulers when the tough old Yorkshire proverb applies to them as strictly as to the lowest of their subjects: "It's dogged as does it." We all know the old saying, "Fire is a good servant, but a bad master." This is equally true of the bicycle: if you give it an inch — nay, a hair — it will take an ell — nay, an evolution — and you a contusion, or, like enough, a perforated knee-cap.

Not a single friend encouraged me to learn the bicycle except an active-minded young schoolteacher, Miss Luther, of my hometown, Evanston, who came several times with her wheel and gave me lessons. I also took a few lessons in a stuffy, semi-subterranean gallery in Chicago. But at fifty-three I was at more disadvantage than most people, for not only had I the impedimenta that result from the unnatural style of dress, but I also suffered from the sedentary habits of a lifetime. And then that small world (which is our real one) of those who loved me best, and who considered themselves largely responsible for my everyday methods of life, did not encourage me, but in their affectionate solicitude — and with abundant reason — thought I should "break my bones" and "spoil my future." It must be said, however, to their everlasting praise, that they opposed no objection when they say that my will was firmly set to do this thing; on the contrary, they put me in the way of carrying out my purpose, and lent to my laborious lessons the light of their countenances reconciled. Actions speak so much louder than words that I here set before you what may be called a feminine bicycler's first position — at least it was mine.

Given a safety-bicycle — pneumatic tires and all the rest of it which renders the pneumatic safety the only safe Bucephalus — the gearing carefully wired in so that we shall not be entangled. "Woe is me!" was my first exclamation, naturally enough interpreted by my outriders "Whoa is me," and they "whoaed" — indeed, we did little but "check up."

(Just here let me interpolate: Learn on a low machine, but "fly high" when once you have mastered it, as you have much more power over the wheels and can get up better speed with a less expenditure of force when you are above the instrument than when you are at the back of it. And remember this is as true of the world as of the wheel.)

The order of evolution was something like this: First, three young Englishmen, all strong-armed and accomplished bicyclers, held the machine in place while I climbed timidly into the saddle. Second, two well disposed young women put in all the power they had, until they grew red in the face, offsetting each other's pressure on the crossbar and thus maintaining the equipoise to which I was unequal. Third, one walked beside me, steadying the ark as best she could by holding the center of the deadly crossbar, to let go whose handles meant chaos and collapse. After this I was able to hold my own if I had the more support of my kind trainers, and it passed into a proverb among them, the short emphatic word of command I gave them at every few turns of the wheel: "Let go, but stand by." Still later everything was learned — how to sit, how to pedal, how to turn, how to dismount; but alas! how to vault into the saddle I found not; that was the coveted power that lingered long and would not yield itself.

That which caused the many failures I had in learning the bicycle had caused me failures in life; namely, a certain fearful looking for of judgment; a too vivid realization of the uncertainty of everything about me; an underlying doubt — at once, however (and this is all that saved me), matched and overcome by the determination not to give in to it.

The best gains that we make come to us after an interval of rest which follows strenuous endeavor. Having, as I hoped, mastered the rudiments of bicycling, I went away to Germany and for a fortnight did not even see the winsome wheel. Returning, I had the horse brought round, and mounted with no little trepidation, being assisted by one of my faithful guides; but behold! I found that in advancing, turning, and descending I was much more at home than when I had last exercised that new intelligence in the muscles which had been the result of repetitions resolutely attempted and practiced long.

Another thing I found is that we carry in the mind a picture of the road; and if it is humpy by reason of pebbles, even if we steer clear of them, we can by no means skim along as happily as when its smoothness facilitates the pleasing impression on the retina; indeed, the whole science and practice of the bicycle is "in your eye" and in your will; the rest is mere manipulation.

As I have said, in many curious particulars the bicycle is like the world. When it had thrown me painfully once (which was the extent of my downfalls during the entire process of learning, and did not prevent me from resuming my place on the back of the treacherous creature a few minutes afterward), and more especially when it threw one of my dearest friends, hurting her knee so that it was painful for a month, then for a time Gladys had gladsome ways for me no longer, but seemed the embodiment of misfortune and dread. Even so the world has often seemed in hours of darkness and despondency; its iron mechanism, its pitiless grind, its swift, silent, on-rolling gait have oppressed to pathos, if not melancholy. Good health and plenty of oxygenated air have promptly restored the equilibrium. But how many a fine spirit, to finest issues touched, has been worn and shredded by the world's mill until in desperation it flung itself away. We can easily carp at those who quit the crowded racecourse without so much as saying "By your leave"; but "let him that thinketh he standeth take heed lest he fall." We owe it to nature, to nurture, to our environments, and, most of all, to our faith in God, that we, too, do not cry, like so many gentle hearts less brave and sturdy, "Anywhere, anywhere, out of the world."

Gradually, item by item, I learned the location of every screw and spring, spoke and tire, and every beam and bearing that went to make up Gladys. This was not the lesson of a day, but of many days and weeks, and it had to be learned before we could get on well together. To my mind the infelicities of which we can see so much in life grow out of lack of time and patience thus to study and adjust the natures that have agreed in the sight of God and man to stand by one another to the last. They will not take the pains, they have not enough specific gravity, to balance themselves in their new environment. Indeed, I found a whole philosophy of life in the wooing and the winning of my bicycle.

Just as a strong and skillful swimmer takes the waves, so the bicycler must learn to take such waves of mental impression as the passing of a gigantic hay-wagon, the sudden obtrusion of black cattle with wide-branching horns, the rattling pace of high-stepping steeds, or even the swift transit of a railway-train. At first she will be upset by the apparition of the smallest poodle, and not until she has attained a wide experience will she hold herself steady in presence of the critical eyes of a coach-and-four. But all this is a part of that equilibrium of thought and action by which we conquer the universe in conquering ourselves.

I finally concluded that all failure was from a wobbling will rather than a wobbling wheel. I felt that indeed the will is the wheel of the mind — its perpetual motion having been learned when the morning stars sang together. When the wheel of the mind went well then the rubber wheel hummed merrily; but specters of the mind there are as well as of the wheel. In the aggregate of perception concerning which we have reflected and from which we have deduced our generalizations upon the world without, within, above, there are so many ghastly and fantastical images that they must obtrude themselves at certain intervals, like filmy bits of glass in the turn of the kaleidoscope. Probably every accident of which I had heard or read in my half-century tinged the uncertainty that by the correlation of forces passed over into the tremor that I felt when we began to round the terminus bend of the broad priory walk. And who shall say by what inherited energy the mind forced itself at once from the contemplation of disaster and thrust into the very movement of the foot on the pedal a concept of vigor, safety, and success? I began to feel that myself plus the bicycle equaled myself plus the world, upon whose spinning wheel we must all learn to ride, or fall into the sluiceways of oblivions and despair.

In Conclusion

If I am asked to explain why I learned the bicycle I should say I did it as an act of grace, if not actual religion.* The cardinal doctrine laid down by my physician was, "Live out of doors and take congenial exercise;" but from the day when, at sixteen years of age, I was enwrapped in the long skirts that impeded every footstep, I have detested walking and felt with certain noble disdain that the conventions of life had cut me off from what in the freedom of my prairie home had been one of life's sweetest joys. Driving is not real exercise; it does not renovate the river of blood that flows so sluggishly in the veins of those who from any cause have lost the natural adjustment of brain to brawn. Horseback riding, which does promise vigorous exercise, is expensive. The bicycle meets all the conditions and will ere long come within the reach of all. Therefore, in obedience to the laws of health, I learned to ride. I also wanted to help women to a wider world, for I hold that the more interests women and men can have in common, in thought, word, and deed, the happier will it be for the home. Besides, there was a special value to women in the conquest of the bicycle by a woman in her fifty-third year, and one who had so many comrades in the white-ribbon army that her action would be widely influential. Then there were three minor reasons:

I did it from pure natural love of adventure — a love long hampered and impeded, like a brook that runs underground, but in this enterprise bubbling up again with somewhat of its pristine freshness and taking its merry course as of old.

Second, from a love of acquiring this new implement of power and literally putting it underfoot.

Last, but not least, because a good many people thought I could not do it at my age. It is needless to say that a bicycling costume was a prerequisite. This consisted of a skirt and blouse of tweed, with belt, rolling collar, and loose cravat, the skirt three inches from the ground; a round straw hat, and walking shoes with gaiters. It was a simple, modest suit, to which no person of common sense could take exception.

As nearly as I can make out, reducing the problem to actual figures, it took me about three months, with an average of fifteen minutes' practice daily, to learn, first, to pedal; second, to turn; third, to dismount; and fourth, to mount independently this most mysterious animal. January 20th will always be a red-letter bicycle day, because although I had already mounted several times with no hand on the rudder, some good friend had always stood by to

---

*The running-in of a separate, complete, noncontiguous section, "In Conclusion," is here indicated by the insertion of a subhead of the same name preceding the run–in material. The sentence here noted represents the first sentence of the run–in section.

lend moral support; but summoning all my force, and most forcible of all, what Sir Benjamin Ward Richardson declares to be the two essential elements — decision and precision — I mounted and started off alone. From that hour the spell was broken; Gladys was no more a mystery: I had learned all her kinks, had put a bridle in her teeth, and touched her smartly with the whip of victory. Consider ye who are of a considerable chronology: in about thirteen hundred minutes, or, to put it more mildly, in twenty-two hours, or, to put it most mildly of all, in less than a single day as the almanac reckons time — but practically in two days of actual practice — amid the delightful surroundings of the great outdoors, and inspired by the birdsongs, the color and fragrance of an English posy garden, in the company of devoted and pleasant comrades, I had made myself master of the most remarkable, ingenious, and inspiring motor ever yet devised upon this planet.

Moral: Go thou and do likewise!

―――― ⌘ ――――

Joshua Slocum on Sailing Alone Around the World (1899)

The victim of an ill-fated expedition and a presumed disappearance at sea, Joshua Slocum's story reminds of Amelia Earhart's, though far less frequently told. A Canadian-American, Slocum attained his U.S. citizenship in the Oregon Territory in 1865, where he had established a reputation as a salmon fisherman. A sports and travel writer, Slocum served as an occasional correspondent for the San Francisco Bee *while hauling freight back and forth between San Francisco and Hawaii. Slocum's practice of book-length participatory journalism began with his 1894 volume* Voyage of the Liberdade, *in which he describes how he recovered from a South American shipwreck by building his own makeshift boat and sailing it back to the States. In 1895 he set sail from Boston, alone, in a voyage that would make him the first man to solo sail around the world and which he recounts in* Sailing Alone Around the World. *The hand-rebuilt craft that took Slocum across the globe, the* Spray, *would later disappear along with its captain in a separate expedition to the Orinoco River in 1909.*

FROM *SAILING ALONE AROUND THE WORLD* "CHAPTER I" AND "CHAPTER III"

I spent a season in my new craft fishing on the coast, only to find that I had not the cunning properly to bait a hook. But at last the time arrived to weigh anchor and get to sea in earnest. I had resolved on a voyage around the world, and as the wind on the morning of April 24, 1895, was fair, at noon I weighed anchor, set sail, and filled away from Boston, where the *Spray* had been moored snugly all winter. The twelve-o'clock whistles were blowing just as the sloop shot ahead under full sail. A short board was made up the harbor on the port tack, then coming about she stood seaward, with her boom well off to port, and swung past the ferries with lively heels. A photographer on the outer pier at East Boston got a picture of her as she swept by, her flag at the peak throwing its folds clear. A thrilling pulse beat high in me. My step was light on deck in the crisp air. I felt that there could be no turning back, and that I was engaging in an adventure the meaning of which I thoroughly understood. I had taken little advice from any one, for I had a right to my own opinions in matters pertaining to the sea. That the best of sailors might do worse than even I alone was borne in upon me not a league from Boston docks, where a great steamship, fully manned, officered, and piloted, lay stranded and broken. This was the *Venetian*. She was broken completely in two over a ledge. So in the first hour of my lone voyage I had proof that the *Spray* could at least do better than this full-handed steamship, for I was already farther on my voyage than she. "Take warning, *Spray*, and have a care," I uttered aloud to my bark, passing fairylike silently down the bay.

The wind freshened, and the *Spray* rounded Deer Island light at the rate of seven knots.

Passing it, she squared away direct for Gloucester to procure there some fishermen's stores. Waves dancing joyously across Massachusetts Bay met her coming out of the harbor to dash them into myriads of sparkling gems that hung about her at every surge. The day was perfect, the sunlight clear and strong. Every particle of water thrown into the air became a gem, and the *Spray*, bounding ahead, snatched necklace after necklace from the sea, and as often threw them away. We have all seen miniature rainbows about a ship's prow, but the *Spray* flung out a bow of her own that day, such as I had never seen before. Her good angel had embarked on the voyage; I so read it in the sea.

Goodbye to the American Coast

I now stowed all my goods securely, for the boisterous Atlantic was before me, and I sent the topmast down, knowing that the *Spray* would be the wholesomer with it on deck.* Then I gave the lanyards a pull and hitched

---

*The running-in of a portion of a separate, noncontiguous chapter, "Chapter Three," is here indicated by the insertion of a subhead suggested by the first descriptive phrase listed by the author (cont.)

them afresh, and saw that the gammon was secure, also that the boat was lashed, for even in summer one may meet with bad weather in the crossing.

In fact, many weeks of bad weather had prevailed. On July 1, however, after a rude gale, the wind came out nor'west and clear, propitious for a good run. On the following day, the head sea having gone down, I sailed from Yarmouth, and let go my last hold on America. The log of my first day on the Atlantic in the *Spray* reads briefly: "9:30 A.M. sailed from Yarmouth. 4:30 P.M. passed Cape Sable; distance, three cables from the land. The sloop making eight knots. Fresh breeze N.W." Before the sun went down I was taking my supper of strawberries and tea in smooth water under the lee of the east coast land, along which the *Spray* was now leisurely skirting.

At noon on July 3 Ironbound Island was abeam. The *Spray* was again at her best. A large schooner came out of Liverpool, Nova Scotia, this morning, steering eastward. The *Spray* put her hull down astern in five hours. At 6:45 P.M. I was in close under Chebucto Head light, near Halifax harbor. I set my flag and squared away, taking my departure from George's Island before dark to sail east of Sable Island. There are many beacon lights along the coast. Sambro, the Rock of Lamentations, carries a noble light, which, however, the liner *Atlantic*, on the night of her terrible disaster, did not see. I watched light after light sink astern as I sailed into the unbounded sea, till Sambro, the last of them all, was below the horizon. The *Spray* was then alone, and sailing on, she held her course. July 4, at 6 A.M., I put in double reefs, and at 8:30 A.M. turned out all reefs. At 9:40 P.M. I raised the sheen only of the light on the west end of Sable Island, which may also be called the Island of Tragedies. The fog, which till this moment had held off, now lowered over the sea like a pall. I was in a world of fog, shut off from the universe. I did not see any more of the light. By the lead, which I cast often, I found that a little after midnight I was passing the east point of the island, and should soon be clear of dangers of land and shoals. The wind was holding free, though it was from the foggy point, south-southwest. It is said that within a few years Sable Island has been reduced from forty miles in length to twenty, and that of three lighthouses built on it since 1880, two have been washed away and the third will soon be engulfed.

On the evening of July 5 the *Spray*, after having steered all day over a lumpy sea, took it into her head to go without the helmsman's aid. I had been steering southeast by south, but the wind hauling forward a bit, she dropped into a smooth lane, heading southeast, and making about eight knots, her very best work. I crowded on sail to cross the track of the liners without loss

prefatory to Chapter III, "Good-by to the American Coast." The sentence here noted represents the first sentence of the run-in chapter.

of time, and to reach as soon as possible the friendly Gulf Stream. The fog lifting before night, I was afforded a look at the sun just as it was touching the sea. I watched it go down and out of sight. Then I turned my face eastward, and there, apparently at the very end of the bowsprit, was the smiling full moon rising out of the sea. Neptune himself coming over the bows could not have startled me more. "Good evening, sir," I cried; "I'm glad to see you." Many a long talk since then I have had with the man in the moon; he had my confidence on the voyage.

About midnight the fog shut down again denser than ever before. One could almost "stand on it." It continued so for a number of days, the wind increasing to a gale. The waves rose high, but I had a good ship. Still, in the dismal fog I felt myself drifting into loneliness, an insect on a straw in the midst of the elements. I lashed the helm, and my vessel held her course, and while she sailed I slept.

During these days a feeling of awe crept over me. My memory worked with startling power. The ominous, the insignificant, the great, the small, the wonderful, the commonplace — all appeared before my mental vision in magical succession. Pages of my history were recalled which had been so long forgotten that they seemed to belong to a previous existence. I heard all the voices of the past laughing, crying, telling what I had heard them tell in many corners of the earth.

The loneliness of my state wore off when the gale was high and I found much work to do. When fine weather returned, then came the sense of solitude, which I could not shake off. I used my voice often, at first giving some order about the affairs of a ship, for I had been told that from disuse I should lose my speech. At the meridian altitude of the sun I called aloud, "Eight bells," after the custom on a ship at sea. Again from my cabin I cried to an imaginary man at the helm, "How does she head, there?" and again, "Is she on her course?" But getting no reply, I was reminded the more palpably of my condition. My voice sounded hollow on the empty air, and I dropped the practice. However, it was not long before the thought came to me that when I was a lad I used to sing; why not try that now, where it would disturb no one? My musical talent had never bred envy in others, but out on the Atlantic, to realize what it meant, you should have heard me sing. You should have seen the porpoises leap when I pitched my voice for the waves and the sea and all that was in it. Old turtles, with large eyes, poked their heads up out of the sea as I sang "Johnny Boker," and "We'll Pay Darby Doyl for his Boots," and the like. But the porpoises were, on the whole, vastly more appreciative than the turtles; they jumped a deal higher. One day when I was humming a favorite chant, I think it was "Babylon's a-Fallin,'" a porpoise jumped higher than the bowsprit. Had the *Spray* been going a little faster she would have scooped him in. The seabirds sailed around rather shy.

July 10, eight days at sea, the *Spray* was twelve hundred miles east of Cape Sable. One hundred and fifty miles a day for so small a vessel must be considered good sailing. It was the greatest run the *Spray* ever made before or since in so few days. On the evening of July 14, in better humor than ever before, all hands cried, "Sail ho!" The sail was a barkantine, three points on the weather bow, hull down. Then came the night. My ship was sailing along now without attention to the helm. The wind was south; she was heading east. Her sails were trimmed like the sails of the nautilus. They drew steadily all night. I went frequently on deck, but found all well. A merry breeze kept on from the south. Early in the morning of the 15th the *Spray* was close aboard the stranger, which proved to be *La Vaguisa* of Vigo, twenty-three days from Philadelphia, bound for Vigo. A lookout from his masthead had spied the *Spray* the evening before. The captain, when I came near enough, threw a line to me and sent a bottle of wine across slung by the neck, and very good wine it was. He also sent his card, which bore the name of Juan Gantes. I think he was a good man, as Spaniards go. But when I asked him to report me "all well" (the *Spray* passing him in a lively manner), he hauled his shoulders much above his head; and when his mate, who knew of my expedition, told him that I was alone, he crossed himself and made for his cabin. I did not see him again. By sundown he was as far astern as he had been ahead the evening before.

There was now less and less monotony. On July 16 the wind was northwest and clear, the sea smooth, and a large bark, hull down, came in sight on the lee bow, and at 2:30 P.M. I spoke the stranger. She was the bark *Java* of Glasgow, from Peru for Queenstown for orders. Her old captain was bearish, but I met a bear once in Alaska that looked pleasanter. At least, the bear seemed pleased to meet me, but this grizzly old man! Well, I suppose my hail disturbed his siesta, and my little sloop passing his great ship had somewhat the effect on him that a red rag has upon a bull. I had the advantage over heavy ships, by long odds, in the light winds of this and the two previous days. The wind was light; his ship was heavy and foul, making poor headway, while the *Spray*, with a great mainsail bellying even to light winds, was just skipping along as nimbly as one could wish. "How long has it been calm about here?" roared the captain of the *Java*, I came within hail of him. "Dunno, cap'n," I shouted back as loud as I could bawl. "I haven't been here long." At this the mate on the forecastle wore a broad grin. "I left Cape Sable fourteen days ago," I added. (I was now well across toward the Azores.) "Mate," he roared to his chief officer—"mate, come here and listen to the Yankee's yarn. Haul down the flag, mate, haul down the flag!" In the best of humor, after all, the *Java* surrendered to the *Spray*.

The acute pain of solitude experienced at first never returned. I had penetrated a mystery, and, by the way, I had sailed through a fog. I had met Neptune in his wrath, but he found that I had not treated him with contempt, and so he suffered me to go on and explore.

In the log for July 18 there is this entry: "Fine weather, wind south-southwest. Porpoises gamboling all about. The S.S. *Olympia* passed at 11:30 A.M., long. W. 34 degrees 50.'"

"It lacks now three minutes of the half-hour," shouted the captain, as he gave me the longitude and the time. I admired the businesslike air of the *Olympia*; but I have the feeling still that the captain was just a little too precise in his reckoning. That may be all well enough, however, where there is plenty of sea-room. But overconfidence, I believe, was the cause of the disaster to the liner *Atlantic*, and many more like her. The captain knew too well where he was. There were no porpoises at all skipping along with the *Olympia*! Porpoises always prefer sailing-ships. The captain was a young man, I observed, and had before him, I hope, a good record.

Land ho! On the morning of July 19 a mystic dome like a mountain of silver stood alone in the sea ahead. Although the land was completely hidden by the white, glistening haze that shone in the sun like polished silver, I felt quite sure that it was Flores Island. At half-past 4:00 P.M. it was abeam. The haze in the meantime had disappeared. Flores is one hundred and seventy-four miles from Fayal, and although it is a high island, it remained many years undiscovered after the principal group of the islands had been colonized.

Early on the morning of July 20 I saw Pico looming above the clouds on the starboard bow. Lower lands burst forth as the sun burned away the morning fog, and island after island came into view. As I approached nearer, cultivated fields appeared, "and oh, how green the corn!" Only those who have seen the Azores from the deck of a vessel realize the beauty of the mid-ocean picture.

At 4:30 P.M. I cast anchor at Fayal, exactly eighteen days from Cape Sable. The American consul, in a smart boat, came alongside before the *Spray* reached the breakwater, and a young naval officer, who feared for the safety of my vessel, boarded, and offered his services as pilot. The youngster, I have no good reason to doubt, could have handled a man-of-war, but the *Spray* was too small for the amount of uniform he wore. However, after fouling all the craft in port and sinking a lighter, she was moored without much damage to herself. This wonderful pilot expected a "gratification," I understood, but whether for the reason that his government, and not I, would have to pay the cost of raising the lighter, or because he did not sink the *Spray*, I could never make out. But I forgive him.

Isabel Savory on Mountaineering in Kashmir (1900)

In the first chapter of A Sportswoman in India, *visiting Englishwoman Isabel Savory finds India to have some of the "finest sport in the world," and she wastes little time going on a "pig-sticking" hunt. Though* A Sportswoman in India *is an overlooked, understudied account of mostly hunting expeditions, in this passage Savory undertakes a rigorous mountain ascent in the Kashmir region. The author, who eschews the presence of a "lady's assistant" on her sporty travels, proves herself unusually intrepid in this excerpt, though scholar Mary A. Procida has pointed out that, in late nineteenth-century India, British women were often, and paradoxically, freer to fully engage in sport than they were back home in Victorian England.*

From "Kashmir"

Mountain climbing grows strangely upon one. You may hardly care for it at first; but if the fascination ever comes, it will last with your life. The scenery responds to your every mood. It is, to begin with, the acme of repose, and repose is one of the greatest latent forces in the world; it is also the expression of form and line in their most soul-satisfying sense; and it is, in Asia at any rate, far removed beyond the reach of man to spoil.

The solemn heights embody the strong and the abiding—those 'everlasting hills'; the weird crags are peopled by the ghosts of fancy; the quiet wastes of snow speak with unearthly voices. Here, at last, the still, sad music of humanity can never weary, nor the sordid stream of life stain.

Five little black dots in the midst of leagues and leagues of snow and ice, we continued our climb, till we were at the top of a ridge. To reach our peak we had to make a sharp descent, then bear away to the right over a level plateau, and finally ascend the west side of our peak by an arête.

Our shortest way lay down a snow couloir—that is, nothing more nor less than a gully partly filled with snow, often a useful institution, and the joy of the mountaineer. Couloirs look prodigiously steep when seen from the front, but snow does not actually lie deeper in them than in other places; this one was like a half section of a sloping chimney, grooved with the passage of stones down in it.

A daring leader is a dangerous thing. F. pronounced our way best to lie down the couloir, and, taking H.'s place, cut footholes for our descent. It certainly was steep. We were going cautiously, moving one at a time, when suddenly we heard *Crack!* and all our hearts stood still. H., just above me, said quietly, "We're done for!" The snow had cracked across just above us, at first only a gape of half an inch; but now the crust of the lower half was slowly beginning to slide downwards, and away we went on it.

"Stop!" we all shouted instantaneously, dashing our axes into the underlying ice. They slid over the hard surface fruitlessly. "Stop!" thundered F., again and again hewing at the ice. But there was no stopping. Slowly at first, faster and faster every moment, we flew down the couloir on our avalanche, driving up clouds of snow in front of it. *Was this the end?*

The couloir, however, turned a corner before it reached the bottom, where a wide terrace ended in a precipice. We all saw that our only chance lay in the angle, and shouting "Jump!" we all threw ourselves, or sprang, or fell, off the moving snow, against the rocks, into the corner; while on rushed the young avalanche — a mad glissade — down the couloir, across the flat, and over — out of sight — below — where we might easily have been lying.

Having waited till we were steady, we turned into the couloir once more, and reaching the flat terrace, we left it on our left. The next snowfield was soon crossed; and then followed the last bit and the worst bit — a steep, rocky arête. Here F. led again, followed by Chowry, and they literally hauled G. and myself up after them. The ridge was completely shattered by frost into nothing more than a heap of piled-up fragments. It was always narrow, and where it was narrowest it was also most unstable and most difficult. We could not ascend it by keeping below the crest, because it was too steep, and if we had sent down one stone, all those above would have tumbled down too; we were therefore forced to keep to the crest of the ridge, and, unable to deviate a single step either to the right or to the left, we were compelled to trust unsteady masses, which trembled under our tread, settled down, and grated in a hollow and ominous way, seeming as though a little shake would send the whole crumbling down in an awful avalanche.

But the top was not far off now. We came to a block which was poised across the ridge, with a gap beyond. We climbed the block, finding it very unsteady, and were faced by a broadish jump to the top of the next crag, which would evidently sway horribly. There was no shame in allowing we were beaten. We went back, and eventually managed to creep around beneath rocks; it was the hardest bit of climbing that day.

At last the rocks were left behind; we all stood, panting, at the top; then almost a run up an easy slope of snow to the summit of all things, and the Silver Throne was ours! Around us and beneath us and on every side were somber, solemn mountain peaks, glittering walls, turrets, pinnacles, pyramids, domes, cones and spires of ice and snow, every combination that the world can give, and every contrast that the heart can desire. We could not linger long, hard though it was to leave. Having eaten some kola biscuits and chocolate, we began to descend by a different route. It proved to be more difficult than the other way, and, worse still, we had no time to spare to come very slowly.

The rocky arête gave place to an ice-slope fully a thousand feet long, across which we moved, as quickly as H., who was once more in front, could cut steps. To save time we managed with as few as possible, and I, for one, fully expected an accident. It came! The nails in H.'s boots had grown rounded and smooth; he suddenly slipped and went flying forwards. I wildly embraced a handy little knob, and the rest clung somehow — somewhere — with axes and fingernails. Taut came the rope with an awful strain — it was an unpleasant moment. We were heading diagonally across the slope, and as we held H. by the rope, he swung to and fro like a pendulum, and finally came to anchor, spread-eagled against the icy face.

He was quite cool — kept hold of his axe, cut himself foot holes, and got back into his place once more. A short time after we were safely off the slope, to our horror a mist came over the mountains, and quickly thickened, blotting out all traces of our whereabouts. It was impossible to go on. O ye immortal gods! Where were we?

However, only a quarter of an hour was passed in despair; shapes began to loom in front of us, and the clouds blew off. Taking to our feet once more, we began to surmount the second ridge; it proved to be slippery rock, and our advance was slow and tedious. The heat at the end of the long afternoons was growing unbearable; there was plenty of air up above, and now and then a refreshing puff quickened us for the moment into life, but for the most part we seemed to be in complete aerial stagnation.

Was life worth living then? It seemed intolerable. We sucked ice to allay our thirst, and only grew more thirsty.

I longed to cast away my alpenstock, to abandon everything, as I mechanically struggled on, caring for nothing, observing nothing, only dimly conscious of the gloomy depths below, floored by cold, hard glaciers, rent with fathomless crevasses. In a dull dream one pictured the ice-steps giving way, and speculated in which crevasse, after falling, falling, falling, one would find oneself.

Thank goodness! The breezy summit brought a reaction, and with the wind in our faces we prepared for the last descent. Putting our "best foot" foremost, we hurried down the slope and over the crisp ice, having unroped. Unexpectedly we came across some awkward corners, which had to be circumvented with care.

I recollect so well, once, on much the same sort of day, we were almost running down the last mile or so into camp, when a bit of bad ground was encountered. I held on to the rock with my right hand, and with my left prodded at the snow with the point of my alpenstock, until I had made a fairly good step. Getting carefully round the rock and standing on the one step, I began to do the same for my other foot, and so on.

The other members of the party were, one following me, the other crossing higher up. Suddenly, in trying to pass the extreme point of the corner, the snow-steps gave way — I slipped and fell. It was upon a steep snow-slope that this took place, at the head of a long, narrow gully. The gully ended in a couple of buttresses leading down to the valley — a great drop — below.

Of course I was whirled down the snow-slope at once, fully thinking that the end had come. All sorts of little, trivial thoughts came into my head, I lost my stick and pitched on the head of the gully, then tumbled off the edge of it, bounding down the slope in great leaps. Luckily it was snowy, and not very hard falling. But the last great bound spun me through the air thirty feet, and landed me at full length on my left side, half buried in snow, on a spot where the slope was less steep, but uncomfortably near the edge of the gully and the precipice. I believe I fainted at that point. At any rate, it was a useful lesson, and not forgotten on the present occasion.

As we tramped downwards, glorious lights and colors were playing upon that most beautiful of mountains — Haramuk. We longed to turn round, to linger, and to enjoy. The sun set behind the gap at Baramoula, sending its brilliant light sweeping over the Wular Lake and bathing Haramuk in glory. Our long shadows hurried before us apace, as though they would hasten towards the wondrous East. Gradually the valley was steeped in purple shadow, the snows lost their fiery tinge, and night came on apace.

Was that the blue smoke of our campfire? Not long, and we were back in our tents, realizing, as one does at the end of a real hard day, such content as is given to few, and to them but seldom in any lifetime.

And over those drinks which are reserved for the faithful, we vowed that Kashmir is the country to visit, that mountain climbing is a game worth the candle.

Frederick G. Aflalo on Hunting the Alligator (1907)

Author or editor of over a half dozen books on fishing and the fishing industry, Aflalo was himself a keen fisherman who traveled from Florida to Canada to California in pursuit of his passion. In addition to authoring individual participatory accounts of angling and hunting, Aflalo coedited the highly regarded Encyclopedia of Sport *in 1897 with Hedley Peek and Henry Charles Howard, the Earl of Suffolk. While fishing consumed most of Aflalo's time, the chapter below, from* Sunshine and Sport in Florida, *describes the author's attempt to assist on an alligator hunt.*

"AN ALLIGATOR HUNT"

One of the *obiter facta* of a holiday in Florida was, so a friend at home assured me, a hunt for alligators, for which purpose he advised me to take one my rifles, preferably a sporting Winchester, in my kit. I did so. The rifle was all but left onboard the *Cunarder* at New York (I devoutly wish that it had been), it involved me in a tedious business with the Customs at Havana, and without firing a single shot throughout my trip, its ultimate fate was to figure in a fancy-dress ball on board the *Tagus* coming home. Had it been in my boat in the Pass on the day of the big shark, the whole magazine might perhaps have been emptied to some purpose into that shagreen hide, but at that moment it reposed unloaded in a corner of my room in Useppa.

One windy day, with the Pass quarantined for fishing, we got up an impromptu alligator hunt on the island of La Costa. The moving spirits in a drama that proved to be Hamlet without the Prince were "Johnny Jack," the Useppa taxidermist, and my guide, Underhill, who has, on his native island of Sanabel, acquired a nose for an alligator that does him credit. Underhill declared that he knew of an immense gator on La Costa, not far from a landing that we could easily reach in Jack's launch, the *Naturalist*; so late on afternoon with darkness not far off, we mustered on the pier as sorry-looking a crowd of filibusters as could well be found outside the pages of Mr. Jack London or Mr. Conrad, both of whom seem to have made strange acquaintances on their walk down life's highway. The general scheme of clothing may be glozed over. Our raiment was cool, but immodest, and we wore indeed a little more clothing than the reptiles we had come so far to unearth. The footwear alone showed individuality; two of the party, fearing rattlesnakes, wore top boots; the rest, indifferent to such risks, went in tennis shoes, or even stocking-foot, and one came forth in a splendid of sealskin slippers, a trophy from an Irish lough, picturesque enough in the smoking room, but in swampy ground a trifle inclined to stay behind.

The launch pushed her nose up on the landing, and one by one the party disembarked. Then Jack and Underhill assumed the leadership, one of them wielding an immense pole, the object of which will soon be appreciated, the other carrying a short-handled gaff to which was attached a coil of rope. I shouldered my rifle, vaguely imagining myself on a punitive expedition in the bush, and another had a revolver stuck in his belt like one of the *Pirates of Penzance*. On the whole, indeed, we made a very effective comic opera combination, and if alligators are gifted with a sense of humor, some of them, peering from behind the dense screen of rank undergrowth, must have chortled happily.

Of path there was no more than that made by those in front hurling themselves against the *chevaux de frise* of sawgrass, three-edged blades of which wave in great tangles as high as the tallest man's eyes, with prickly pear to detain keepsakes from the breeches, and stunted palmetto to trip the feet. The shortest ramble on those islands, the moment you leave the beach, is one continuous battle with vegetation, which is, in fact, far more formidable than the animal life.

Hush! Underhill has struck a trail. With head lowered, like a Cherokee brave tracking his enemy, he pushes on, his eyes never off the ground, and from time to time halts to consult with his confederate. At accelerated pace these backwoods men press on through that miserable maze of vegetables mimicking barbed wire, and we unfortunates struggle torn and breathless in pursuit, not liking to call a respite, not daring to be left behind in the gathering gloom. If only Underhill had offered me at that moment five shillings for my rifle, which he had much admired, it would not now be mine! The final consultation lasted long enough for the stragglers to come up with the vanguard, and there, sure enough, was the spoor evidently a large alligator, with other indications of where its tail and body had ploughed their lonely furrow over half a mile of oozy haunts, leading unmistakably to a large swamp, in the bank of which was a low hole. This looked to our unpracticed eyes scarcely large enough to accommodate a well-fed eel, but Underhill declared that it was the front door of the gator's family mansion.

We had him safe, the experts agreed, unless there was another way out. Alligators, it appears, often leave a back way, like burglars, and the reptile at whose front door we now unmasked our batteries had, it soon transpired, not overlooked this essential condition of safety. The excitement was tense. Pole, gaff, rifle and revolver were requisitioned, and a large and powerful spade now made its appearance for the first time, having been carried by one who brought up the rear. Forgotten were the troubles with sawgrass and red bugs, the blisters and the bumps even then rising on tender limbs. The pole was now thrust within the "cave." Underhill then informed us that the passage within turned off at right angles six or eight feet from the entrance. Often, he assured us, the naughty reptile is found close to daylight, when the gaff, with its coil of rope, does the rest in surprisingly short time, someone standing by with a stick to give the hermit his quietus as soon as his head emerges. On this occasion the end of our adventure at this particular cave was less dramatic. Someone of an inquiring turn of mind discovered another exit to this underworld, where, sure enough, the footmarks pointed away from home. Pole and gaff and other weapons were once more shouldered, and our indefatigable guides led the way to fresh pastures.

Another "cave" was reached within a few minutes, and here, they said, the conditions were very promising. Underhill knelt before the entrance in a gesture that suggested that he was vastly enjoying the effluvium of marsh gas arising from the threshold with an odor that indicated less the residence of alligators than their burial-ground. Presently, however, we found that his object was business, not pleasure, for he began to utter a series of low and fearful grunts, placing his hand before his mouth, apparently to render his imitation of the alligator's trills yet more realistic. I was at once reminded of the way in which our Portuguese fisherman at Madeira used to whistle and sing for the *muraenas* to come forth from their lairs in the rocks, and the analogy struck another member of the party, him of the sealskin slippers, who had fished with me in that distant isle. The only difference was that the *muraenas* used to come forth in response to the invitation, while the alligators did not. Yet Underhill was quite sure someone was at home. The spade was accordingly got to work, since the pole failed, and we presently had the satisfaction of securing a magnificent alligator of about three feet. It was for this monster that I brought a rifle that would, in other hands than mine, bring down an elephant at five hundred yards.

At a neighboring health resort of the species, where the stench was almost overpowering to the untrained nose, Underhill secured two more, which actually did, to their own undoing, respond to his motherly cry. These ponderous reptiles, either of which would have gone at the time in my breast pocket, accompanied me via the West Indies to Devonshire, whence, after a month of incarceration in a small box in the drawing room, they were eventually dispatched to happier quarters in the Reptile House at the Zoo.

Such were the slender fruits of a hunt that promised such episodes as were to have consoled us for our banishment from the Pass. Alas! we returned to Useppa an even more disreputable looking band of tatterdemalions than we had set out, the state of our clothing having been aggravated by the fact that the launch struck thrice on the mud and we had to get out, waist-deep, and shove her off.

For him of the sealskin slippers, at any rate, the experience was too much, for he saw alligators the whole time. These infant creations of this heated brain were by tacit consent given the benefit of the doubt. True, someone on the return journey unfeelingly recalled an anecdote. It was that of the man, returning from a city dinner, who fancied that he saw a monkey in his hall.

"If," he said, "shading his eyes with his left hand, while his right grasped his heaviest stick, "if that is a monkey, then it's in for a devil of a time. If it is *not* a monkey, then, oh Lord! *I'm* in for a devil of a time! "The man in the sealskin slippers, which had with difficulty been rescued from the last morass, looked as if he considered the narrative in bad taste. He said that seeing was believing. Someone retorted that believing was sometimes seeing. It depended on the mood. Then the party relapsed into silence. It was quite dark, and everyone was wet and cold and tingling with the onslaught of plant and insect enemies. We had, we found next morning, unanimously resolved that our first hunt for alligators would also be our last. We agreed that alligator hunting was the limit!

Jack London on Surfing (1908)

> *A controversial figure in sports journalism for his mostly disparaging coverage of black heavyweight champion Jack Johnson, Jack London's larger oeuvre nevertheless contains some of the best sportswriting of its era. Called America's "first celebrity sportswriter" by London anthologist Howard Latchman, London is credited with helping to create "a new awareness and popular interest in surfing at a time when it was in some danger of dying out." An all-around sportsman who was a participant in boxing and fencing in addition to shotputing, swimming, sailing, surfing, and shooting, London, author of the classic fiction* The Call of the Wild, *was one the most popular, most versatile writers of his time, largely because of what Latchman calls his "spirited portrayal of the sports world and his equally enthusiastic participation in it." London wrote the first-person surfing account that follows, drawn from* The Cruise of the Snark, *about his visit to Hawaii.*

"A Royal Sport"

That is what it is, a royal sport for the natural kings of earth. The grass grows right down to the water at Waikiki Beach, and within fifty feet of the everlasting sea. The trees also grow down to the salty edge of things, and one sits in their shade and looks seaward at a majestic surf thundering in on the beach to one's very feet. Half a mile out, where is the reef, the white-headed combers thrust suddenly skyward out of the placid turquoise-blue and come rolling in to shore. One after another they come, a mile long, with smoking crests, the white battalions of the infinite army of the sea. And one sits and listens to the perpetual roar, and watches the unending procession, and feels tiny and fragile before this tremendous force expressing itself in fury and foam and sound. Indeed, one feels microscopically small, and the thought that one may wrestle with this sea raises in one's imagination a thrill of apprehension, almost of fear. Why, they are a mile long, these bull-mouthed monsters, and they weigh a thousand tons, and they charge in to shore faster than a man can run. What chance? No chance at all, is the verdict of the shrinking ego; and one sits, and looks, and listens, and thinks the grass and the shade are a pretty good place in which to be.

And suddenly, out there where a big smoker lifts skyward, rising like a sea-god from out of the welter of spume and churning white, on the giddy, toppling, overhanging and downfalling, precarious crest appears the dark head of a man. Swiftly he rises through the rushing white. His black shoulders, his chest, his loins, his limbs — all is abruptly projected on one's vision. Where but the moment before was only the wide desolation and invincible roar, is now a man, erect, full-statured, not struggling frantically in that wild movement, not buried and crushed and buffeted by those mighty monsters, but standing above them all, calm and superb, poised on the giddy summit, his feet buried in the churning foam, the salt smoke rising to his knees, and all the rest of him in the free air and flashing sunlight, and he is flying through the air, flying forward, flying fast as the surge on which he stands. He is a Mercury — a brown Mercury. His heels are winged, and in them is the swiftness of the sea. In truth, from out of the sea he has leaped upon the back of the sea, and he is riding the sea that roars and bellows and cannot shake him from its back. But no frantic outreaching and balancing is his. He is impassive, motionless as a statue carved suddenly by some miracle out of the sea's depth from which he rose. And straight on toward shore he flies on his winged heels and the white crest of the breaker. There is a wild burst of foam, a long tumultuous rushing sound as the breaker falls futile and spent on the beach at your feet; and there, at your feet steps calmly ashore a Kanaka, burnt, golden and brown by the tropic sun. Several minutes ago he was a speck a quarter of a mile away. He has "bitted the bull-mouthed breaker" and ridden it in, and the pride in the feat shows in the carriage of his magnificent body as he glances for a moment carelessly at you who sit in the shade of the shore. He is a Kanaka — and more, he is a man, a member of the kingly species that has mastered matter and the brutes and lorded it over creation.

And one sits and thinks of Tristram's last wrestle with the sea on that fatal morning; and one thinks further, to the fact that that Kanaka has done what Tristram never did, and that he knows a joy of the sea that Tristram never knew. And still further one thinks. It is all very well, sitting here in cool shade of the beach, but you are a man, one of the kingly species, and what that Kanaka can do, you can do yourself. Go to. Strip off your clothes that are a nuisance in this mellow clime. Get in and wrestle with the sea; wing your heels with the skill and power that reside in you; bit the sea's breakers, master them, and ride upon their backs as a king should.

And that is how it came about that I tackled surf-riding. And now that I have tackled it, more than ever do I hold it to be a royal sport. But first let me explain the physics of it. A wave is a communicated agitation. The water that composes the body of a wave does not move. If it did, when a stone is thrown into a pond and the ripples spread away in an ever widening circle, there would appear at the center an ever increasing hole. No, the water that composes the body of a wave is stationary. Thus, you may watch a particular portion of the ocean's surface and you will see the same water rise and fall a thousand times to the agitation communicated by a thousand successive waves. Now imagine this communicated agitation moving shoreward. As the bottom shoals, the lower portion of the wave strikes land first and is stopped. But water is fluid, and the upper portion has not struck anything, wherefore it keeps on communicating its agitation, keeps on going. And when the top of the wave keeps on going, while the bottom of it lags behind, something is bound to happen. The bottom of the wave drops out from under and the top of the wave falls over, forward, and down, curling and cresting and roaring as it does so. It is the bottom of a wave striking against the top of the land that is the cause of all surfs.

But the transformation from a smooth undulation to a breaker is not abrupt except where the bottom shoals abruptly. Say the bottom shoals gradually for from quarter of a mile to a mile, then an equal distance will be occupied by the transformation. Such a bottom is that off the beach of Waikiki, and it produces a splendid surf-riding surf. One leaps upon the back of a breaker just as it begins to break, and stays on it as it continues to break all the way in to shore.

And now to the particular physics of surf-riding. Get out on a flat board, six feet long, two feet wide, and roughly oval in shape. Lie down upon it like a small boy on a coaster and paddle with your hands out to deep water, where the waves begin to crest. Lie out there quietly on the board. Sea after sea breaks before, behind, and under and over you, and rushes in to shore, leaving you behind. When a wave crests, it gets steeper. Imagine yourself, on your board, on the face of that steep slope. If it stood still, you would slide down just as a boy slides down a hill on his coaster. "But," you object, "the wave doesn't stand still." Very true, but the water composing the wave stands still, and there you have the secret. If ever you start sliding down the face of that wave, you'll keep on sliding and you'll never reach the bottom. Please don't laugh. The face of that wave may be only six feet, yet you can slide down it a quarter of a mile, or half a mile, and not reach the bottom. For, see, since a wave is only a communicated agitation or impetus, and since the water that composes a wave is changing every instant, new water is rising into the wave as fast as the wave travels. You slide down this new water, and yet remain in your old position on the wave, sliding down the still newer water that is rising and forming the wave. You slide precisely as fast as the wave travels. If it travels fifteen miles an hour, you slide fifteen miles an hour. Between you and shore stretches a quarter of mile of water. As the wave travels, this water obligingly heaps itself into the wave, gravity does the rest, and down you go, sliding the whole length of it. If you still cherish the notion, while sliding, that the water is moving with you, thrust your arms into it and attempt to paddle; you will find that you have to be remarkably quick to get a stroke, for that water is dropping astern just as fast as you are rushing ahead.

And now for another phase of the physics of surf-riding. All rules have their exceptions. It is true that the water in a wave does not travel forward. But there is what may be called the send of the sea. The water in the overtoppling crest does move forward, as you will speedily realize if you are slapped in the face by it, or if you are caught under it and are pounded by one mighty blow down under the surface panting and gasping for half a minute. The water in the top of a wave rests upon the water in the bottom of the wave. But when the bottom of the wave strikes the land, it stops, while the top goes on. It no longer has the bottom of the wave to hold it up. Where was solid water beneath it, is now air, and for the first time it feels the grip of gravity, and down it falls, at the same time being torn asunder from the lagging bottom of the wave and flung forward. And it is because of this that riding a surfboard is something more than a mere placid sliding down a hill. In truth, one is caught up and hurled shoreward as by some Titan's hand.

I deserted the cool shade, put on a swimming suit, and got hold of a surfboard. It was too small a board. But I didn't know, and nobody told me. I joined some little Kanaka boys in shallow water, where the breakers were well spent and small — a regular kindergarten school. I watched the little Kanaka boys. When a likely-looking breaker came along, they flopped upon their stomachs on their boards, kicked like mad with their feet, and rode the breaker in to the beach. I tried to emulate them. I watched them, tried to do everything that they did, and failed utterly. The breaker swept past, and I was not on it. I tried again and again. I kicked twice as madly as they did, and failed. Half a dozen would be around. We would all leap on our boards in front of a good breaker. Away our feet would churn like the sternwheels of river steamboats, and away the little rascals would scoot while I remained in disgrace behind.

I tried for a solid hour, and not one wave could I persuade to boost me shoreward. And then arrived a friend, Alexander Hume Ford, a globetrotter by profession, bent ever on the pursuit of sensation. And he had found it at Waikiki. Heading for Australia, he had stopped off for a week to find out if there were any thrills in surf-riding, and he had become wedded to it. He had been at it every day for a month and could not yet see any symptoms of the fascination lessening on him. He spoke with authority.

"Get off that board," he said. "Chuck it away at once. Look at the way you're trying to ride it. If ever the nose of that board hits bottom, you'll be disembowelled. Here, take my board. It's a man's size."

I am always humble when confronted by knowledge. Ford knew. He showed me how properly to mount his board. Then he waited for a good breaker, gave me a shove at the right moment, and started me in. Ah, delicious moment when I felt that breaker grip and fling me. On I dashed, a hundred and fifty feet, and subsided with the breaker on the sand. From that moment I was lost. I waded back to Ford with his board. It was a large one, several inches thick, and weighed all of seventy-five pounds. He gave me advice, much of it. He had had no one to teach him, and all that he had laboriously learned in several weeks he communicated to me in half an hour. I really learned by proxy. And inside of half an hour I was able to start myself and ride in. I did it time after time, and Ford applauded and advised. For instance, he told me to get just so far forward on the board and no farther. But I must have got some farther, for as I came charging in to land, that miserable board poked its nose down to bottom, stopped abruptly, and turned a somersault, at the same time violently severing our relations. I was tossed through the air like a chip and buried ignominiously under the downfalling breaker. And I realized that if it hadn't been for Ford, I'd have been disembowelled. That particular risk is part of the sport, Ford says. Maybe he'll have it happen to him before he leaves Waikiki, and then, I feel confident, his yearning for sensation will be satisfied for a time.

When all is said and done, it is my steadfast belief that homicide is worse than suicide, especially if, in the former case, it is a woman. Ford saved me from being a homicide. "Imagine your legs are a rudder," he said. "Hold them close together, and steer with them." A few minutes later I came charging in on a comber. As I neared the beach, there, in the water, up to her waist, dead in front of me, appeared a woman. How was I to stop that comber on whose back I was? It looked like a dead woman. The board weighed seventy-five pounds, I weighed a hundred and sixty-five. The added weight had a velocity of fifteen miles per hour. The board and I constituted a projectile. I leave it to the physicists to figure out the force of the impact upon that poor, tender woman. And then I remembered my guardian angel, Ford. "Steer with your legs!" rang through my brain. I steered with my legs, I steered sharply, abruptly, with all my legs and with all my might. The board sheered around broadside on the crest. Many things happened simultaneously. The wave gave me a passing buffet, a light tap as the taps of waves go, but a tap sufficient to knock me off the board and smash me down through the rushing water to bottom, with which I came in violent collision and upon which I was rolled over and over. I got my head out for a breath of air and then gained my feet. There stood the woman before me. I felt like a hero. I had saved her life. And she laughed at me. It was not hysteria. She had never dreamed of her danger. Anyway, I solaced myself, it was not I but Ford that saved her, and I didn't have to feel like a hero. And besides, that leg steering was great. In a few minutes more of practice I was able to thread my way in and out past several bathers and to remain on top my breaker instead of going under it.

"Tomorrow," Ford said, "I am going to take you out into the blue water."

I looked seaward where he pointed, and saw the great smoking combers that made the breakers I had been riding look like ripples. I don't know what I might have said had I not recollected just then that I was one of a kingly species. So all that I did say was, "All right, I'll tackle them tomorrow."

The water that rolls in on Waikiki Beach is just the same as the water that laves the shores of all the Hawaiian Islands; and in ways, especially from the swimmer's standpoint, it is wonderful water. It is cool enough to be comfortable, while it is warm enough to permit a swimmer to stay in all day without experiencing a chill. Under the sun or the stars, at high noon or at midnight, in midwinter or in midsummer, it does not matter when, it is always the same temperature — not too warm, not too cold, just right. It is wonderful water, salt as old ocean itself, pure and crystal-clear. When the nature of the water is considered, it is not so remarkable after all that the Kanakas are one of the most expert of swimming races.

So it was, next morning, when Ford came along, that I plunged into the wonderful water for a swim of indeterminate length. Astride of our surfboards, or, rather, flat down upon them on our stomachs, we paddled out through the kindergarten where the little Kanaka boys were at play. Soon we were out in deep water where the big smokers came roaring in. The mere struggle with them, facing them and paddling seaward over them and through them, was sport enough in itself. One had to have his wits about him, for it was a battle in which mighty blows were struck, on one side, and in which cunning was used on the other side — a struggle between insensate force and intelligence. I soon learned a bit. When a breaker curled over my head, for a swift instant I could see the light of day through its emerald body; then down would go my head, and I would clutch the board with all my strength. Then would come the blow, and to the onlooker on shore I would be blotted out. In reality the board and I have passed through the crest and emerged in the respite of the other side. I should not recommend those smashing blows to an invalid or delicate person. There is weight behind them, and the impact of the driven water is like a sandblast. Sometimes one passes through half a dozen combers in quick succession, and it is just about that time that he is liable to discover new merits in the stable land and new reasons for being on shore.

Out there in the midst of such a succession of big smoky ones, a third man was added to our party, one Freeth. Shaking the water from my eyes as I emerged from one wave and peered ahead to see what the next one looked like, I saw him tearing in on the back of it, standing upright on his board, carelessly poised, a young god bronzed with sunburn. We went through the wave on the back of which he rode. Ford called to him. He turned an airspring from his wave, rescued his board from its maw, paddled over to us and joined Ford in showing me things. One thing in particular I learned from Freeth, namely, how to encounter the occasional breaker of exceptional size that rolled in. Such breakers were really ferocious, and it was unsafe to meet them on top of the board. But Freeth showed me, so that whenever I saw one of that caliber rolling down on me, I slid off the rear end of the board and dropped down beneath the surface, my arms over my head and holding the board. Thus, if the wave ripped the board out of my hands and tried to strike me with it (a common trick of such waves), there would be a cushion of water a foot or more in depth, between my head and the blow. When the wave passed, I climbed upon the board and paddled on. Many men have been terribly injured, I learn, by being struck by their boards.

The whole method of surf-riding and surf-fighting, I learned, is one of nonresistance. Dodge the blow that is struck at you. Dive through the wave that is trying to slap you in the face. Sink down, feet first, deep under the surface, and let the big smoker that is trying to smash you go by far overhead. Never be rigid. Relax. Yield yourself to the waters that are ripping and tearing at you. When the undertow catches you and drags you seaward along the bottom, don't struggle against it. If you do, you are liable to be drowned, for it is stronger than you. Yield yourself to that undertow. Swim with it, not against it, and you will find the pressure removed. And, swimming with it, fooling it so that it does not hold you, swim upward at the same time. It will be no trouble at all to reach the surface.

The man who wants to learn surf-riding must be a strong swimmer, and he must be used to going under the water. After that, fair strength and common-sense are all that is required. The force of the big comber is rather unexpected. There are mix-ups in which board and rider are torn apart and separated by several hundred feet. The surf-rider must take care of himself. No matter how many riders swim out with him, he cannot depend upon any of them for aid. The fancied security I had in the presence of Ford and Freeth made me forget that it was my first swim out in deep water among the big ones. I recollected, however, and rather suddenly, for a big wave came in, and away went the two men on its back all the way to shore. I could have been drowned a dozen different ways before they got back to me.

One slides down the face of a breaker on his surf-board, but he has to get started to sliding. Board and rider must be moving shoreward at a good rate before the wave overtakes them. When you see the wave coming that you want to ride in, you turn tail to it and paddle shoreward with all your strength, using what is called the windmill stroke. This is a sort of spurt performed immediately in front of the wave. If the board is going fast enough, the wave accelerates it, and the board begins its quarter-of-a-mile slide.

I shall never forget the first big wave I caught out there in the deep water. I saw it coming, turned my back on it and paddled for dear life. Faster and faster my board went, till it seemed my arms would drop off. What was happening behind me I could not tell. One cannot look behind and paddle the windmill stroke. I heard the crest of the wave hissing and churning, and then my board was lifted and flung forward. I scarcely knew what happened the first half-minute. Though I kept my eyes open, I could not see anything, for I was buried in the rushing white of the crest. But I did not mind. I was chiefly conscious of ecstatic bliss at having caught the wave. At the end, of the half minute, however, I began to see things, and to breathe. I saw that three feet of the nose of my board was clear out of water and riding on the air. I shifted my weight forward, and made the nose come down. Then I lay, quite at rest in the midst of the wild movement, and watched the shore and the bathers on the beach grow distinct. I didn't cover quite a quarter of a mile on that wave, because, to prevent the board from diving, I shifted my weight back, but shifted it too far and fell down the rear slope of the wave.

It was my second day at surf-riding, and I was quite proud of myself. I stayed out there four hours, and when it was over, I was resolved that on the morrow I'd come in standing up. But that resolution paved a distant place. On the morrow I was in bed. I was not sick, but I was very unhappy, and I was in bed. When describing the wonderful water of Hawaii I forgot to describe the wonderful sun of Hawaii. It is a tropic sun, and, furthermore, in the first part of June, it is an overhead sun. It is also an insidious, deceitful sun. For the first time in my life I was sunburned unawares. My arms, shoulders, and back had been burned many times in the past and were tough; but not so my legs. And for four hours I had exposed the tender backs of my legs, at right angles, to that perpendicular Hawaiian sun. It was not until after I got ashore that I discovered the sun had touched me. Sunburn at first is merely warm; after that it grows intense and the blisters come out. Also, the joints, where the skin wrinkles, refuse to bend. That is why I spent the next day in bed. I couldn't walk. And that is why, today, I am writing this in bed. It is easier to than not to. But tomorrow, ah, tomorrow, I shall be out in that wonderful water, and I shall come in standing up, even as Ford and Freeth. And if I fail tomorrow, I shall do it the next day, or the next. Upon one thing I am resolved: the *Snark* shall not sail from Honolulu until I, too, wing my heels with the swiftness of the sea, and become a sun-burned, skin-peeling Mercury.

John Muir on Glaciering (1909)

> *Published by Doubleday in 1909 and selected by editor Joyce Carol Oates for the* Best American Essays of the Century *in 2000,* Stickeen *can rightly be called a classic. The title of the piece when it first appeared in* Century *magazine, "An Adventure with a Dog and a Glacier," better represents the adventure sports themes implicit in the narrative. In fact, "glaciering" as a sport is now routinely offered visiting sportsmen and women by Alaskan guides. Muir's adventure occurred in 1880; the story of the dog's loyalty moved him so much that he spent nearly two decades processing the expedition's momentous events for publication.*

"Stickeen"

In the summer of 1880 I set out from Fort Wrangell in a canoe to continue the exploration of the icy region of southeastern Alaska, begun in the fall of 1879. After the necessary provisions, blankets, etc., had been collected and stowed away, and my Indian crew were in their places ready to start, while a crowd of their relatives and friends on the wharf were bidding them goodbye and good luck, my companion, the Rev. S. H. Young, for whom we were waiting, at last came aboard, followed by a little black dog, that immediately made himself at home by curling up in a hollow among the baggage. I like dogs, but this one seemed so small and worthless that I objected to his going, and asked the missionary why he was taking him.

"Such a little helpless creature will only be in the way," I said; "you had better pass him up to the Indian boys on the wharf, to be taken home to play with the children. This trip is not likely to be good for toy dogs. The poor silly thing will be in rain and snow for weeks or months, and will require care like a baby." But his master assured me that he would be no trouble at all; that he was a perfect wonder of a dog, could endure cold and hunger like a bear, swim like a seal, and was wondrous wise and cunning, etc., making out a list of virtues to show he might be the most interesting member of the party.

Nobody could hope to unravel the lines of his ancestry. In all the wonderfully mixed and varied dog tribe, I never saw any creature very much like him, though in some of his sly, soft, gliding motions and gestures he brought the fox to mind. He was short-legged and bunch-bodied, and his hair, though smooth, was long and silky and slightly waved, so that when the wind was at his back it ruffled, making him look shaggy. At first sight his only noticeable feature was his fine tail, which was about as airy and shady as a squirrel's, and was carried curling forward almost to his nose. On closer inspection you might notice his thin sensitive ears, and sharp eyes with cunning tan spots above them. Mr. Young told me that when the little fellow was a pup about the size of a woodrat he was presented to his wife by an Irish prospector at Sitka, and that on his arrival at Fort Wrangell he was adopted with enthusiasm by the Stickeen Indians as a sort of new good-luck totem, was named "Stickeen" for the tribe, and became a universal favorite; petted, protected, and admired wherever he went, and regarded as a mysterious fountain of wisdom.

On our trip he soon proved himself a queer character — odd, concealed, independent, keeping invincibly quiet, and doing many little puzzling things that piqued my curiosity. As we sailed week after week through the long intricate channels and inlets among the innumerable islands and mountains of the coast, he spent most of the dull days in sluggish ease, motionless, and apparently as unobserving as if in deep sleep. But I discovered that somehow he always knew what was going on. When the Indians were about to shoot at ducks or seals, or when anything along the shore was exciting our attention, he would rest his chin on the edge of the canoe and calmly look out like a dreamy-eyed tourist. And when he heard us talking about making a landing, he immediately roused himself to see what sort of a place we were coming to, and made ready to jump overboard and swim ashore as soon as the canoe neared the bench. Then, with a vigorous shake to get rid of the brine in his hair, he ran into the woods to hunt small game. But though always the first out of the canoe, he was always the last to get into it. When we were ready to start he could never be found, and refused to come to our call. We soon found out, however, that though we could not see him at such times, he saw us, and from the cover of the briers and huckleberry bushes in the fringe of the woods was watching the canoe with wary eye. For as soon as we were fairly off he came trotting down the beach, plunged into the surf, and swam after us, knowing well that we would cease rowing and take him in. When the contrary little vagabond came alongside, he was lifted by the neck, held at arm's length a moment to drip, and dropped aboard. We tried to cure him of this trick by compelling him to swim a long way, as if we had a mind to abandon him; but this did no good; the longer the swim the better he seemed to like it.

Though capable of great idleness, he never failed to be ready for all sorts of adventures and excursions. One pitch-dark rainy night we landed about ten o'clock at the mouth of a salmon stream when the water was phosphorescent. The salmon were running, and the myriad fins of the onrushing multitude were churning all the stream into a silvery glow, wonderfully beautiful and impressive in the ebon darkness. To get a good view of the show I set out with one of the Indians and sailed up through the midst of it to the foot of a rapid about half a mile from camp, where the swift current dashing over rocks made the luminous glow most glorious. Happening to look back down the stream, while the Indian was catching a few of the struggling fish, I saw a long spreading fan of light like the tail of a comet, which we thought must be made by some big strange animal that was pursuing us. On it came with its magnificent train, until we imagined we could see the monster's head and eyes; but it was only Stickeen, who, finding I had left the camp, came swimming after me to see what was up.

When we camped early, the best hunter of the crew usually went to the woods for a deer, and Stickeen was sure to be at his heels, provided I had not gone out. For, strange to say, though I never carried a gun, he always followed me, forsaking the hunter and even his master to share my wonderings. The days that were too stormy for sailing I spent in the woods, or on the adjacent mountains, wherever my studies called me; and Stickeen always insisted on going with me, however wild the weather, gliding like a fox through dripping huckleberry bushes and thorny tangles of *panax* and *rubus*, scarce stirring their rain-laden leaves; wading and wallowing through snow, swimming icy streams, skipping over logs and rocks and the crevasses of glaciers with the patience and endurance of a determined mountaineer, never tiring or getting discouraged. Once he followed me over a glacier the surface of which was so crusty and rough that it cut his feet until every step was marked with blood; but he trotted on with Indian fortitude until I noticed his red track, and, taking pity on him, made him a set of moccasins out of a handkerchief. However great his troubles he never asked help or made any complaint, as if, like a philosopher, he had learned that without hard work and suffering there could be no pleasure worth having.

Yet none of us was able to make out what Stickeen was really good for. He seemed to meet danger and hardships without anything like reason, insisted on having his own way, never obeyed an order, and the hunter could never set him on anything, or make him fetch the birds he shot. His equanimity was so steady it seemed due to want of feeling; ordinary storms were pleasures to him, and as for mere rain, he flourished in it like a vegetable. No matter what advances you might make, scarce a glance or a tail-wag would you get for your pains. But though he was apparently as cold as a glacier and about as impervious to fun, I tried hard to make his acquaintance, guessing there must be something worthwhile hidden beneath so much courage, endurance, and love of wild-weathery adventure. No superannuated mastiff or bulldog grown old in office surpassed this fluffy midget in stoic dignity. He sometimes reminded me of a small, squat, unshakable desert cactus. For he never displayed a single trace of the merry, tricksy, elfish fun of the terriers and collies that we all know, nor of their touching affection and devotion. Like children, most small dogs beg to be loved and allowed to love; but Stickeen seemed a very Diogenes, asking only to be let alone: a true child of the wilderness, holding the even tenor of his hidden life with the silence and serenity of nature. His strength of character lay in his eyes. They looked as old as the hills, and as young, and as wild. I never tired of looking into them: it was like looking into a landscape; but they were small and rather deep-set, and had no explaining lines around them to give out particulars. I was accustomed to look into the faces of plants and animals, and I watched the little sphinx more and more keenly as an interesting study. But there is no estimating the wit and wisdom concealed and latent in our lower fellow mortals until made manifest by profound experiences; for it is through suffering that dogs as well as saints are developed and made perfect.

After exploring the Sum Dum and Tahkoo fiords and their glaciers, we sailed through Stephen's Passage into Lynn Canal and thence through Icy Strait into Cross Sound, searching for unexplored inlets leading toward the great fountain icefields of the Fairweather Range. Here, while the tide was in our favor, we were accompanied by a fleet of icebergs drifting out to the ocean from Glacier Bay. Slowly we paddled around Vancouver's Point, Wimbledon, our frail canoe tossed like a feather on the massive heaving swells coming in past Cape Spenser. For miles the sound is bounded by precipitous mural cliffs, which, lashed with wave-spray and their heads hidden in clouds, looked terribly threatening and stern. Had our canoe been crushed or upset we could have made no landing here, for the cliffs, as high as those of Yosemite, sink sheer into deep water. Eagerly we scanned the wall on the north side for the first sign of an opening fiord or harbor, all of us anxious except Stickeen, who dozed in peace or gazed dreamily at the tremendous precipices when he heard us talking about them. At length we made the joyful discovery of the mouth of the inlet now called "Taylor Bay," and about five o'clock reached the head of it and encamped in a spruce grove near the front of a large glacier.

While camp was being made, Joe the hunter climbed the mountain wall on the east side of the fiord in pursuit of wild goats, while Mr. Young and I went to the glacier. We found that it is separated from the waters of the inlet by a tide-washed moraine, and extends, an abrupt barrier, all the way across from wall to wall of the inlet, a distance of about three miles. But our most interesting discovery was that it had recently advanced, though again slightly receding. A portion of the terminal moraine had been plowed up and shoved forward, uprooting and overwhelming the woods on the east side. Many of the trees were down and buried, or nearly so, others were leaning away from the ice-cliffs, ready to fall, and some stood erect, with the bottom of the ice plow still beneath their roots and its lofty crystal spires towering huge above their tops. The spectacle presented by these century-old trees standing close beside a spiry wall of ice, with their branches almost touching it, was most novel and striking. And when I climbed around the front, and a little way up the west side of the glacier, I found that it had swelled and increased in height and width in accordance with its advance, and carried away the outer ranks of trees on its bank.

On our way back to camp after these first observations I planned a far-and-wide excursion for the morrow. I awoke early, called not only by the glacier, which had been on my mind all night, but by a grand flood-storm. The wind was blowing a gale from the north and the rain was flying with the clouds in a wide passionate horizontal flood, as if it were all passing over the country instead of falling on it. The main perennial streams were booming high above their banks, and hundreds of new ones, roaring like the sea, almost covered the lofty gray walls of the inlet with white cascades and falls. I had intended making a cup of coffee and getting something like a breakfast before starting, but when I heard the storm and looked out I made haste to join it; for many of Nature's finest lessons are to be found in her storms, and if careful to keep in right relations with them, we may go safely abroad with them, rejoicing in the grandeur and beauty of their works and ways, and chanting with the old Norsemen, "The blast of the tempest aids our oars, the hurricane is our servant and drives us whither we wish to go." So, omitting breakfast, I put a piece of bread in my pocket and hurried away.

Mr. Young and the Indian were asleep, and so, I hoped, was Stickeen; but I had not gone a dozen rods before he left his bed in the tent and came boring through the blast after me. That a man should welcome storms for their exhilarating music and motion, and go forth to see God making landscapes, is reasonable enough; but what fascination could there be in such tremendous weather for a dog? Surely nothing akin to human enthusiasm for scenery or geology. Anyhow, on he came, breakfastless, through the choking blast. I stopped and did my best to turn him back. "Now don't," I said, shouting to make myself heard in the storm. "now don't, Stickeen. What has got into your queer noddle now? You must be daft. This wild day has nothing for you. There is no game abroad, nothing but weather. Go back to camp and keep warm, get a good breakfast with your master, and be sensible for once. I can't carry you all day or feed you, and this storm will kill you."

But Nature, it seems, was at the bottom of the affair, and she gains her ends with dogs as well as with men, making us do as she likes, shoving and pulling us along her ways, however rough, all but killing us at times in getting her lessons driven hard home. After I had stopped again and again, shouting good warning advice, I saw that he was not to be shaken off; as well might the earth try to shake off the moon. I had once led his master into trouble, when he fell on one of the topmost jags of a mountain and dislocated his arm; now the turn of his humble companion was coming. The pitiful wanderer just stood there in the wind, drenched and blinking, saying doggedly, "Where thou goest I will go." So at last I told him to come on if he must, and gave him a piece of the bread I had in my pocket; then we struggled on together, and thus began the most memorable of all my wild days.

The level flood, driving hard in our faces, thrashed and washed us wildly until we got into the shelter of a grove on the east side of the glacier near the front, where we stopped awhile for breath and to listen and look out. The exploration of the glacier was my main object, but the wind was too high to allow excursions over its open surface, where one might be dangerously shoved while balancing for a jump on the brink of a crevasse. In the meantime the storm was a fine study. There the end of the glacier, descending an abrupt swell of resisting rock about five hundred feet high, leans forward and falls in ice-cascades. And as the storm came down the glacier from the north, Stickeen and I were beneath the main current of the blast, while favorably located to see and hear it. What a psalm the storm was singing, and how fresh the smell of the washed earth and leaves, and how sweet the still small voices of the storm! Detached wafts and swirls were coming through the woods, with music from the leaves and branches and furrowed boles, and even from the splintered rocks and ice crags overhead, many of the tones soft and low and flute-like, as if each leaf and tree, crag and spire were a tuned reed. A broad torrent, draining the side of the glacier, now swollen by scores of new streams from the mountains, was rolling boulders along its rocky channel, with thudding, bumping, muffled sounds, rushing toward the bay with tremendous energy, as if in haste to get out of the mountains; the winters above and beneath calling to each other, and all to the ocean, their home.

Looking southward from our shelter, we had this great torrent and the forested mountain wall above it on our left, the spiry ice crags on our right, and smooth gray gloom ahead. I tried to draw the marvelous scene in my notebook, but the rain blurred the page in spite of all my pains to shelter it, and the sketch was almost worthless. When the wind began to abate, I traced the east side of the glacier. All the trees standing on the edge of the woods were barked and bruised, showing high-ice mark in a very telling way, while tens of thousands of those that had stood for centuries on the bank of the glacier farther out lay crushed and being crushed. In many places I could see down fifty feet or so beneath the margin of the glacier-mill, where trunks from one to two feet in diameter here being ground to pulp against outstanding rock-ribs and bosses of the bank.

About three miles above the front of the glacier I climbed to the surface of it by means of axe-steps made easy for Stickeen. As far as the eye could reach, the level, or nearly level, glacier stretched away indefinitely beneath the gray sky, a seemingly boundless prairie of ice. The rain continued, and grew colder, which I did not mind, but a dim snowy look in the drooping clouds made me hesitate about venturing far from land. No trace of the west shore was visible, and in case the clouds would settle and give snow, or the wind again become violent. I feared getting caught in a tangle of crevasses. Snow-crystals, the flowers of the mountain clouds, are frail, beautiful things, but terrible then flying on storm winds in darkening, benumbing swarms or when welded together into glaciers full of deadly crevasses. Watching the weather, I sauntered about on the crystal sea. For a mile or so out I found the ice remarkably safe. The marginal crevasses mere mostly narrow, while the few wider ones were easily avoided by passing around them, and the clouds began to open here and there.

Thus encouraged, I at last pushed out for the other side; for Nature can make us do anything she likes. At first we made rapid progress, and the sky was not very threatening, while I took bearings occasionally with a pocket compass to enable me to find my way back more surely in case the storm should become blinding; but the structure lines of the glacier were my main guide. Toward the west side we came to a closely crevassed section in which we had to make long, narrow tacks and doublings, tracing the edges of tremendous traverse and longitudinal crevasses, many of which were from twenty to thirty feet wide, and perhaps a thousand feet deep — beautiful and awful. In working a way through them I was severely cautious, but Stickeen came on as unhesitating as the flying clouds. The widest crevasse that I could jump he would leap without so much as halting to take a look at it. The weather was now making quick changes, scattering bits of dazzling brightness through the wintry gloom at rare intervals, when the sun broke forth wholly free, the glacier was seen from shore to shore with a bright array of encompassing mountains partly revealed, wearing the clouds as garments, while the prairie bloomed and sparkled with irised light from myriads of washed crystals. Then suddenly all the glorious show would be darkened and blotted out.

Stickeen seemed to care for none of these things, bright or dark, nor for the crevasses, wells, moulins, or swift flashing streams into which he might fall. The little adventurer was only about two years old, yet nothing seemed novel to him. Nothing daunted him. He showed neither caution nor curiosity, wonder nor fear, but bravely trotted on as if glaciers were playgrounds. His stout, muffled body seemed all one skipping muscle, and it was truly wonderful to see how swiftly and to all appearance heedlessly he flashed across nerve-trying chasms six or eight feet wide. His courage was so unwavering that it seemed to be due to dullness of perception, as if he were only blindly bold; and I kept warning him to be careful. For we had been close companions on so many wilderness trips that I had formed the habit of talking to him as if he were a boy and understood every word.

We gained the west shore in about three hours; the width of the glacier here being about seven miles. Then I pushed northward in order to see as far back as possible into the fountains of the Fairweather Mountains, in case the clouds should rise. The walking was easy along the margin of the forest, which, of course, like that on the other side, had been invaded and crushed by the swollen, overflowing glacier. In an hour or so, after passing a massive headland, we came suddenly on a branch of the glacier, which, in the form of a magnificent ice cascade two miles wide, was pouring over the rim of the main basin in a westerly direction, its surface broken into wave-shaped blades and shattered blocks, suggesting the wildest updashing, heaving, plunging motion of a great river cataract. Tracing it down three or four miles, I found that it discharged into a lake, filling it with icebergs.

I would gladly have followed the lake outlet to tidewater, but the day was already far spent, and the threatening sky called for haste on the return trip to get off the ice before dark. I decided therefore to go no farther and, after taking a general view of the wonderful region, turned back, hoping to see it again under more favorable auspices. We made good speed up the canyon of the great ice-torrent, and out on the main glacier until we had left the west shore about two miles behind us. Here we got into a difficult network of crevasses, the gathering clouds began to drop misty fringes, and soon the dreaded snow came flying thick and fast. I now began to feel anxious about finding a way in the blurring storm. Stickeen showed no trace of fear. He was still the same silent, able little hero. I noticed, however, that after the storm darkness came on he kept close up behind me. The snow urged us to make still greater haste, but at the same time hid our way. I pushed on as best I could, jumping innumerable crevasses, and for every hundred rods or so of direct advance traveling a mile in doubling up and down in the turmoil of chasms and dislocated ice-blocks. After an hour or two of this work we came to a series of longitudinal crevasses of appalling width, and almost straight and regular in trend, like immense furrows. These I traced with firm nerve, excited and strengthened by the danger, making wide jumps, poising cautiously on their dizzy edges after cutting hollows for my feet before making the spring, to avoid possible slipping or any uncertainty on the farther sides, where only one trial is granted — exercise at once frightful and inspiring. Stickeen followed seemingly without effort.

Many a mile we thus traveled, mostly up and down, making but little real headway in crossing, running instead of walking most of the time as the danger of being compelled to spend the night on the glacier became threatening. Stickeen seemed able for anything. Doubtless we could have weathered the storm for one night, dancing on a flat spot to keep from freezing, and I faced the threat without feeling anything like despair; but we were hungry and wet, and the wind from the mountains was still thick with snow and bitterly cold, so of course that night would have seemed a very long one. I could not see far enough through the blurring snow to judge in which general direction the least dangerous route lay, while the few dim, momentary glimpses I caught of mountains through rifts in the flying clouds were far from encouraging either as weather signs or as guides. I had simply to grope my way from crevasse to crevasse, holding a general direction by the ice structure, which was not to be seen everywhere, and partly by the wind. Again and again I was put to my mettle, but Stickeen followed easily, his nerve apparently growing more unflinching as the danger increased. So it always is with mountaineers when hard beset. Running hard and jumping, holding every minute of the remaining daylight, poor as it was precious, we doggedly persevered and tried to hope that every difficult crevasse we overcame would prove to be the last of its kind. But on the contrary, as we advanced they became more deadly trying.

At length our way was barred by a very wide and straight crevasse, which I traced rapidly northward a mile or so without finding a crossing or hope of one; then down the glacier about as far, to where it united with another uncrossable crevasse. In all this distance of perhaps two miles there was only one place where I could possibly jump it, but the width of this jump was the utmost I dared attempt, while the danger of slipping on the farther side was so great that I was loath to try it. Furthermore, the side I was on was about a foot higher than the other, and even with this advantage the crevasse seemed dangerously wide. One is liable to underestimate the width of crevasses where the magnitudes in general are great. I therefore stared at this one mighty keenly, estimating its width and the shape of the edge on the farther side, until I thought that I could jump it if necessary, but that in case I should be compelled to jump back from the lower side I might fail. Now, a cautious mountaineer seldom takes a step on unknown ground which seems at all dangerous that he cannot retrace in case he should be stopped by unseen obstacles ahead. This is the rule of mountaineers who live long, and, though in haste, I compelled myself to sit down and calmly deliberate before I broke it.

Retracing my devious path in imagination as if it were drawn on a chart, I saw that I was recrossing the glacier a mile or two farther upstream than the course pursued in the morning, and that I was now entangled in a section I had not before seen. Should I risk this dangerous jump, or try to regain the woods on the west shore, make a fire, and have only hunger to endure while waiting for a new day! I had already crossed so broad a stretch of dangerous ice that I saw it would be difficult to get back to the woods through the storm, before dark, and the attempt would most likely result in a dismal night-dance on the glacier; while just beyond the present barrier the surface seemed more promising, and the east shore was now perhaps about as near as the west. I was therefore eager to go on. But this wide jump was a dreadful obstacle.

At length, because of the dangers already behind me, I determined to venture against those that might be ahead, jumped and landed well, but with so little to spare that I more than ever dreaded being compelled to take that jump back from the lower side. Stickeen followed, making nothing of it, and we ran eagerly forward, hoping we were leaving all our troubles behind. But within the distance of a few hundred yards we were stopped by the widest crevasse yet encountered. Of course I made haste to explore it, hoping all might yet be remedied by finding a bridge or a way around either end. About three fourths of a mile upstream I found that it united with the one we had just crossed, as I feared it would. Then, tracing it down, I found it joined the same crevasse at the lower end also, maintaining throughout its whole course a width of forty to fifty feet. Thus to my dismay I discovered that we were on a narrow island about two miles long, with two barely possible ways to escape: one back by the way we came, the other ahead by an almost inaccessible sliver-bridge that crossed the great crevasse from near the middle of it!

After this nerve-trying discovery, I ran back to the sliver-bridge and cautiously examined it. Crevasses, caused by strains from variations in the rate of motion of different parts of the glacier and convexities in the channel, are mere cracks when they first open, so narrow as hardly to admit the blade of a pocket-knife, and gradually widen according to the extent of the strain and the depth of the glacier. Now some of these cracks are interrupted, like the cracks in wood, and in the opening the strip of ice between overlapping ends is dragged out, and may maintain a continuous connection between the side, just as the two sides of a slivered crack in wood that is being split are connected. Some crevasses remain open for months or even years, and by the melting of their sides continue to increase in width long after the opening strain has ceased; while the sliver-bridges, level on top at first and perfectly safe, are at length melted to thin, vertical, knife-edged blades, the upper portion being most exposed to the weather; and since the exposure is greatest in the middle, they at length curve downward like the cables of suspension bridges. This one was evidently very old, for it had been weathered and wasted until it was the most dangerous and inaccessible that ever lay in my way. The width of the crevasse was here about fifty feet, and the sliver crossing diagonally was about seventy feet long; its thin knife-edge near the middle was depressed twenty-five or thirty feet below the level of the glacier, and the up-curving ends were attached to the sides eight or ten feet below the brink. Getting down the nearly vertical wall to the end of the sliver and up the other side were the main difficulties, and they seemed all but insurmountable. Of the many perils encountered in my years of wandering on mountains and glaciers none seemed so plain and stern and merciless as this. And it was presented when we were wet to the skin and hungry, the sky dark with quick driving snow, and the night near. But we were forced to face it. It was a tremendous necessity.

Beginning, not immediately above the sunken end of the bridge, but a little to one side, I cut a deep hollow on the brink for my knees to rest in. Then, leaning over, with my short-handled axe I cut a step sixteen or eighteen inches below, which on account of the sheerness of the wall was necessarily shallow. That step, however, was well made; its floor sloped slightly inward and formed a good hold for my heels. Then, slipping cautiously upon it, and crouching as low as possible, with my left side toward the wall, I steadied myself against the wind with my left hand in a slight notch, while with the right I cut other similar steps and notches in succession, guarding against losing balance by glinting of the axe, or by wind gusts, for life and death were in every stroke and in the niceness of finish of every foothold.

After the end of the bridge was reached I chipped it down until I had made a level platform six or eight inches wide, and it was a trying thing to poise on this little slippery platform while bending over to get safely astride of the sliver. Crossing was then comparatively easy by chipping off the sharp edge with short, careful strokes, and hitching forward an inch or two at a time, keeping my balance with my knees pressed against the sides. The tremendous abyss on either hand I studiously ignored. To me the edge of that blue sliver was then all the world. But the most trying part of the adventure, after working my way across inch by inch and chipping another small platform, was to rise from the safe position astride and to cut a stepladder in the nearly vertical face of the wall — chipping, climbing, holding on with feet and fingers in mere notches. At such times one's whole body is eye, and common skill and fortitude are replaced by power beyond our call or knowledge. Never before had I been so long under deadly strain. How I got up that cliff I never could tell. The thing seemed to have been done by somebody else. I never have held death in contempt, though in the course of my explorations I have oftentimes felt that to meet one's fate on a noble mountain, or in the heart of a glacier, would be blessed as compared with death from disease, or from some shabby lowland accident. But the best death, quick and crystal-pure, set so glaringly open before us, is hard enough to face, even though we feel gratefully sure that we have already had happiness enough for a dozen lives.

But poor Stickeen, the wee, hairy, sleekit beastie, think of him! When I had decided to dare the bridge, and while I was on my knees chipping a hollow on the rounded brow above it, he came behind me, pushed his head past my shoulder, looked down and across, scanned the sliver and its approaches with his mysterious eyes, then looked me in the face with a startled air of surprise and concern, and began to mutter and whine; saying as plainly as if speaking with words, "Surely, you are not going into that awful place." This was the first time I had seen him gaze deliberately into a crevasse, or into my face with an eager, speaking, troubled look. That he should have recognized and appreciated the danger at the first glance showed wonderful sagacity. Never before had the daring midget seemed to know that ice was slippery or that there was any such thing as danger anywhere. His looks and tones of voice when he began to complain and speak his fears were so human that I unconsciously talked to him in sympathy as I would to a frightened boy, and in trying to calm his fears perhaps in some measure moderated my own. "Hush your fears, my boy," I said, "we will get across safe, though it is not going to be easy. No right way is easy in this rough world. We must risk our lives to save them. At the worst we can only slip, and then how grand a grave we will have, and by and by our nice bones will do good in the terminal moraine."

But my sermon was far from reassuring him: he began to cry, and after taking another piercing look at the tremendous gulf, ran away in desperate excitement, seeking some other crossing. By the time he got back, baffled of course, I had made a step or two. I dared not look back, but he made himself heard; and when he saw that I was certainly bent on crossing he cried aloud in despair. The danger was enough to haunt anybody, but it seems wonderful that he should have been able to weight and appreciate it so justly. No mountaineer could have seen it more quickly or judged it more wisely, discriminating between real and apparent peril.

When I gained the other side, he screamed louder than ever, and after running back and forth in vain search for a way of escape, he would return to the brink of the crevasse above the bridge, moaning and wailing as if in the bitterness of death. Could this be the silent, philosophic Stickeen? I shouted encouragement, telling him the bridge was not so bad as it looked, that I had left it flat and safe for his feet, and he could walk it easily. But he was afraid to try. Strange so small an animal should be capable of such big, wise fears. I called again and again in a reassuring tone to come on and fear nothing; that he could come if he would only try. He would hush for a moment, look down again at the bridge, and shout his unshakable conviction that he could never, never come that way; then lie back in despair, as if howling, "O-o-oh! what a place! No-o-o, I can never go-o-o down there!" His natural composure and courage had vanished utterly in a tumultuous storm of fear. Had the danger been less, his distress would have seemed ridiculous. But in this dismal, merciless abyss lay the shadow of death, and his heart-rending cries might well have called Heaven to his help. Perhaps they did. So hidden before, he was now transparent, and one could see the workings of his heart and mind like the movements of a clock out of its case. His voice and gestures, hopes and fears, were so perfectly human that none could mistake them; while he seemed to understand every word of mine. I was troubled at the thought of having to leave him out all night, and of the danger of not finding him in the morning. It seemed impossible to get him to venture. To compel him to try through fear of being abandoned, I started off as if leaving him to his fate, and disappeared back of a hummock; but this did no good; he only lay down and moaned ill utter hopeless misery. So, after hiding a few minutes, I went back to the brink of the crevasse and in a severe tone of voice shouted across to him that now I must certainly leave him, I could wait no longer, and that, if he would not come, all I could promise was that I would return to seek him next day. I warned him that if he went back to the woods the wolves would kill him, and finished by urging him once more by words and gestures to come on, come on.

He knew very well what I meant, and at last, with the courage of despair, hushed and breathless, he crouched down on the brink in the hollow I had made for my knees, pressed his body against the ice as if trying to get the advantage of the friction of every hair, gazed into the first step, put his little feet together and slid them slowly, slowly over the edge and down into it, bunching all four in it and almost standing on his head. Then, without lifting his feet, as well as I could see through the snow, he slowly worked them over the edge of the step and down into the next and the next in succession in the same way, and gained the end of the bridge. Then, lifting his feet with the regularity and slowness of the vibrations of a seconds pendulum, as if counting and measuring one-two-three, holding himself steady against the gusty wind, and giving separate attention to each little step, he gained the foot of the cliff, while I was on my knees leaning over to give him a lift should he succeed in getting within reach of my arm. Here he halted in dead silence, and it was here I feared he might fail, for dogs are poor climbers. I had no cord. If I had had one, I would have dropped a noose over his head and hauled him up. But while I was thinking whether an available cord might be made out of clothing, he was looking keenly into the series of notched steps and finger holds I had made, as if counting them, and fixing the position of each one of them in his mind. Then suddenly up he came in a springy rush, hooking his paws into the steps and notches so quickly that I could not see how it was done, and whizzed past my head, safe at last!

And now came a scene! "Well done, well done, little boy! Brave boy!" I cried, trying to catch and caress him; but he would not be caught. Never before or since have I seen anything like so passionate a revulsion from the depths of despair to exultant, triumphant, uncontrollable joy. He flashed and darted hither and thither as if fairly demented, screaming and shouting, swirling round and round in giddy loops and circles like a leaf in a whirlwind, lying down, and rolling over and over, sidewise and heels over head, and pouring forth a tumultuous flood of hysterical cries and sobs and gasping mutterings. When I ran up to him to shake him, fearing he might die of joy, he flashed off two or three hundred yards, his feet in a mist of motion; then, turning suddenly, came back in a wild rush and launched himself at my face, almost knocking me down, all the while screeching and screaming and shouting as if saying, "Saved! saved! saved!" Then away again, dropping suddenly at times with his feet in the air, trembling and fairly sobbing. Such passionate emotion was enough to kill him. Moses's stately song of triumph after escaping the Egyptians and the Red Sea was nothing to it. Who could have guessed the capacity of the dull, enduring little fellow for all that most stirs this mortal frame? Nobody could have helped crying with him!

But there is nothing like work for toning down excessive fear or joy. So I ran ahead, calling him in as gruff a voice as I could command to come on and stop his nonsense, for we had far to go and it would soon be dark. Neither of us feared another trial like this. Heaven would surely count one enough for a lifetime. The ice ahead was gashed by thousands of crevasses, but they were common ones. The joy of deliverance burned in us like fire, and we ran without fatigue, every muscle with immense rebound glorying in its strength. Stickeen flew across everything in his way, and not till dark did he settle into his normal fox-like trot. At last the cloudy mountains came in sight, and we soon felt the solid rock beneath our feet, and were safe. Then came weakness. Danger had vanished, and so had our strength. We tottered down the lateral moraine in the dark, over boulders and tree trunks, through the bushes and devil-club thickets of the grove where we had sheltered ourselves in the morning, and across the level mud-slope of the terminal moraine. We reached camp about ten o'clock, and found a big fire and a big supper. A party of Hoona Indians had visited Mr. Young, bringing a gift of porpoise meat and wild strawberries, and Hunter Joe had brought in a wild goat. But we lay down, too tired to eat much, and soon fell into a troubled sleep. The man who said, "The harder the toil, the sweeter the rest," never was profoundly tired. Stickeen kept springing up and muttering in his sleep, no doubt dreaming that he was still on the brink of the crevasse; and so did I, that night and many others long afterward, when I was over-tired.

Thereafter Stickeen was a changed dog. During the rest of the trip, instead of holding aloof, he always lay by my side, tried to keep me constantly in sight, and would hardly accept a morsel of food, however tempting, from any hand but mine. At night, when all was quiet about the campfire, he would come to me and rest his head on my knee with a look of devotion as if I were his god. And often as he caught my eye he seemed to be trying to say, "Wasn't that an awful time we had together on the glacier?"

Nothing in after years has dimmed that Alaska storm day. As I write it all comes rushing and roaring to mind as if I were again in the heart of it. Again I see the gray flying clouds with their rain-floods and snow, the ice cliffs towering above the shrinking forest, the majestic ice cascade, the vast glacier outspread before its white mountain-fountains, and in the heart of it the tremendous crevasse — emblem of the valley of the shadow of death — low clouds trailing over it, the snow falling into it; and on its brink I see little Stickeen, and I hear his cries for help and his shouts of joy. I have known many dogs, and many a story I could tell of their wisdom and devotion; but to none do I owe so much as to Stickeen. At first the least promising and least known of my dog-friends, he suddenly became the best known of them all. Our storm-battle for life brought him to light, and through him as through a window I have ever since been looking with deeper sympathy into all my fellow mortals.

None of Stickeen's friends knows what finally became of him. After my work for the season was done, I departed for California, and I never saw the dear little fellow again. In reply to anxious inquiries his master wrote me that in the summer of 1883 he was stolen by a tourist at Fort Wrangell and taken away on a steamer. His fate is wrapped in mystery. Doubtless he has left this world — crossed the last crevasse — and gone to another. But he will not be forgotten. To me Stickeen is immortal.

John Neihardt on Paddling the Missouri River (1910)

Poet, philosopher, folklorist, mystic, and journalist-sportsman John Neihardt was one of the true Renaissance men of the Golden Age. Best known for transcribing the now canonical book Black Elk Speaks, *Neihardt began his career as a Nebraska journalist editing the Bancroft Blade. Restless as a small town newsman, Neihardt and a small crew canoed 2000 miles from Fort Benton, Montana to Sioux City, Iowa, the result of which was one of the earliest American sports participatory accounts of its kind,* The River and I. *In 1921, the Nebraska legislature elected Neihardt the state poet laureate. He would go on to hold professorships at the University of Nebraska and the University of Missouri-Columbia.*

From "Getting Down to Business"

It all came back there by the smoldering fires — the wonder and the beauty and the awe of being alive. We had eaten hugely — a giant feast. There had been no formalities about the meal. Lying on our blankets under the smoke drift, we had cut with our jackknives and tender morsels from a haunch as it roasted. When the haunch was at last cooked to the bone, only the bone was left.

Heavy with the feast, I lay on my back watching the gray smoke brush my stars that seemed so near. *My stars!* Soft and gentle and mystical! Like a dark-browed Yotun woman wooing the latent giant in me, the night pressed down. I closed my eyes, and through me ran the sensuous surface fires of here dream-wrought limbs. Upon my face the weird magnetic lure of ever-nearing, never-kissing lips made soundless music. Like a sister, like a mother, she caressed me, lazy with the giant feast; and yet, a drowsy, half-voluptuous joy shimmered and rippled in my veins.

Drowsing and dreaming under the drifting smoke-wrack, I felt the sense of time and self drop away from me. No now, no tomorrow, no yesterday, no I! Only eternity, one vast whole — sun-shot, star-sprent, love-filled, changeless. And in it all, one spot of consciousness more acute than other spots; and that was something that had eaten hugely, and that now felt the inward-flung glory of it all; the swooning, half-voluptuous sense of awe and wonder, the rippling, shimmering, universal joy.

And then suddenly and without shock — like the shifting of the wood smoke — the mood veered, and there was nothing but I. Space and eternity where I — vast projections of myself, tingling with my consciousness to the remotest fringe of the outward swinging atom-drift; through immeasurable night, pierced capriciously with shafts of paradoxic day; through and beyond the awful circle of yearless duration, my ego lived and knew itself and thrilled with the glory of being. The slowly revolving Milky Way was only a glory with me; the great woman-star jewelling the summit of a cliff, was only an ecstasy within me; the murmuring of the river out in the dark was only the singing of my heart; and the deep, deep blue of the heavens was only the splendid color of my soul.

The *Atom*, very fast under power, was, with paddles, the slowest boat imaginable.* There was no lift to her prow, no exhilarating leap as with the typical light canoe driven by regulation paddles. And she was as unwieldy as a log. A light wind blew upstream, and the current was very slow. After dark we caught up with Bill and Frank, who had supper waiting. I had been tasting venison all day; but there was none left for supper. In spite of the night's smoking, all if it had spoiled. This left us without meat. Our provisions now consisted mostly of flour. We had a few potatoes and some toasted wind called "breakfast food." During six or seven hours of hard work at the paddles, we had covered no more than fifteen miles. These facts put together gave no promising result. In addition to this, it was impossible to stir up a song. Even the liquor wouldn't bring it out. And the flapjacks were not served *à la chansonette* that night. I tried to explain why the trip was only beginning to get interesting; but my words fell flat. And when the irrepressible Kid essayed a joke, I alone laughed at it, though rather out of gratitude than mirth.

There are many men who live and die with the undisputed reputation of being good fellows — your friends and mine — who, if put to the test — would fail miserably. Fortunate is that man to whom it is not given to test all of his friends. This is not cynicism; it is only human nature, being myself possessed of so much of it. I admire it when it stands firmly upon its legs,

---

*Excision of material from the original chapter is here indicated by the insertion of a line space. The noted sentence marks the first sentence of the fourth full paragraph on page 192.

and I love it when it wobbles. But when it gains power with increasing odds, grows big with obstacles, I worship it.

> To thrill with the joy of girded men,
> To go on forever and fail, and go on again —
> With the half of a broken hope for a pillow at night —

Thus it should have been. But that night, staring into the faces of three of the four, I saw the yellow streak. The Kid was not one of the three. The first railroad station would hold out no temptation to him. He was a kid, but manhood has little to do with age. It must exist from the first like a tang of iron in the blood. Age does not really create anything — it only develops. Your wonderful and beautiful things often come as paradoxes. I looked for a man and found him in a boy.

Bill talked about home and stared into the twilight. The "floaters" were irritable, quarrelling with the fire, the grub, the cooking utensils, and verbally sending the engine to the devil.

Seeing about 1800 miles of paddle work ahead, knowing that at that season of the year the prevailing winds would be headwinds, and having very little faith in the engine under any conditions, I decided to travel day and night, for the water was falling steadily and already the channels were at times hard to find. Charley and Frank grumbled. I told them we would split the grub fairly, a fifth to a man, and that they might travel as slowly as they liked, the skiff being their property. They stayed with us.

We lashed the boats together and put off into the slow current. A haggard, eerie fragment of moon slinked westward. Stars glinted in the flawless chilly blue. The surface of the river was like polished ebony — a dream-path wrought of gloom and gleam. The banks were lines of dusk, except where some lone cottonwood loomed skyward like a giant ghost clothed with a mantle that glistened and darkled in the chill star-sheen.

There was the feel of moving in eternity about it all. The very limitation of the dusk gave the feeling of immensity. There was no sense of motion, yet we moved. The sky seemed as much below as above. We seemed suspended in a hollow globe. Now and then the boom of a diving beaver's tail accented the clinging quiet; and by fits the drowsy muttering of waterfowl awoke in the adjacent swamps, and droned back into the universal hush.

Frank and I stood watch, the three others rolling up in their blankets among the luggage. It occurred to me for the first time that we had a phonograph under the cargo. I went down after it. At random I chose a record and set the machine going. It was a Chopin *Nocturne* played on a cello — a vocal yearning, a wailing of frustrate aspirations, a brushing of sick wings across the gates of heavens never to be entered; and then the finale — an insistent, feverish repetition of the human ache, ceasing as with utter exhaustion.

I looked about me drinking in the night. How little this music really expressed itself. It seemed too humanly near-sighted, too egotistic, too petty to sound out under those far-seeing stars, in that divine quiet.

I slipped on another record. This time it was a beautiful little song, full of the sweet melancholy of love. I shut it down. The thing wouldn't do. In the evening — yes. But *now!* Truly there is something womanly about Night, something loverlike in a vast impersonal way; but too big — she is too terribly big to woo with human sentiment. Only a windlike chant would do — something with an undertone of human despair, outsoared by brave, savage flights of invincible soul-hope — great virile singing man-cries, winged as the starlight, weird as space — Whitman sublimated, David's soul poured out in symphony.

I started another going. This time I did not stop it, for the Night was singing — through its nose perhaps, but still it was singing — out of that machine. It was Wagner's *Evening Star* played by an orchestra. It filled the night, swept the glittering reaches, groped about in the glooms; and then, leaving the human theme behind, soul-like the upward yearning violins took flight, dissolving at last into starlight and immensity. Ages swept by me like a dream-wind. When I got back, the machine, all but run down, was scorching hideously.

Slowly we swung about in the scarcely perceptible current. Down among the luggage the three snored discordantly. Frank's cigarette glowed intermittently against the dim horizon, like a bonfire far off. Somewhere out in the gloom coyotes chattered and yelped, and from far across the dusky valley others answered — a doleful tension.

I dozed. Frank awoke us all with a shout. We leaped up and stared blinkingly into the north. That whole region of the sky was aflame from zenith to horizon with spectral fires. It was the aurora. Not the pale, ragged glow, sputtering like the ghost of a huge, lamp-flame, which is familiar to every one, but a billowing of color, rainbows gone mad! In the northeast the long rolling columns formed — many-colored clouds of spectral light whipped up as by a whirlwind — flung from eastward to westward, devouring Polaris and the Wain — rapid sequent towers of smokeless fire!

It dazzled and whirled and mounted and fell like the illumined filmy skirts of some invisible Titanic serpentine dancer, madly pirouetting across a carpet of stars. Then suddenly it all fell into a dull ember-glow and flashed out. The ragged moon dropped out of the southwestern sky. In the chill of the night, gray, dense fog wraiths crawled upon the hidden face of the waters.

Again I dozed and awakened with the sense of having stopped suddenly. A light wind had arisen and we were fast on a bar. Frank and I took our blankets out on the sand, rolled up, and went to sleep.

The red of dawn awoke us as though someone had shouted. Frank and

I sat up and stared about. A white-tail deer was drinking at the river's edge three hundred yards away. So far as we were concerned, it was a dream-deer. We had blinked complacently at it until it disappeared in the brush. Then we thought of the rifle.

We were all stiff and chilled. The boats were motionless in the shallow water. We all got out in the stream that felt icy to us, and waded the crafts into the channel. Incidentally we remembered Texas and his wisdom.

The time was early August; but nevertheless there was a tang of frost in the air and the river seemed to flow not water but a thick frore fog. I smelled persimmons distinctly — it was that cold; brown spicy persimmons smashed on crisp autumn leaves down in old Missouri! The smell haunted me all morning like the a bittersweet regret.

We breakfasted on flapjacks and, separating the boats, put off. The skiff left us easily and disappeared. A headwind arose with the sun and increased steadily. By eleven o'clock it blew so strongly that we could make no headway with the rude paddles, and the waves, rolling at least four feet from trough to crest, made it impossible to hold the boat on course. We quit paddling, and got out in the water with the line. Two pulled and one pushed. All day we waded, sometimes up to our necks; sometimes we swam a bit, and sometimes we clung to the boat and kicked it on to the next shallows. Our progress was ridiculously slow, but we kept moving. When we stopped for a few minutes to smoke under the lee of a bank, our legs cramped.

To lay up one day would be only to establish a precedent for day after day of inactivity. The prevailing winds would be headwinds. We clung to the shoddy hope held out by that magic name — Milk River. We knew too well that Milk River was only a snare and a delusion; but one must fight toward something — it makes little difference what you call that something. A goal, in itself, is an empty thing; all the virtue lies in the moving toward the goal.

Often we sank deep in the mud; often at the bends we could scarcely forge against the blast that held us leaning to the pull. Noon came and still we had not overtaken the skiff. Dark came, and we had not yet sighted it. But with the sun, the wind fell, and we paddled on, lank and chilled. About ten o'clock we sighted the campfire.

We ate flapjacks once more — delicious, butterless flapjacks! — and then once more we put off into the chill night air. We made twelve miles that day, and every foot had been a fight. I wanted to raise it to twenty-five before sunrise. No one grumbled this time; but in the light of the campfire the faces looked cheerless — except the Kid's face.

We huddled up in our blankets and, naturally, all of us went to sleep. A great shock brought us to our feet. The moon had set and the sky was overcast. Thick night clung around us. We saw nothing, but by the rocking of the boats and the roaring of the river, we knew we were shooting rapids.

Still dazed with sleep, I had a curious sense of being whirled at a terrific spped into some subterranean suck of waters. There was nothing to do but wait. We struck rocks and went rolling, shipping buckets of water at every dip. Then there was a long sickening swoop through utter blackness. I ended abruptly with a thud that knocked us down.

We found that we were no longer moving. We got out, hanging to the gunwales. The boats were lodged on a reef or rock, and we were obliged to "walk" them for some distance, when suddenly the water deepened, and we went up to our necks. And the night seemed bitterly cold. I never shivered more in January.

It was yet too dark to find a camping place; so we drifted on until the east paled. Then we built a great log fire and baked ourselves until sunrise.

Day after day my log-book begins with the words, "Heavy headwinds," and ends with the words, "Drifted most of the night," We covered about twenty-five miles every twenty-four hours. Every day the cooks grumbled more; and Bill had a way of staring wistfully into the distance talking about home that produced in me an odd mixture of anger and pity.

We had lost our map: we had no calendar. Time and distance, curiously confused, were merely a weariness in the shoulders.

Edward Lydell Fox on Ice-Boating (1912)

A well-respected yachtsman in his day and a contributor to Outing *magazine, among others, Edward Lydell Fox attempts, in the excerpt below, to transfer his sailing skills to the mostly undiscovered sport of ice-boating. Conspicuous in this article is Fox's substitution of the first-person with the autobiographical sobriquet "a Man," a technique not uncommon for nineteenth and twentieth century personal journalists uneasy with the subjectivities implied by the "I" pronoun.*

From "Learning to Sail an Ice-boat"

To frozen Great South Bay — that still, inland sea washing Long Island's southern shore — there came one bright midwinter morning, a Man. A yachtsman, master of his sailing from carboat to forty-footer, from keel to masthead, he came on scoffing bent. For at his club, the week before, the conversation had strayed to iceboating and fastening there had blazed suddenly into discussion vituperative. This, because the Man had ridiculed the sport before a friend, the latter one of its most zealous pursuers. And so in the course of lurid argument it simply had to be that the Man was dared by his friend to go down to Moriches and there sail an iceboat, alone.

All of which explains why we find the lonely figure this day, whereof we know, standing on the edge of the sedgy, frozen bay. Back, beyond the field somewhere, his friend had stopped to instruct the chauffeur about the returning hour and had bidden the Man to go ahead and await him down on the shore. And so we see the Man admiring the shifting white picture spread out before him — the sweep of glistening ice over which moved in the distance a flock of sails, careening in steady flight, like some great birds of winter; the gray line of Fire Island with its dunes piled high, and beyond, the curve of the ocean, faintly blue where the sun shone — dull, like a sheet of steel. Nearby an inlet was mumbling; in the cove, black water flowed sluggishly under the frost-feathered edges of the ice and over the white reaches of the bay, the distant drumming of the surf on the outer bar fluttered in faint and vague whimperings.

The friend appeared — appeared unexpectedly from behind the flapping wings of a strange shape right on the ice before the Man. It had come swooping from behind a bend and wheeling suddenly, had lit, all motionless, almost at his very feet — an enormous gull come to rest. But he had little time to examine its lines, for the friend was gesticulating rigidly, like a frozen semaphore, bidding him hurry. And he did, picking his way over the ice toward this oddest of ships.

Never mind what they said and thought when they met — it concerns us not. Also, their personalities we can blissfully ignore. For we shall follow them through this winter day simply so that by observing their every move and eavesdropping (if the subject of their conversation warrants) we may learn how to sail iceboats — learn with the Man.

But unfortunately for him, he was not as patient as we. Remember, however, that the friend had dared him to sail an iceboat alone. Is it any wonder then that he jumped in before being asked and with frantic assistance from his friend made before a brisk wind? Picture his sensations — the craft behaving beautifully, the exuberance given by the air and the knowledge that he who dared him to do it stood, doubtless, stupefied, back on the ice somewhere. Fine! Then an imp lit on his shoulder and whispered: "It's time to come about and sail back to show your friend how well you can handle her already."

So with his knowledge of water-sailing and his ignorance of ice sailing, the Man luffed up suddenly dead into the wind. The runners scraped, the sails flapped overhead, the bowsprit wavered from right to left — all motion ceased. Becalmed, as it were, because ice sailing conditions are so different from those of the water, he now knew why the dare had been given. As on all sides of him, across the glassy sheet, flocks of white sails were skimming off the wind at high speed, all satisfaction of the moment before rose vapory, vanishing into air like the breath he exhaled. More, he made out the grinning face of his friend moving toward him over the ice.

While awaiting this second coming of the friend, it is permissible for us to reflect with the Man. Obviously his reflections were of what he had just experienced.

"A yachtsman!" thought he moodily. "A yachtsman isn't necessarily an iceboater. Anyone can sail to leeward on one of these things (he kicked the runner plank spitefully) — the secret is to learn to sail to windward."

Meanwhile the friend had come up offering him warm condolences that froze under the Man's glare. He rambled on, however, and his ramblings will tell us some things we want to know, we'll play eavesdroppers for the moment.

"You admit, then, the friend was saying, "that from now until this ice-boating demonstration has been finished, you're the greenest thing that ever came down these icy mountains the hymn book used to tell about? Very well. Now listen. In the first place you haven't got nearly enough clothes on. No wonder you're chattering there. That overcoat would look great in town, but remember that you're up against the frostiest proposition this side of Baffin's Bay. You'll want this extra sweater (he handed the Man a thick woolen jacket slung over his arm) and then you won't be any too warm.

"Grab these woolen gloves, too, or you'll lose your grip and take a bump on the ice when we come about, swinging round bow to the wind. I'm sorry I haven't another pair of felt boots. If you don't get cold feet in those otherwise good shoes, you belong in a museum as the original human stove. All fixed? Fine!"

Before them, the boat looked like a huge Grecian cross, encumbered by many trappings. At either end of the crossbar, beneath it, iron skates almost three feet long were fastened and rested on the ice. This was the rudder, and just before it, fastened to the underside of the beam, was an oval platform of wood known by courtesy as the cockpit. At the intersection of the crossbar and the longer pole rose the mast, mainsail-jib rigged with bowsprit where it is on any respectable sloop. But the friend was talking again —

"Move that runner a bit, will you? (this impatiently) Yes! Yes! That's it, the long skate-like effect at the end of the plank. Got to change the position of this boat if you're going to get going again. By the way, child, if you ever meet a runner struck to the ice by an overnight freeze and it's too deep to be shoved, try this method: Alternate on the position of the helm and pry on the end of the main boom. She'll twist around so that the wind'll be caught slightly around on the port or starboard side. That'll wrench the runner loose. Then straighten your tiller again. Get that?"

The Man, still being cold, nodded savagely, but his friend, undisturbed, continued with all the suavity of the barber who tells you that your hair needs singeing.

Walter Camp on Coaching Football (1912)

Known as the "Father of American Football," Walter Camp captained the Yale football squad from 1879 to 1880, coached the squad from 1888 to 1891, and in the early 1900s served on the rules committees that gradually divorced football from its parent sport, rugby. Credited with replacing the rugby scrum with the football scrimmage in addition to other inventions and adaptations, Camp was, first and foremost, a writer, as he published over 30 books and more than two hundred periodical articles in his lifetime. In the excerpt below, Camp manages to artfully avoid the first person while speaking directly from his firsthand participation as the Yale varsity coach. The public pressure Camp describes he well knew in yet another pioneering pigskin post: selector of the All-American football team.

From "Making a Football Team"

Mr. Lee McClung, Treasurer of the United States, gave a little dinner in New York last fall that was unique in its own way, and I doubt if it can ever be equaled or repeated by anyone else. When he was at Yale he was captain of the university football team. That team was one of the most remarkable on record, going through the season without being scored upon by anyone and running up 488 points against their opponents. That was twenty years ago, and as we sat at that table and looked over the faces of these men we could not help feeling that the playtime of life had in it the most valuable lessons for all these men in future years. In those days of the making of that team the writer was brought in very close contact with Mr. McClung and saw much of the young man's spirit injected into the individual members of his eleven and then saw, and may perhaps have helped somewhat, the welding of the individual self-reliance into a general spirit of team play. And to say that this was an interesting study was to put it mildly, for the making of a football team has in it certain elements of development that cannot be surpassed if one has any interest at all in the development of character.

I have known the head coach of a big university football team who weighed 182 pounds in September tip the scales at 157 at the end of November on the eve of his important game! And the captain has almost equal responsibilities! Now this gives one some idea of what it means in the way of expenditure of nervous energy to accomplish what is known as "making a modern football team." No sooner will these lines have been read than some will arise with the contention. "There! That is just what we have been saying right along; that there is too much of the coach or captain and too little of the individual player in the modern American game of football." These critics are all the time advocating a sort of game where each individual player runs about the field, picks up the ball as he has opportunity, kicks, passes, or runs with it according as the mood of the moment possesses him; as some of these advisers say, "Make it a game that any man can play any day with any set of men; a game that will not require signals and team play."

Now a good deal depends upon what kind of training one wishes to get for these boys at all modern games. If he just wishes them to make a happy lark of playtime perhaps some such game as that above suggested would be good, but if he wishes through the instrumentality of sport to introduce a certain amount of modern discipline and to secure for boys the development of some characteristics which will be valuable to them in later life, it is far better to take the more complicated modern team game.

I once talked with a retired manufacturer who did not at all approve of the present detailed methods of organization and specialization in any first-class plant. He told me about the good old times when he had only twenty-five or fifty men working for him and he used to show each one what to do by doing it himself then saying, "Now, come on, boys." He had no respect for and little appreciation of the modern method where one man or set of men repeats an operation over and over again while others do their part so that the net result is a product of specialization. Now, it does not make any great amount of difference what walk of life our boys are going into; they will certainly find that efficiency is the watchword and that efficiency can only be obtained through organization and team play, as it were.

Coaches in football do not by any means monopolize the principal work of the team, and although they may be commented upon in the newspapers and much appreciated by the boys themselves they represent only the combined and tabulated knowledge given from year to year through the experience of captains and individuals on teams. In other words, these coaches are the repository of information which without them might be frittered away or neglected. Coaches are the ones who should see that an experience once gained is made valuable for the future. In other words, when a method or play has been thoroughly exploited, certain conclusions should be derived as to the wisdom of developing it further or of abandoning it so that succeeding teams and captains may not have to repeat the work all over again in order to find out whether the play or method will prove successful.

Joseph Knowles on Trapping a Bear (1913)

The story of illustrator turned "caveman" Joseph Knowles is one of the most compelling, and little-told tales of the 1910s. Celebrated as a hero by tens of thousands and a fraud by more than a few, Knowles claimed to have lived the life of a "primitive man" in Maine's north woods for two months before making his triumphant return to Boston bedecked in the very same bearskin he obtains in the passage that follows. Historian Roderick Nash reports that Knowles's sporting achievement upstaged the October 1913 World Series, earned him an interview with the governor of Massachusetts, and sold 300,000 copies of his participatory account Alone in the Wilderness. *Unable to repeat his back-to-nature, hunting and gathering experiment despite calls that he do so, Knowles retreated to a remote cabin in coastal Washington and died in 1942. In the excerpt anthologized here, consisting of a portion of the book's explanatory first chapter, a section break, and the controversial Chapter V "Trapping a Bear" in its entirety, Knowles describes the call to adventure and the improvisations necessary to a life in the wilderness.*

From "An Idea and a Birthday" and "Trapping a Bear"

On the Saturday afternoon of October fourth, nineteen hundred and thirteen, just at the time when sunshine marked the end of two days' heavy rain, I emerged from the Canadian forest on the shores of Lake Megantic, having lived the life of a primitive man for two months in the wilderness of northern Maine.

I was tanned to the color of an Indian. I had a matted beard, and long, matted hair. I was scratched from head to foot by briers and underbrush.

Over the upper part of my body I wore the skin of a black bear which I had fastened together in front with deerskin thongs. My legs were encased in crudely tanned deerskin chaps, with the hair inside. On my feet I wore moccasins of buckskin, sewed together with sinew. I wore no hat. On my back was a pack, made from woven lining bark of the cedar, in which I carried various implements from the forest.

I had a rude bow and arrows, and a crude knife, made from the horn of a deer, dangled at my waist.

It was thus that I entered the little French-Canadian town of Megantic — back to the civilized world.

I received a welcome that I had not dreamed of, and I was very happy, for it proved to me at that time that the people were really interested. However, as the hours went on, I began to realize that they considered that I had done a wonderful thing.

It is because of this impression, which seems to have taken hold of many people since my return, that I will begin this narrative by saying that it was not wonderful. Above all else I want to emphasize that my living alone in the wilderness for two months without clothing, food, or implements of any kind was not a wonderful thing. It was an interesting thing; but it was not wonderful.

Any man of fair health could do the same thing, provided he meant business and kept his head. But, to the best of my knowledge, no other man in the history of civilization ever did what I did; and for that reason the people are marveling at it. To be sure, doing a thing for the first time has its usual and mysterious side; but it is not necessarily wonderful.

The idea of this experiment came to me about a year ago, while I was spending a few weeks at Bradford, Vermont. At the time I was painting pictures of outdoor life in a little log cabin on what is known in that locality as Saddleback Mountain. I was painting a moose, and, as I added a touch of color to the canvas, I began to wonder how many people would notice that particular bit of color, which, from a standpoint of faithful portrayal, was as important as the eye of the creature itself.

From this thought my mind wandered on to the realization that the people of the present time were sadly neglecting the details of the great book of nature.

And, as I thought, I forgot the picture before me. I said to myself, "Here, I know something about nature. I wonder if it would not be possible for me to do something for the benefit of others."

Then I would laugh at the idea of my doing anything for the world! Probably all of us have wild dreams now and then. I am beginning to think that wild dreams are wonderful things to have. I have always hoped, more than anything else, that I might sometime do something which would benefit mankind, even in a small way.

The idea of "nature and myself" stuck in my mind, and I began to wonder what I might do to turn the attention of the public back to nature. I knew that art appealed to only a part of the people. I couldn't do it by art alone; no one ever had. A new impetus was needed.

I believed there was too much artificial life at the present day in the cities. I found myself comparing our present mode of living with the wild rugged life of the great outdoors. Then, all of a sudden, I wondered if the man of the present day could leave all his luxury behind him and go back into the wilderness and live on what nature intended him to have.

In that thought came the birth of the idea.

That night I went down to the hotel in Bradford and began talking it over with several of my friends. At first they laughed at the absurdity of today going back to the life of the primitive man of yesterday. I remember, as we sat around the fireplace, they asked me all kinds of questions.

I told them that in order to make such an experiment interesting it would be necessary for a man to enter the woods entirely naked, without even a match or a knife, and live in a stipulated time without the slightest communication or aid from the outside world.

"What would you do for fire?" one man asked me.

I replied to that very quickly.

Another wanted to know what food I would be able to get in the wilderness and how I would get it without weapons. I mentioned a dozen ways.

Then the conversation became like a game. Everyone wanted to see if he couldn't stick me in some way.

That night I couldn't think of a single thing that would keep me from undertaking such an experiment.

In the busy days which followed I promptly forgot all about the idea, just as nine tenths of all ideas are forgotten. Not until the beginning of last summer did the thought take hold of me again.

From time to time my friends would jokingly inquire when I was going to leave them and become a wild man.

Then, all of a sudden, it hit me hard. Another mood seized me like the one I had felt in the cabin while painting the picture of the moose. I said — and this time I meant it—"I'll try this stunt, and demonstrate to the people that there are marvelous things to be derived from life in the great outdoors."

When I told my friends that I really was going to try the experiment during the months of August and September, they became serious indeed. They were not joking now, when they cried, "Do not think of such a thing!" They reminded me that it might be easy enough to answer all of their theoretical questions satisfactorily; but to actually find fire and food and clothing would be impractical and, indeed, utterly impossible.

But my mind was fully made up. I left Bradford immediately for Boston, to make preparations for the trip. By preparations I do not mean that I went back to the city to train for the trip. I went to Boston simply to discuss with other friends the plans that were in my mind.

First of all it was necessary for me to choose a location for the experiment. This was some task, inasmuch as I desire to enter a wilderness far away from civilization, where I would not be bothered by people from the outside world.

Finally I decided that I would go into the forest on the fourth of August, in what is known in the northwest Maine country as the Dead River Region.

This county is covered with heavy black-growth timber. Directly north is Bear Mountain, below which stretches Spencer Lake. To the east is Little Spencer, with the Heald Mountain just beyond. Horseshoe Pond and the Spencer Stream lie to the southward, and the domain is bounded on the west by King and Bartlett Lake.

I selected this particular time for the experiment because I wanted it to be the most severe kind of a test.

I was handicapped by civilization's habits and comforts: my skin was not tough; my muscles were not firm; and my stomach was used to seasoned and well-cooked food.

However, I still retained my knowledge of the woods, and it was on that alone I placed dependence. It is in the mind, I claim, the mind that has been trained to know nature, that the spark of complete independence is retained down through the ages.

As August fourth drew near some of my closest friends literally begged me to abandon the idea. They warned me that I might become ill and wreck my future health, or even lose my life, and all that kind of talk. They were good to me, and I appreciated their feelings, but I knew they did not understand.

I knew better. I was confident.

Trapping a Bear

That night it was colder than usual. I began to realize that, sooner or later, I would be forced to break the game laws and get some sort of skins for protection.*

During the day, while I was on the move, I really didn't need anything on my body. In fact, through the entire trip, even up to the very last day, I went around the forest, rain or shine, absolutely naked. But at night I did need something for a covering.

It was also time for me to be thinking about what I should wear when I

---

*The running-in of a separate, complete, noncontiguous chapter, "Trapping a Bear," is here indicated by the insertion of a subhead of the same name preceding the run-in material. The sentence here noted represents the first sentence of the run-in chapter.

came back to civilization. I could scarcely return to the world naked! I thought of the deer I had obtained and then lost.

In my wanderings I had seen many signs of bears. Once, in the burnt lands, I saw three feeding on the berries, shortly after the deer episode.

A bearskin would mean much to me. Then, too, I could utilize the sinew and meat to good advantage.

A man little dreams what he can accomplish until he is put to the test. I fully believe that necessity, coupled with determination and confidence, makes failure impossible.

From the first moment the idea of getting a bear came into my head I felt confident I could trap one. I carefully went over in my mind various ways I might make the attempt, and when morning came I had my plan all mapped out.

I didn't even wait that day to see if my friends, the red deer and the white fawn, would come to the spring. I was all bear now, and was anxious to get to work constructing a trap.

For over an hour I walked about searching for a suitable spot and finally found the right place.

A deadfall was impractical, so my plan was to build a combination pit and deadfall, much after the plan of the Indian way of trapping grizzly bears in the West.

Digging a pit meant a lot of work. I started in my loosening the ground with sharp pointed stones and hornbeam sticks. It was slow work, but I made progress, scooping the earth out with flat shale from the ledges.

I worked for several hours that day, returning to my partially excavated hole the next day and again setting to work.

I don't know how many hours I worked on that pit; it might have been ten or fifteen during the two or three days I kept at it.

Once during the digging I thought I should have to give up that spot, for I came across some heavy rock and buried, petrified wood. It took the most arduous labor to dislodge that rock and chip my way through the wood until I found earth again.

At last the hole was large enough to hold a bear, being about three and a half or four feet deep.

I bedded two logs — one on each side — in the earth I had scooped from the hole.

I next made a kind of deadfall over the pit with logs and sticks, covering this with rocks I had taken out of the hole.

Then I set a spindle trip, which resembled the figure four, under the deadfall. This spindle I baited with stale fish. I arranged the bait quite high up so that the bear would have to stand on his hind legs to get it.

The trap was done at last, and I was pleased with it.

The covering loaded with rocks fitted securely just inside the bed logs. This would make it impossible to move the top from side to side when once it was down.

I didn't get a bear that night, but the next night as I passed by the pit I thought I heard a rustle as if some animal were moving away from the trap. I didn't go any nearer, because through the trees I could just make out the slant of the roof. It hadn't been sprung yet.

The next night I "looked" the trap and found a bear in it.

While I had been confident all along that I would be able to land a bear, there was more or less surprise attached to the capture of this one.

Coming up the side of the pit I saw, through the roof cover, a young bear, making every effort to get out.

"This is great luck," I said to myself. "Everything is coming my way." There would be the skin, and the meat, and I began to think of everything about the animal that I could use.

I made up my mind that he must not get away from me. I can't describe to you my feelings just then. I imagine they were something like those of a miser when there is a possibility of his losing his gold.

At that time the bear was worth more to me than all the gold in the world.

Considering the situation carefully, I found that I would have to break away some of the lashing in order to get at the animal. But I had to be careful not to break away too much, so I made an aperture just big enough for him to stick his head out.

Before doing this I got a hornbeam club, which I held in readiness.

Presently out came the nose of the bear. I made a vicious swing and missed him. My presence so enraged the animal that he struggled around trying frantically to escape. Again his head came up through the torn place in the cover, and this time I landed squarely on top if it!

But you can't kill a bear by hitting him over the head. You must strike him on the nose. I knew that, and waited my chance. As I looked down at him a feeling of pity came over me at the method I was forced to use. But how else could I do it? Pretty soon he struck out his front paws. I swung and hit them. With a cry of pain he pulled them back.

Keeping my eyes on the bear every minute I backed away to a tree and broke off a small limb covered with leaves. Returning to the trap I tore away another lashing.

With my left hand I began to dangle the leaves on the end of the branch in his face to divert his attention so that I could deliver a blow with the club.

In his anger a good part of his nose came out. I swung my club, landing on the side of the bear's nose. The animal toppled over in the pit and lay perfectly still.

Knowing bears of old, I did not take any chances even then. I prodded him with the stick. There was no question about it — he was dead!

It had been pretty strenuous work, so I decided to put off the task of skinning the creature until the next day. I knew what that would mean without any knife! It would take me hours to complete the work.

Catching that bear was the biggest thing I had yet accomplished in the forest.

I think every man who has accomplished something a bit bigger than the ordinary things of his daily routine has a right to feel proud. It is a part of his reward.

However, there was a great deal of luck attached to my catching that bear. Anyway I had him, and I was pleased beyond measure.

The red deer and the little white fawn came up to my spring the next morning.

By seven o'clock I was at the trap again. On the way I picked up the sharpest-edged rocks I could find, throwing away those I had as I came across the better ones. These rocks are surprisingly sharp, and abound everywhere in this region.

I was ready for a hard day's work.

Pulling away the covering, I broke down the side of the pit and forced a couple of logs under the body of the bear, raising him slightly. I should estimate that he weighed close to two hundred pounds.

By getting a good hold and tugging and hauling I managed to drag him up the side of the pit I had just broken down. Then I rolled him over on his back. I would have given anything for a knife just then! In its place I took one of the sharp rocks and began sawing back and forth on the inside of one of his hind legs.

After a seemingly endless time the hair began to curl up under the rock. It worked hard at first, but by putting all my muscle back of it I finally broke the skin.

Not until later had I worked down the hind legs, up to the stomach, and then up and down the inside of the front legs.

While it was a crude piece of work, the skin was now ready to be taken off.

I was tired after finishing this stunt. A few moments' rest and I was at work again. Then for hours I tugged and pulled at that skin trying to remove it from the carcass. Alternately working and resting for short periods, I took hold of the skin with one hand while I ripped it away from the flesh by scraping between the two with the sharpest stones I had.

Of course, quantities of meat came off with the skin, but that didn't bother me for I knew I could scrape it off later.

Not until late in the afternoon — judging by the sun — did I finally pull that skin entirely off. And I had started to work about seven that morning!

As Lost Pond was not very far from where I had made the trap I decided to go there, and afterwards to my first lean-to, which was in that vicinity.

First I sawed off with my rock a large proportion of the bear meat for food, gathering the sinew. Slinging the meat and skin over my shoulder, I started for camp.

I confess I was pretty much "all in" when I arrived at the pond. My hands were cramped and scratched, and every muscle in my back and arms ached.

Throwing the skin and meat down on the shore, I plunged into the water. The bath was very refreshing; it made a new man out of me. After I came out I lay down in the sun to rest.

The beavers were busy over on the dam, and I watched them a long time.

With visions of an early bed I went back into the woods in the direction of my lean-to, where I built a new fire and ate a supper of dried berries and smoked trout, which I had previously stored away for just such an emergency.

I slept soundly that night.

In the morning the first thing I determined to do was to get that skin into some sort of condition. I laid it out on some cedar logs and fleshed it clean, by scraping it off with the rock and pulling it over the logs.

Next I took a sheet of birch bark and made a watertight dish. Filling this with water, I threw in some small pieces of rotten wood, and began to steep it over the fires. A birchbark dish will never burn below the water line.

When the mixture had stepped enough, I spread the bear hide flat on the ground, with the hair side down, and poured the liquid from the birchbark dish upon it. By repeating this process several times the skin became tanned to a certain extent.

A thorough drying was needed now. I singled out two saplings about the proper distance apart, and, stretching the skin as much as I could, I laced it to the slender trunks with cedar bark.

I had yet to work the skin and make it pliable and soft.

Off and on I worked on that hide for about three days. During those days I walked back to the trap and brought the remainder of the meat to my camp.

Tearing with the grain, I ripped the meat into strips with my hands, roasting some for immediate use, and putting the rest in the smoke hole. I used quantities of dirty wood in this smoking process, as I could get up a lot of smoke that way. This smoked meat wasn't particularly pleasing to look at, but it would keep and was nourishing.

While this was not the first time I had ever trapped a bear in my life, it was the first time I had ever eaten any of the meat.

In my years of experience as a guide I had hunted and trapped all kinds of game — animals and birds. But I had never eaten a pound of wild meat in my life, because I never liked it particularly. In fact, I had never eaten much fresh meat.

Now I was compelled to eat it. I didn't relish it a bit; but, after I devoured some, I always felt stronger, and knew that it was just what I needed.

Aside from the comfort of having that bear skin to throw over me at night, and the supply of food I had obtained, I had secured in the sinews of that creature a lasting cord for my fire kindler. The inner lining bark of the cedar, while it had answered the purpose after a fashion, was not the best thing for sawing back and forth. It wore out too quickly.

With the sinew string I would not have to use any care for fear of its breaking. I could work the bow with all my strength, and the cord would not be affected in any way, producing the friction in much less time.

There is no known substance for sinew that can equal its toughness and lasting qualities. The Indians have a way of chewing it and stripping it into thin fibers, which they use as thread to sew moccasins and rawhide.

I hadn't reached the sewing stage just yet.

Since I had trapped the bear something had been prowling around my camp at night. I could tell by the sound that it wasn't a very large animal, but as it kept coming I became curious to see what it might be.

First I thought that the meat in my lean-to might have attracted a wildcat. Then the idea of a bear cub came into my mind.

Anyway, I was bound to find out just what it was, so one night, just before getting ready to turn in, I let my fire burn pretty low and sat up watching for some signs of the visitor.

On the other nights the sound of crackling twigs had always come just after my fire had burned out.

Scarcely had the last glimmer of my fire flickered away when, off in the darkness to my right, came the expected sound. I had almost dozed off as I sat there, but I woke up quickly and listened.

Straining my eyes in the direction of the noise, I could barely make out the outline of some animal. It was impossible to tell what it was, but I knew it was dark colored.

As if suddenly switched on by an unseen electric current, two balls of light flashed in the darkness. The creature was looking at me too! The fire was between us, and as a lazy flame sputtered a moment before fading away I could see the reflection of the firelight dancing in those eyes!

Presently the eyes disappeared. I seized a smoldering brand, and, fanning it into flame, rushed toward the spot.

I was now convinced that the animal was a bear cub by the way it acted. Through the dim light from my brand, which was already burning low again, I saw that the creature was black. I couldn't see clearly enough to determine the head and the hind; but I felt sure that my company was a clumsy young bear.

The first thought was to catch him alive.

The little fellow made a sudden turn and almost dodged past me, but I hurled the brand at him and drove him back toward the fire. He was literally between two fires!

As the brand struck the ground it went out. With that the animal turned and ran directly toward me. Again he tried to rush by me, but I jumped in front of him and stopped him with my legs.

Then I jumped again, but in a different direction! My supposed bear cub had turned out to be a hedgehog, and for some moments I was fully occupied removing quills from my legs. My bark chaps were ample protection against the briers and brush, but not against quills of hedgehogs.

My third week in the wilderness was already drawing to a close. Physically I was perfectly well. I had plenty of food and a comfortable bearskin. But mentally I was suffering.

I was terribly lonesome!

Gertrude Buffington Phillips on Salmon Fishing (1913)

Gertrude Buffington Phillips's career as a journalist seemed destined for drama; in May 1910 The New York Times *reported that she accompanied sportswoman Blanche Stuart Scott on an automobile endurance trip across the United States from New York City to San Francisco at a time when, according to the National Air and Space Museum, there were only a couple hundred miles of paved roads outside America's major cities. Scott's trip, dutifully recorded by Phillips in her official role as trip documentarian, was reported to have been the first westward, coast-to-coast trip in an automobile by an American woman. Later Blanche Stuart Scott, "The Tomboy of the Air" would turn to aviation, becoming, by some accounts, the first woman to solo pilot an airplane.*

Two years after publishing the following article in Outing, *Phillips married noted post–Impressionist and Modernist painter Middleton Manigault, whose brief participation in World War I as an ambulance driver, à la Hemingway, forever darkened his art. After Manigault was discharged and returned home suffering from acute depression, Phillips became his primary caregiver. Her personal courage and evocative power as a writer are both on display in her account of catching her first salmon in Newfoundland. "This is the story," she writes, "of adventures in search of them alone — the narrative of a novice, and if I got excitement and met misfortune, well — I laid myself open to it."*

From "My First Salmon"

Salmon-killing in the far rough countries has always been considered a man's work. True, many women have caught many salmon, but most of them have been ably abetted by big husbands, brothers, and friends. This is the story of adventures in search of them alone — the narrative of a novice, and if I got excitement and met misfortune, well — I laid myself open to it.

Because the Newfoundland streams and pools are the best, they were my choice, and with an outfit selected according to the best print authorities, plus my own more adequate knowledge in hunting lake trout, bass, tarpon, muskellunge, etc., I landed in quaint old fish-odoriferous St. John's, and bumped forthwith into a fountain of salmon wisdom in the person of an old enthusiast just from the pools. He was little, short, and fat, and I first saw him one sunset as he sat swinging his bandy legs from the parapet at the top of the ascent to the squat old cathedral that wards over the sleepy town. This is the queer but illuminating lecture he delivered on salmon — truly the best I have ever heard:

"Miss, them is the fish of mystery. They is the gypsies of the salt and fresh water, contrary as you women, and got a memory like a Scotchman. I run an engine on the Erie all year long just to get enough extra money to come up here and let them make faces at me. You say you never took one yet? Well, let me tell you a little bit about them, leastways these fellers in Newfoundland and the Maritime Provinces. Maw Salmon gets the family idea just about the time we begin to eat strawberries in New York. The first piece of strawberry shortcake you see it's time to shellac the roughed spots on your salmon rod and put your fly books in order."*

Easy Laws for the Fisherman

As often happens, my first incursion was the most satisfactory. I had pitched on the Little Codroy on account of its ready accessibility, which is a great item with a woman, though I am too proud to confess to any lack of courage before a long, rough hike or days of jolting on the wooden seat of a springless wagon. The railway runs down the wonderful faces of the Cape Ray mountains, and when on the pools almost any quiet hour I could hear the distant clatter and roar and the wailing whistle of a passing train.

At the time I went out, the coaches looked like the assemblage of all the mad enthusiasts from the Sportsmen's Show. There were parties and parties, and yet more parties, but station by station they melted away, till at last I

Following the sentence here noted, eleven contiguous paragraphs — in which the old codger explains the habits of Salmon family as well as local game laws and licensing — have been excised for concision.

realized that in those vast, lonely regions the entire population of New York City could go fishing at one and the same time without crowding. Having left St. John's in the early evening, the whole train-load, almost, dwindled down till there was nothing left to distract one's attention from the marvelous scenery of the next day's crossing of the island. Though it was nine at night when I got down at Little River, having passed two or three hundred miles of the finest fishing water in the world, there was still a blue glow of light from the west, and the scene was so enchanting that I had no misgivings or regrets for the possible fish left behind.

Out of the purple gloom, with the soft, swaying tread of the born canoeman, came a short, lithe, broad-shouldered man. He moved out of a group speaking a tongue I had never heard. It was pure Gaelic! Pulling his cap, he stood before me, speaking my name. He was my guide, one of a family of famous brothers and cousins who always figure large in the annual reports by the Game and Inland Fisheries Board of the trout and salmon taken.

Crude, clean, and comfortable was the place in which I slept, and when the pink and green dawn cut clear against the east the great bulk of Table Mountain, I was up and we were on our way to the pools. In the heavy rains a month before, there had been a slide of rocks and earth just above Kid's Pool, and soil was still dropping in every now and then, so that we rounded it past Country Path and came to the brink of Island Pool from the north.

When I had brought down my tackle before starting, my guide, losing the dull, sleepy look from his little blue eyes and, puffing more quickly on his short pipe, had walked around it two or three times, looking at it with sidelong glances, before he said at last: "Tham bain't inssential—nowt all, Miss. One pound is ten eventime, Miss."

Everything had been bought and brought on advice, so most meekly I opened up my bandoliered rod case and my tackle box, and with fingers that were deft and sensitive for all their clumsy, stubby look, he had gone over every part. In the end there were two piles. In one was the bulk of my tackle, including the box. In the other was my second from heaviest, double-handed, full-agated rod, with a spare tip, a ten-fly book, a simple hundred-yard reel, and the small accessories which he palmed and scrutinized carefully before he knotted them in a big blue handkerchief for me to fasten to a loop at the belt of my short khaki skirt. Later I understood why he did not take even an extra rod section. When one broke he cut a section of a green withe, set the ferrules, and inserted it.

On the Pools

The chill of the morning still hung in the valley as we came into the second pool. The wind was gusty and with a March-like temper and sting. Setting up and rigging, I was soon on a broad shaly ledge that commanded the deeper water, and essayed my first cast, the guide, crouched low on the ground at my left, directing my efforts. Wielding a salmon rod and an ordinary fly rod have the differences that lie between using an axe and handling a hatchet, but control of the line and judgment of direction being the same, I was soon doing fairly well. Half an hour only brought, however, one silvery, quickly vanishing flash from behind a split boulder on the lower side.

Once the guide touched my arm with his pipe and pointed quickly. What he had seen I was too slow to catch, but it was salmon leaving the pool and going up. We, too, moved on to Tompkins Pool, finding indications that late the night before, or perhaps even that morning, someone had been there. I was getting my first comprehension of what it meant to traverse such bulks of rock.

The second cast I made across the head of the pool my fly, a Durham Ranger, was hovering at the limit when I heard the guide's breath indrawn sharply, and at the same instant saw what looked like a curving bolt of bright metal swing up with incredible speed from the cold, dark green depths. A whirl of spray and spindle and my drop-fly was gone, while the line was cutting down to the left. I struck in insane rapture — my good fortune was astounding. The barb went home somewhere in the jaw of one of the great fish of mystery.

If the pool had been broader I should never have turned him. Time and again I thought my tip or second section would go owing to my eager handling. Ten mad minutes and he began to sulk.

"He bain't a wearied, Miss," chuckled the guide. "Change forefoot to rest yornself."

Game to the Last

Indeed, he was not wearied, for as soon as he realized that the new enemy that had bitten him was not to be conquered by such methods, he tried other and took the air. I could have shouted with joy when I saw that great body leaving the sunshine, but my teeth were too close set, and the only sound that issued was something akin to a strangling man's call for help. Some persons recommend a down and out draught on the line when the fish is leaping, but my habit is to slack as swiftly as possible when he strikes back into the water. How many times I did this, and how many times he tried to throw the hook from his mouth, I cannot tell. I had lost all track of time and all thought of anything else on earth except that beauty.

After a while I was able to bring him to my side of the pool, and at last he came to the top of the water without leaving it for the air. For the first time the guide looked about to see where he had dropped the gaff. It was thirty feet away. Leisurely he ambled over, filled and lit his pipe, picked up the gaff, and ambled back. He seemed to know just what my process was, as I realized with a sense of humiliation.

"Brang him by that yon bowder, Miss," admonished the guide.

I did so just an instant before the man leaped like a cat from the water edge, lit on the boulder, balanced, and struck down. My salmon was gaffed! Also I saw that my hook was fast and deep in his jaw, and I drew him out on the shingle and shale.

When the guide held him up, and I saw what a splendid specimen my first salmon was, and I had figured the man's estimates in stones and fractions into pounds, a silly smile came on my face. It was impossible, it was incredible! Without mishap and unaided, I had landed my first salmon, one weighing more than twenty pounds. Then I knew I must have been a very long time doing it, but as I had not looked at my wristwatch since leaving the lower pool, there was no way of telling. All I know is that the sun seemed an hour or two higher in the heavens, and it was getting hotter with a vengeance.

It was only with an effort that I recovered myself sufficiently to go on fishing. Also my casting was now hopeless, and I had more line and reel trouble than would come in an ordinary month.

Past Dugget's Pool, Tompkins Nose, Rock Pool, McQuarrie's Pool, Aggravation, and Long Turn Pools we went, reaching the latter without having hooked anything more. Tired as I was I would not give up till between us we had taken two grilse, which we did not gaff, but turned back. As a matter of fact, since that first salmon, I have never gaffed one of the fish of mystery save as a means to saving tackle or when it was necessary to do so to land him at all.

It was nearly dark when we came to the Tompkins Inn. As soon as I had my smoking-hot supper, I tried to write a letter to a sister enthusiast about my first take, but when I came to with my face on the sheet and smeared with ink from nodding, I crawled into bed, face unwashed, and slept like a rock.

Wilma Anderson-Gilman on Pistol Shooting (1914)

Seldom studied sportswoman Wilma Anderson-Gilman remains a cipher. A contributor to Outing *as well as other sports periodicals of her era, Gilman's prose ode to the pistol that follows rings with an exuberance bordering on zealotry. While rightly classified as a sports article, this short excerpt anticipates many contemporary issues: the benefits of self-defense for women and the case for carried and concealed weapons, to name just two.*

From "The Woman's Weapon"

"God," says an old toast, "made big men, and God made little men; but God bless Col. Colt, who made all men equal." A pistol will shoot just as straight and hit just as hard in the hands of a woman as it will for the most brawny and brutal of men. As between these two, it gives each an equal power to inflict injury upon the other and leaves the victory to the one having the more coolness, courage, and skill. And the day when woman was willing to admit that she was inferior to man in these qualities is long past.

I do not like to dwell upon this phase of the pistol question. But, to the average person, man or woman the pistol undoubtedly appears first and foremost a weapon of combat. The subject is one which will not down and might as well be touched and disposed of at once, thus clearing the air for a consideration of the wider and more pleasant field of the pistol's usefulness.

The knowledge that she has a pistol and knows how to use it certainly does tend to reassure the woman alone in camp or cabin and enable her to face things very confidently. It is true that the rifle or shotgun are even better weapons of defense, but the pistol is so much more portable that it is the arm she can most easily keep where it will be in her hand at the first instant she needs it.

I can imagine no more morbid, fear-fraught situation than that of a woman alone save for a pistol she is afraid of, which simply serves to remind her that, in some remote, improbably contingency, she might have to rely on it for protection.

To be a real safeguard the pistol to her should be an article of familiar, everyday use; something which she can utterly forget until the time she wants to use it — and then pick up and use as naturally as a saucepan or a curling iron.

It was my entire innocence of the romantic, dime-novel idea of firearms which led to the practical, commonplace use of this arm by my husband as well as myself. A thievish red squirrel had earned the death sentence and I, in my very ignorance, turned to a little .22-caliber revolver as the instrument of execution. Here was a squirrel to be shot and here was a pistol which, as I understand it, was made to shoot things. So I took the pistol and shot him.

That very simple act saved us both from the "gun-toter" state of mind. We kept up target practice and tried to improve our marksmanship, but it was not at all with the idea of preparing for a possible "gun fight." In the woods, whether on canoe trips or around the shack, we both wear the pistol — because it is convenient and always at hand when we want it. The use may be a marauding porcupine inside the "deadline," a rabbit or a brace of partridges desired for the table, a fish to be quieted before he is taken aboard the canoe, a signal shot to give information of our whereabouts — or a provoking tin can may move the spirit to a little target practice.

Lewis R. Freeman on Swimming, Sprints, Canoe Races, Shot Put, Cricket, Long- and High Jumping, and Marathoning Versus the Fijians (1914)

Lewis Ransome Freeman stands as one of the most prolific, most historically neglected sportsmen of his era. The author of over twenty books, Freeman was a consummate, virtuoso athlete, earning letters in football, baseball, tennis, and track at Stanford University and, remarkably, coaching the U.S.C. Trojans football team while a student in 1897. From 1899 to 1912, Freeman traveled all over the world as an adventurer, athlete and war correspondent in the 1905 Russo Japanese War. On occasional trips home to Pasadena during the period, Freeman somehow managed to earn the doubles and singles tennis titles in the Ojai Valley Tennis Tournament in 1903. In World War I, Freeman was a correspondent for the Allied armies in Europe and, as a participant, earned the rank of lieutenant in the Royal Navy Volunteer Reserve. A member of the elite Explorer's Club at his death in 1960, Freeman's sports legacy was noted in the Los Angeles Times, *among other major newspapers, and his achievements earned mention in* Who's Who of California.

The excerpt that follows finds Freeman and friends immersed in an impromptu sports challenge they instigated while traveling Polynesia in the early 1910s. Exhibiting an unselfconscious racist tendency typical of the post–Victorian era, the editors of Outing *magazine billed Freeman's piece as "How Three Caucasians Battled Valiantly for the Glory of Their Race." Though painfully dated in its racial attitudes, Freeman's unorthodox and mostly good-humored multi-sport competition reminds of the more palatable "immunity challenges" of the popular contemporary reality television program* Survivor.

FROM "A FIJIAN FIELD DAY"

The natives of Mbau, probably on account of the patronage extended by their distinguished chief, have the reputation of being keener on outdoor sports than those of any other part of the Fiji, and it was this circumstance which inspired my young friends with the idea of holding a field day in which the white race should compete with the brown. The honor of the Caucasian was to be upheld by Bertie, Tom, and myself, while that of the Polynesian would be maintained by a selection from all the Fijians on the island. The natives accepted eagerly, although the team with which we were finally confronted was not made up entirely of Mbau, nor even of Polynesians. That, however, transpired later.

Most of the first day was spent arranging the program. The natives wanted a tug-of-war, but our captain — Bertie — realizing that we lacked the "beef" for such a contest, agreed to its inclusion only in the event that the missionary — with whom South Sea life had agreed so well that he weighed in the vicinity of 250 pounds — could be induced to pull with us for the honor of his race. Needless to say, the event was not scheduled.

We did the sporting thing, though, however, by offering to oppose an eleven made up of the island's best cricketers with a "team" composed of Bertie, Tom, and myself. The other events decided upon were two swimming races, two sprints, two canoe races, shot put, throwing the cricket ball, broad and high jumps, a "modified Marathon" and three boxing contests.

The Three-Man "Team"

The second day we spent in practice and "elimination trials" to decide which particular events each of us was best fitted to compete in, as, except for the cricket and one canoe race, the finals were to be strictly "man-to-man" affairs. Luckily, our respective abilities dovetailed perfectly. Tom was an adept at swimming and no novice in handling the outrigger canoe, while his splendid endurance made him a natural if inexperienced distance runner; Bertie had given promise of developing into one of the fastest amateur sprinters in England before the Gaiety girl supervened, and had recently bested some of the speediest men in Australia at the "hundred" and "two-twenty."

My experience in my old varsity events, the shot put and broad jump, and the remnants of a fair throwing arm, made me our logical representative in the remaining contests we had scheduled. Each of us was slated to box in his respective class — Bertie in lightweight, Tom in the middleweight, and I — "because I weighed a good fourteen stone and looked jolly fit," as my teammates put it — in the heavyweight.

The elimination trials of the Fijians, on account of the wealth of candidates, were more complicated. They were astir before sunrise, and fought and wrangled from morn till dewy eve and on into the moonlight in an earnest endeavor to pick the likeliest representatives to uphold the honor of their race. The final list was not handed to Bertie till near midnight, and even then, as became apparent next day, was not quite complete.

Every soul on the island except the immediate members of the missionary's household was on the beach in the morning when the canoe races were started, and what with beaten war drums and coal-oil cans raised a pandemonium that would have made a varsity "rooting" section appear like a Quaker meeting when their man splashed across the line an easy winner in the one-paddle event. Tom made a good fight, but his opponent had too many generations of training behind him.

Won by a Wreck

The "open" canoe race was one of the events which our opponents had forced upon us, and in it Bertie, Tom, and I were to paddle against any hand-propelled craft that the Fijians could put in the water. It was their original idea to launch the old hundred-foot double outrigger of the great Thakambau — the same that it was customary to push down the beach over human rollers in the good old days — man it with fifty paddlers and swamp all opposition in the backwash. When the Mbuli vetoed the use of that sacred relic for so frivolous a purpose, they cheerfully compromised on the absent Roko Kandavu's state barge, which had thwarts for twenty paddlers. This was ready on the morning of the meet, but after the Fijians had seen the effort required on the part of Bertie and myself even to keep balanced in our sliver-like outrigger, they did the sporting thing by entering a high-sterned old headhunting canoe with but a quartette of paddlers.

The odds were still a hundred to one against us, or rather they would have been had our confident opponents picked anything better than a dugout that had been rotting and cracking in the rains and suns of the last thirty years. As it was the change cost them the race, for though they got away at a gait that carried them out of sight around a point while we were still serpentining in the vicinity of the starting line, the speed and the flailing paddles put the old canoe under too much of a strain, and it disintegrated and sank before half the circuit of the little island had been made. Under Tom's careful coaching, Bertie and I rounded into form sufficiently to allow the three of us to nurse our reeling outrigger over the course and across the finish line, where we arrived just in time to see our bedraggled opponents being "drummed out of town" by the oil-can brigade.

In the high jump we were weak, and Bertie, who had never essayed the event before, was no match for a slender Fijian youth who had been to school in Auckland. A few minutes later, however, he evened up things by sprinting the length of the village green a good twenty feet ahead of his dusky opponent, and my victory in the broad jump put us in the lead for the first time.

Tom, who was really a marvel at the Australian "crawl," had his revenge in swimming for his defeat in the outrigger contest, beating his man almost two to one in a dash of about a hundred year across a bight in the sea wall.

The vanquished Fijian, who had also been picked to swim in the race of a half mile or more to the mainland and back, was so crushed by the completeness of his defeat that he refused to compete again, the event being called off.

In the shot puting contest we used an old, rust-eaten, twenty-pound cannonball which had been thrown into Mbau away back in the '40s by a British gunboat on a punitive expedition against the natives for killing and eating a family of missionaries. My opponent made up in strength what he lacked in "form," and by dint of following the missile out of the "ring," threw it to a distance which I was able to beat only by resorting to the same unorthodox experiment. Bertie added to our score by romping to another easy victory in the sprint around an approximate 220-yard circle which had been marked with coconuts along the inside of the village green.

The last event of the forenoon was the "Modified Marathon" to be run over a course once around the island again to finish in front of the council house, a distance of about three miles. We had counted on Tom to win this event handily — the Fijian, as a rule, runs to strength rather than speed — but the natives sprang a "ringer" on us by entertaining one Moti Lal, the lanky East Indian coolie employed by the Roku to hoe his taro patch and carry messages between Mbau and Rewa.

This human greyhound sprang away at the report of the "pistol" — in this instance a blow on the hollow-log war drum — and had loped around the island and half way to the mainland before poor Tom, winded already, staggered out by Thakambau's old outrigger on the leeward beach. Here Bertie and I headed him off and took him out of the race to save his strength for the trails of the afternoon. The natives, who appeared to figure the importance of a race in direct proportion to its length, beat their hollow-log drums and sang chesty, sonorous war chants all through the rest hour in celebration of this victory.

While Bertie was winning the first event of the afternoon, the cricket ball-throwing contest — a competition in which he substituted for me who had originally qualified for it — I essayed to give the Fijians an exhibition of the hammer throwing, with the technique of which they were still unfamiliar. In the absence of a regulation hammer, a network of fiber was woven around the twenty-pound cannonball we had used in the shot put, and into this mesh the end of a three-foot strand of cocoa husk rope was fixed. This contrivance looked decidedly flimsy, and, as transpired presently, did not belie its appearance. It held together for a couple of tentative tosses, and even through the preliminary swings of a real throw; but when I whirled into the first circle of what was to have been a triple turn, the fibrous mesh gave way and, while I did a double back somersault, the ponderous old missile went hurtling through the air and banged against the side of the great council house.

The stout woven wall was not breached, but a muffled crash told of havoc among the tribal relics which adorned the interior. A few minutes later the Mbuli, who with several of the elders of the village had hurried to investigate, emerged with a baleful look on his face to announce that the great *yangoona* bowl, out of the sacred depths of which kava had been served even to royal Thakambau himself, was split across the middle from the jar received when it struck the floor.

The Fijians appeared rather awed at the magnitude of the catastrophe, but the unquenchable Bertie, after placing his "field" for the cricket match, called out to the Mbuli to ask if it did not seem like old times to have the walls of Mbau battered down with cannonballs.

The one-inning cricket game was a Caucasian walk-over. The dazzling work of Tom and Bertie, who alternated between bowling and wicket-keeping, finished man after man with a "goose-egg," and, in spite of the inexperienced "field"—myself, whose "cricket" had all been learned in baseball—retired the bewildered Fijians with less than two score of runs. This total that versatile pair, batting in partnership, exceeded in a quarter of an hour.

Acknowledging that they were outclassed in cricket, the Fijians now demanded that a game of soccer football should be played upon the same terms—a full team of them to the three of us—and to this proposal the game Bertie, displaying better sportsmanship than judgment, consented. Of course, after a severe buffeting which left us all rather groggy and winded for the boxing contests, we were overwhelmingly defeated.

Kathrene Gedney Pinkerton on Women's Canoeing (1914)

Kathrene Gedney Pinkerton and her husband Robert E. Pinkerton might legitimately be called the first family of North American, twentieth-century canoeing. More than perhaps any sporting pair in the Golden Age, the Pinkertons lived their creed. With the large sum they made from selling a novelette to Munsey's *magazine, they built a cabin in the Ontario bush, a place they made their permanent home except for the weeks around the birth of their daughter, Bobs. Accessible only by canoe in the summer and dogsled during the winter, the cabin made canoe navigation an essential skill for Kathrene Pinkerton. Once established, the log home served as base camp for the couple, as both continued to sell outdoor nonfiction to magazines such as* The Country Gentleman *and* Outing *and fiction to a variety of pulp magazines. A Minnesota native, Kathrene Pinkerton was fond of the north woods, an affinity she makes clear in this one-of-a-kind article. In sum, she authored dozens of books based on her experience in the North, including nonfiction, fiction, and young adult literature, the most popular of which describes her unorthodox, back-to-nature family,* Wilderness Wife *(1939) and* Three's a Crew *(1940). Incidentally, Robert Pinkerton's* The Canoe, Its Selection, Care, and Use *(1914), while not his most popular work, is nevertheless considered a classic of its genre.*

From "Paddling Her Own Canoe"

Ans-ee-quay-gee-sick and his squaw, Teck-ee-mash-ee, stopped at our cabin last fall to make a portage into a string of nameless lakes in the big swamp behind the ridge. They had paddled twelve miles that morning, and there were two miles of hard portaging and more paddling between them and the lake where they would camp that night.

Teck-ee-mash-ee placed almost the entire outfit — dishes, clothing, food, tent and bedding, perhaps one hundred pounds in all — in a blanket, knotted the four corners, and swung it to her back, one strip of blanket acting as a head strap. Anse took a smaller pack, laid the paddles across the thwarts of their birch canoe, and lifted it to his shoulders. A few days later they appeared suddenly on the trail behind the cabin, set their canoe in the water, placed their packs in it, and were off again.

They were making the journey together, sharing in the work on portage, in canoe, in camp. And as I watched them down the lake, I thought of white men from the cities I have seen on canoe trips in our country, men who travel through a wonderful land of forest and lake and stream, always in parties of two or more and almost never with a woman.

"I'd give anything if she'd come," many have told me. "I know she would like it when she understood it. Perhaps, if I got a good guide and took an easy trip, do you think she could stand it?"

And here I always say: "Don't. Guide-paddled and guide-served, she will be shut out forever from the real wilderness. Let her learn it as you have learned it. Let her be your comrade, not your passenger."

For paddling is one of the easiest and most fascinating means of traversing the trail to the real spirit of the wilderness. And it is as possible to the woman as to the man. What she may lack in physical strength she may more than overbalance by her nerve force, her endurance. Even before her paddling may take her to the real wilderness it can afford her pleasure. There is as much joy in the quick, effectual stroke as in any other well-played game of the out-of-doors. Wind and current are as worthy adversaries as one finds on links or courts, and the victory is as satisfying.

I shall never forget my first rapids. I had ascended them by tracking line and had done much steering in the bow while the canoe was being poled up long stretches of white water. I had learned all the rocks and currents in that rapids thoroughly and had absorbed the principles, and much of the practice, of steering from the bow.

But with the stern man standing, ready with the pole to snub the craft, and upon me resting almost alone the guiding, I had a sudden desire, when the current gripped us, to jump, to scream, to do anything but accept the responsibility. Ahead was a large boulder, around and over which the water boiled. We seemed to be rushing straight upon it. Desperately I plunged my paddle in and drew the canoe to one side. Now I know that the parting of the current by the rock helped me. Then I felt only that I had conquered my fear, controlled my nerves, and met the situation. A feeling of exultant triumph and new confidence came to me.

And that is only one of the many things canoeing has done for me. It has brought a greatly increased physical efficiency and a new joy in the possession thereof. It has brought calm and controlled nerves, not only on the water but with the rifle, the road, and on the long snowshoe tramp.

It has taught me to love the northland and to feel its lure, as men love it and feel it. This, for women, means another of those rare planes upon which they can meet as comrades. It means that they can understand men where they have not understood before, and that men can find a new quality to appreciate. It does not mean a corresponding loss in womanliness, even though the woman ceases to expect the usual little attentions made difficult by the toil of portage and paddle.

A joy in maps has come, an understanding of the attraction of the wide spaces for men. The adventurous, exploring spirit has been aroused, and dim trails have beckoned.

And the canoe has made possible an intimate acquaintance with that strange, silent, hard-shelled, lovable individual, the woodsman. I have learned to know his point of view, to understand his life, his work, the type, and the canoe has made it possible for me to talk to him and, far better, to loosen his tongue and open a storehouse of interesting, intimate little bits of forest wisdom. I have spent many pleasant hours with trappers, talking paddle blades, canoes, traps, fur, snowshoes, dogs, toboggans, woods, foods and clothing, and out-of-the-way places which even men seldom visit.

Hiram Connibear on Coaching College Crew (1914)

Like Walter Camp, rower Hiram Connibear's historical reputation rests largely on his unparalleled record as an intercollegiate coach, mentor, and innovator. A former bicycle racer and Chicago White Sox trainer, Connibear had never even rowed a boat when he was appointed the University of Washington head coach in 1908. Together with famed Canadian boatbuilder George Pocock, who Connibear singlehandedly convinced to immigrate to Seattle, Connibear built a rowing dynasty at Washington while revolutionizing, even in his ignorance, rowing technique. Though the University of Washington faculty knew him to be a novice and tried to oust him before his first big race, Connibear and his team prevailed and he became a hero, eventually earning a reputation as the "grandfather of U.S. crew racing." In 1937 no less than Time *magazine hailed the Connibear crew dynasty in opening the article "Compton Cup and Connibear" with the following analogy: "What Notre Dame is to intercollegiate football, the University of Washington (Seattle) is to intercollegiate rowing." Like several of the other unlikely sports heroes of the Golden Age, Connibear died tragically, falling from a plum tree and suffering a broken neck in 1917.*

From "Coaching a Varsity Crew"

I am not a rowing professional oarsman. Neither was I a professional coach of rowing before the beginning of my experience at the University of Washington. What I know about rowing has been learned largely as a result of observation and study. I began with no theories except the common-sense belief that a man who knew the best methods of training and the fundamentals facts of condition could teach other men the principles of any sport in which condition enters as an important factor.

Personally, I have never had much patience with the attitude that regards any kind of athletics as requiring mysterious knowledge in order to win success. If a sport is so complicated that the average man who applies himself to it cannot soon understand its basic principles, I think it shows that the pastime is not one suited for general interest. Of course, after the first requirement — mastery of technique — has been satisfied, the rest comes down to the ability of a coach to bring out the best which is in his material and of keeping the men in condition.

I have been a coach and conditioner of men since 1894 and now that Mike Murphy is dead, I take off my hat to no one in the world in this field of effort. It has always been natural with me to observe and experiment, arriving at my own conclusion in Yankee style.

One thing that has impressed me is that there is never an end to the knowledge which a rowing coach can acquire. I learn something new every day and the fact that I know there are many more things to learn is one of the principal reasons why my interest in the sport never fails to keep up.

To my mind rowing of the college variety is the highest type of sport. There is never any question about amateur standing of an oarsman in a university boat. The patience required and the fact that there is rarely any individual glory to distribute, limits the candidates for a crew to men with a high ideal of athletics. The fact that large sums of money are spent upon rowing when there are no receipts and all the colleges get out of it is a few boat races shows that it is a sport for sport's sake.

Ever since Dr. A. L. Sharpe, now coaching at Cornell, gave me my first lesson in the art of pulling a shell, what I have seen of the rowing game has made me feel that it is the cleanest, manliest branch of athletics. It was at Chautauqua Lake, New York, that I met Sharpe and he was good enough to inspire me with an enthusiasm for rowing and some of the knowledge gained from his own rowing experience at New Haven, which have stood me in good stead since.

There has been a lot of talk this spring about the advisability of reducing the distance of the Eastern races from four miles to three. A good many critics seem to feel that lessening the distance would reduce the strain on the men. To my mind it makes very little if any difference. The proposition comes down to two essentials; First, material, and, second, faithfulness of the men in carrying out training instructions. At almost all the colleges I know anything about, there are enough strong, hearty young men to man the crews. These fellows can be taught to row four miles, without injuring themselves, just as well as three.

I do not think there is any coach who would put a man in a boat who is not physically strong enough to stand the strain of rowing. And this speaks pretty well for the standards of character among coaches. For at every university there are some people who want the coach to drive home a winning crew, regardless of everything else. They are likely not to care how he wins, provided he does win, and they don't care how much good he may be doing for the physical upbuilding of undergraduates, if he does not win.

Given a fair-sized squad of able-bodied young men who can be counted upon to train faithfully, and a four-mile race can be entered without fear of any bad effects on the individual oarsmen. I have trained men for six-day and six-night bicycle races where one man rode all of this time and I have trained them for twenty-four-hour races. I have trained sprinters for fifty- and one-hundred-yard dashes and for the mile and two-mile, as well as for the twenty-five-mile races. I have seen men run until they were all in and drop at the finish of a one hundred yard dash, just as I have seen them drop at the end of distance races.

The distance does not make a bit of difference to my way of looking at it — provided a man has trained properly and is fit for his event. The key to whole educational system is concentration and determination. The part which athletics has in the larger work is that of teaching undergraduates to bring the body under the control of the will.

Keeping men under lock and key is not my idea of a good coaching program. If they are impressed with the need for building themselves up into the best condition possible and made to understand that if they aren't willing to do so they had best not compete for places on teams, they can be relied upon to do the square thing. I take it for granted that the candidates are turning out for rowing because they want to and not because they have to. I tell my freshman to spend twenty minutes a day in a room all by himself, looking himself squarely in the eye.

"Have I done all I could to raise my standard as a man in the past twenty-four hours? Have I been fair and square with those that I have had dealings with?"

These are the questions I tell them to ask of themselves and if the answers are right all around, I know I have the makings of some good crew men.

Horace Kephart on Spelunking (1914)

> One of the most fascinating, and prolific, outdoor writers of the Golden Age, Horace Kephart likely wrote this piece as a memoir recalling a caving expedition taking place between 1890 and 1903, the period in which Kephart served as director of the prestigious Mercantile Library in St. Louis, Missouri, and during which he made many trips to the Ozarks. After 1903, Kephart, claiming nervous exhaustion exacerbated by urban St. Louis, recouped at his father's house in Ohio for a short time before moving on to western North Carolina's Smoky Mountains. From there the unassuming and largely reclusive woodsman-author wrote more than 100 articles for sports and outdoor recreation periodicals and published two classic books, Our Southern Highlanders *and* Camping and Woodcraft. *The piece following, from* Outing *magazine exemplifies the exhilarating sense of discovery available to the participatory sportswriter attempting a new skill, in this case caving/spelunking. Even though the Ozark cavern Kephart and companion explore turns out to be only one of a type, the author, in a perfect summation of the esprit de corps of the participatory journalist, writes, "This remains the most interesting cavern in the world; for it was here we passed our novitiate. After all, it is not the magnitude of results, but the uncertainty about them, that makes a game worth playing."*

From "Adventures in a Cavern"

There are many to whom the bare suggestion of exploring vast natural cavities in the earth is horrible and mad. Whoso ventures into such places without a guide must be subject, they think, to some strange perversion that makes him vain of fearsome and foolhardy experiences. To a sensitive mind unfortified by scientific training, an unexplored cavern is charged with fantastic perils. Superstitions long in abeyance are revived. One may not believe in specters and earth demons when the sun is shining; he may flaunt ghouls and goblins even at night if he has room for a swift escape; but what might not exist in a region of eternal blackness and silence deeper and more uncanny than any grave? If not the chimera that breathes fire and the basilisk that exhales death, why not horrible living things: snakes, slimy lizards, panthers, bears, wolves, or even scaly antediluvian monsters, long belated underground and still snapping their fangs in these Plutonian depths?

Whoever, on the contrary, is keen to observe natural phenomena, even though he be a novice in cave work, will smile at such childish fears. And yet he is alert to real dangers that may test his fortitude to the limit. The abruptness of the change from world to underworld, the sudden descent from sunshine or starlight into a cold void blacker than any gloom on earth, is a strain upon one's self-possession.

One's very life hangs on the proper functioning of his lantern. There is no means of forecasting whither his steps may lead, nor how shocking may be the next minute's adventure. The rays of his light cannot penetrate a hundred feet; for the cave atmosphere, being optically as well as chemically pure, does not transmit the rays so well as our outer air. There may be pitfalls ahead, slippery ledges, hazardous passages over gulfs that no torch can fathom, rotten rock crumbling in one's grasp. You may wedge fast in a crack. The light may fail. You may be lost in the bowels of the earth!

All these risks are real enough, and we pondered them in silence as we eyed those somber portals on which fancy might well inscribe: *Abandon all hope, ye who enter.*

But there is a fascination in solving the mystery of what has lain for untold ages beyond human ken; in venturing, as we were about to venture, where no foot of man has ever trod. What was there within those forbidding arches? Vast chambers, perhaps, hung with weird pendants, walls glittering with crystals, forests of stalagmites, columns of alabaster or of "onyx." There might be relics of prehistoric races buried in stone since some past geological epoch, petrifactions of plants and animals that died ages before man was born, living species unknown to the upper world. There might be dripping springs trickling through crannies in the rock, rills tumbling from ledge to ledge in fairy waterfalls and gathering far below in some subterranean river that ran "Through caverns measureless to man/Down to a sunless sea."

Our advance was menaced at the outset by a deep fissure that could only be crossed by leaping. On the farther brink there was no other place to land than a large slab that had fallen from the roof. This slab sloped toward us and looked perfectly smooth. I regretted having no hobnails in my shoes. However, we struck without slipping, and then found that the rock was really rough from corrosion, its apparent smoothness being due to a thin layer of cavern dust. In the dry upper galleries of caves, the dust on the floors is peculiar. It never rises when stirred, does not stick to clothing, nor does it even soil one's shoes.

We chose one of the passages leading from the antechamber, and soon emerged into a second room not markedly different from the first. Onward, then, through devious ways, until we came up against a blank wall and had to retrace our steps. Another corridor was chosen, generous at first, but soon the vault descended and the walls close in to a mere crack where we had to edge and crawl. Then we came out upon a space strewn wildly with uptilted slabs and debris. The sides of this chamber gaped with crevices and looked tottery weak, as though at any moment they might collapse. I think the fall of a pebble behind us would have made our knees totter, too.

We toiled over a jumble of sharp-edged rocks that skinned our hands as we helped ourselves along, and thus came, on the farther side, to a chasm down which the beam of our little searchlight could show no bottom. Shuddering on the brink of this abyss, we seemed balked until one of us espied, above and to the right, a narrow ledge that skirted the gulf. This lead to a jagged passage upward, then down to a fair hallway and into a domed rotunda.

It would be tedious to describe our wanderings in detail. Always we were seeking a course running downward; for I was convinced that we were in an ancient upper gallery, and that there must be a lower tier in which the filtration and occasional floods could gather, and through which a regular watercourse must flow to its debouchment in the Mississippi.

One unpleasant fact impressed us more and more as we advanced, namely: the cave was a labyrinth. We lost count of the openings we had passed. They went up, down, right, left. The whole rocky mass was perforated in every direction like worm-eaten wood. The reader may recall his bewilderment when seeking the exit from some artificial maze in a city park. But that was all on one level, and in the light of day. Imagine, then, a labyrinth of three dimensions, in the pit blackness under the earth! Several times we must have followed passages that crossed over or under others that we had traversed before.

We lost all sense of direction, and had no measure of the distance traveled. We had a compass, to be sure; but what would a compass be good for in the interior of a sponge that was magnified ten thousand times? A pedometer, likewise, would have been of no avail, since much of our progress was by crawling or by leaping from rock to rock, and we never went a hundred feet in steady cadence.

Wherever, in our wanderings, we noticed that it might be difficult to retrace our steps, we left marks on the cavern wall; yet in several places we had been too interested in our surroundings or too eager to push on. Sometimes, on entering a chamber, we had neglected to turn round and mark which passage we had come in by, where there were two more leading in various directions. It is unpleasant to admit such recklessness; but in this strange underworld it was written that we should pay for our experience.

The Silence of Ages

We traveled generally without other talk than the necessary consultations. Each of us was busy enough with his own scrutinies and speculations. And it seemed almost sacrilege to disturb the awful silence that had brooded for ages in this inviolate realm. There is not stillness comparable to it on earth — not even in the desert, at night, when no faintest zephyr stirs. One sitting at rest could hear the beat of his normally pulsing heart.

Once only, exhilarated by the surplus of oxygen in the air, we challenged the invisible keepers of the cavern by shouting aloud. The answer abashed us. Instead of the intermittent echoes that we expected, there arose a continuous horrible din that seemed to leap zigzag from wall to wall, changing its pitch according to the surface or cavity encountered. This medley of uncouth sounds was prolonged for a surprising time; then, instead of dying away in the distance, it was caught by some dome or wall and came back as if on the rebound.

After two hours of tortuous wandering, I was sure that we had not progressed toward the Mississippi; for the drainage level below our "blowing-hole" could not be very deep. On the contrary, we had worked back in the other direction, and were now somewhere far underneath the crown of one of the neighboring hills. Gradually we had come into an old formation, where the stalactites and stalagmites sometimes met in pillars, where the walls were deeply incrusted with deposits of dripstone, and the floors were smooth. Once upon a time a considerable stream had flowed through these passages, but, long ago, it had cut down through the stratum we were following and had found a new channel on a lower level.

Some of the rooms were wet. We were showered with dripping springs. There was a series of saucer-shaped depressions in the floor, into the first of which I slipped and fell prostrate, receiving, to my astonishment, a complete ducking in icy water. The liquid was so crystal clear that we had not seen there was any water there at all.

Then we came suddenly into the most beautiful grotto! White — brilliantly, dazzlingly white! Every square inch of the walls and ceilings was coated with frosty mineral efflorescence and snowy nodules. It was like frozen mist at Niagara, or fog congealed on the trees and shrubbery of a mountain top. Myriads of tiny transparent crystals, set in the immaculate white of the incrustation, flashed and sparkled as if rejoicing in the creation of Light. It was fairyland awakened after a thousand years of sleep. The splendor of this welcoming radiance, bursting upon us after our long toil through the blackness of cavernous depths, was inexpressibly cheering. We sank upon alabaster seats, and here we had luncheon with the fairies.

But what a world was this of contrasts and contradictions! My hand, feeling along the glittering wall for some crystal large enough to keep as a specimen, touched something that was soft and *alive*. Two feet from my nose I had not distinguished it from the snowy decorations. The thing did not try to escape, and I lifted it from the wall — a white bat! Who ever heard of such a creature? I was used to white mice, white rabbits, white deer, and even human albinos, but never had I imagined an albino bat. I put the little animal in my empty lunchbox, and sat down to examine it at my leisure.

Was this really an albino freak? Its eyes, instead of being pink, were beady black. Ah — more interesting — this must be an example of coloration adapted to a change of environment. Not protective coloration (nothing would pursue a cave bat) but a mask assumed with the design of catching prey. Wonderful! I would not have taken a new greenback for that white bat.

But my comrade either was indifferent to my high-flown zoology or impatient to make discoveries of his own — anyway, he was gone. The last of him that I had noticed was his feet disappearing in a small round orifice high in the wall of a vestibule beyond. This has been some minutes ago. A trifle vexed at his quiet departure, I likened his exit to a toad vanishing in a rathole.

In the Real Dark

The aperture through which Sidney had left me was scarcely bigger than a barrel head, and could only be reached by skirting a treacherous ledge, past a deep fissure, and then climbing upward. I shoved my tall lantern into the hole and followed it headforemost. There was barely room to work my elbows and knees, and continually I was bumping my head. Why had that scapegrace chosen such a nasty, damp, crooked tube? Suppose one should get his clothing caught on one of the spiny projections — that might easily happen, especially if he tried to back out.

Had Sidney really got through, or was he stuck and helpless somewhere in the labyrinth beyond? Perhaps he had fallen into a pit and lay there stunned or dead.

I pushed along as fast as I could. In squirming around a bend of the tube

I upset my lantern, and that bothersome but indispensable utensil instantly went out.

The shock of utter darkness was followed by one of pain as I butted my head against the rock while fumbling for my matchbox. A good thing that the box was waterproof, for I was so soaking wet that the lining of my pocket clung to my hand.

Then a creepy horror suffused me as I realized that there was nothing dry to light a match on. From head to foot I was wet, and the rock all about me was wet. I tried one match on the checked side of the matchbox, but that too was wet. I studied, and studied, but it was no use. Nervously I screwed back the cap of the box tight upon its rubber gasket. If Sidney did not return (and could he ever find the way again?) my life depended upon those matches.

I yelled lustily for my comrade; but not even a mocking echo answered. At intervals I called again. It was incredible that Sidney should not hear me in that tomb-like silence where one could almost have heard the crawling of a snail. Did he indeed lie helpless with shattered bones, or had he wedged fast and fainted from very horror?

As I lay there on my belly, cruelly cramped in that black inferno, it seemed I could feel the rock shrinking to compress me. The very darkness seemed solidified, as though I were a petrifaction bedded forever in a mass of coal. For moments that were ages I lay as in a nightmare, trying but failing to struggle against doom.

To retreat without a light was madness; for how should I ever pass that chasm in the rear? To advance in utter blindness was a hazard reserved for the last extremity. I realized how it must feel to be buried alive in a graveyard; and yet a coffin would be preferable to this, for soon it would mercifully stifle one to death.

It is easy enough, as one sits comfortably at home, to think of several ways by which a match might have been lighted. Why did I not strike one across the edge of my knife? Any hero of romance would have done so at once. But I was no hero, nor was this romance. I had all I could do, just then, to fight off panic. In revulsion I was seized with anger and swore that I would get out of that man-trap, blind though I was. Anything was better than inaction.

I started to crawl forward. "This," thought I to myself, "is enough to make a fellow grit his teeth." At that last word a trick popped back into my head that had been forgotten ever since I was a bad little boy setting the good little schoolgirls' nerves atwitter. I took out a match, placed its head end between my teeth, jerked sharply forward, and had a flame instantly. I relighted the lantern and went ahead.

The descent proved difficult, even with a light. My old kerosene lantern was like a glowworm in the garden on a pitch-dark night. The tunnel corkscrewed downward to a considerable depth and then came out amid tumbled angular rocks that were hard to pass. Beyond was easy travel through a winding gallery.

I kept calling for my comrade, but still there was no reply. It was impossible to track him, for his smooth-shod feet had left no imprint on the dustless floor. The solitude was most depressing. I was alone where time was measured only by the slow drip of water, and no hour had ever struck. In this colossal and mysterious void there was no day, no night; no summer, no winter; no life, no death, save maybe for a few pitiable minikins forever imprisoned in silence and darkness that had made them colorless and mute and blind.

Back to Daylight

Then my hail was answered! Pressing eagerly forward, I found my partner in a byway where he was groping for water. The reservoir in his little acetylene lamp was nearly dry, and the light was dying. He had spare carbide to recharge the lantern, but had not provided a flask of water to go with it. That was why he had not come back to learn my whereabouts.

We went on along the lower gallery searching for water, but luck at first was against us. There was none but the slow, slow drip. Then a small supply was found. We set forth on a hunt for some easier route to the upper gallery, but became bewildered and had to admit to each other that we were lost.

Sidney discussed our situation with admirable coolness. As for myself, it was so good to have light and companionship, and our present dilemma was so small in comparison with what I had just been through, that I took good heart.

Fate favored us now by revealing a shaft through which we could climb aloft without serious risk. We emerged into the upper tier of passages, found our old trail, and the rest of the trip was uneventful. Four hours after we had lowered ourselves into the "blowing-hole" we were back in the blessed light of day, and there we reclined gasping for a while in the sultry change of air on the surface.

The snowy nodules that I had collected in our fairy grotto were brilliant, at first, in the sunlight, but soon they began turning to a rusty and dirty brown. My "albino" (must I tell it?) turned rusty, too; and the next day, having meantime licked or rubbed herself clean of the white cave-powder with which she had disguised her complexion, my incredible contribution to science was shockingly revealed as a common mouse-colored bat!

It might be thought that our misadventures on this first real exploration underground would discourage us from every trying such a trip again. But had we not met and conquered them? We were not longer tenderfoots. The first lesson in any art is how *not* to go about it; and this we had surely learned.

Thereafter we looked well to our lighting equipment; and we carried balls of light twine, taking turnabout in paying it out behind us as we advanced — a simple and infallible guide for retracing our way.

Two other expeditions we made into this same cavern, of five hours and seven hours, respectively, taking five other men with us on the last trip. We discovered several new routes, and finally did get down to the true drainage level, or so near it we could hear where the unseen waters flowed; but we found no outlet that was practicable for man.

Our cave turned out to be nothing remarkable as compared with many another. Yet for us two blundering adventurers who were the first to open and explore it, this remains the most interesting cavern in the world; for it was here we passed our novitiate. After all, it is not the magnitude of results, but the uncertainty about them, that makes a game worth playing.

Malcolm Ross on Alpining (1914)

Praised by Davis Oswald William Hall as "one of the most enterprising amateurs of his day above snow line" Malcolm Ross was a successful Kiwi journalist and record-setting alpinist credited with being the first to traverse and the fourth to climb New Zealand's Mount Cook. The author of several books, most famously A Climber in New Zealand, *and a founder of the New Zealand Alpine Club, Ross covered his country's Parliament for several Wellington newspapers as well as the* The Times *of London. Like his contemporary Lewis R. Freeman, Ross traveled the world as a war correspondent from 1914 to 1918 and excelled at athletic endeavors including running, rowing, cycling, tennis, and golf. Significantly, Malcolm Ross was a soccer player (footballer) of renown, playing for the Otago team in 1885–86. In the excerpt that follows, Ross describes overcoming injury to attempt what would become his record-setting traverse of Mount Cook.*

From "The First Crossing of Mt. Cook"

"Tighten the muscle, feel the strong blood flow, And set your foot upon the utmost crest!"
 — Geoffrey Winthrop Young

It was decided not to go to sleep that evening, but to start for the traverse of Mount Cook before midnight. We, however, crept into our sleeping bags inside the tent in order to keep warm. Turner had complained of the dampness at the end of the tent the night before, so I took his place, and gave him an inside berth. At 10 P.M. Fyfe was astir boiling us a billy of tea, and at 10:20 we breakfasted! The sky was clear, and the moon was shining; but, higher up the range, the clouds were pouring over between Haidinger and De la Beche. This did not augur well for success. On going through our rucksacks again, we discarded a few things to make them lighter, but, what with cameras, spare clothing, food, and the two aluminum water bottles, one filled with claret and the other with water, we had to carry from 15 lb. to 20 lb., each rather heavy loads for so long and difficult a climb.

Our provisions consisted of half a loaf, one large tin of ox tongue, one tin of sheep's tongues, one tin of sardines, two tins of jam, some butter, two oranges, two lemons, a few raisins, and about a pound of brown sugar, upon which latter I subsisted almost entirely on all our climbs. I had remembered reading about the virtues of brown sugar in one of Sir Martin Conway's books, and my wife had obtained some special brown Demerara sugar for me from our grocer. Then I looked the subject up in Conway's book on the ascent of Aconcagua. After mentioning the necessity for light foods, such as soup and jam, for high ascents, he states that on the Aconcagua climb more important than all these was a great tin of coarse brown Demerara sugar, the finest heat-producing, muscle-nourishing food in the world. For men taking violent exercise, such as soldiers on active service or athletes in training, a plentiful supply of sugar was, he stated, far better than large meat rations. A quarter of a pound per day per man was his allowance on the mountainside, and he was inclined to think that this might be increased to nearly half a pound with advantage, cane sugar, of course, being selected for this purpose.

We were aware that on such a climb, what with the great exertion, the want of water, and the reduced atmospheric pressure, we should be able to eat very little, and that, if we were successful, most of the provisions we were taking would not be needed. Still there was the danger, in consequence of a sudden storm, or other unforeseen difficulties, of our having to spend the night out on an exposed ledge of rock at an altitude of 10,000 or 11,000 feet, in which case our lives would depend upon a supply of extra clothing and food. Therefore we dared not with prudence make our loads any lighter.

At 11.15 P.M. on the night of Tuesday, January 9, we started, having rolled up all our belongings that we did not require in the sleeping bags, and these, in turn, in the tent. This made one big bundle, which we jammed under the rock as far as possible and weighted down with stones, so that it should not be blown away. We took with us also one 65-foot length and one 50-foot length of Alpine rope made by Buckingham, of London, and tested to a breaking strain of 2000 lb. In single file, in the moonlight, we toiled up the snow slopes leading to the Glacier Dome, 1300 feet above our bivouac. For the most part we climbed upwards in solemn silence, each one being busy with his own thoughts, and wondering, no doubt, what the day would bring about. Ten minutes after midnight we had left the final steep snow slope of the Dome behind, and looked across the great plateau that stretches, at an altitude of over 7000 feet, for a distance of some four miles, at the foot of the precipitous slopes of Mounts Cook and Tasman. From the Dome we had now to descend 700 feet, and then cross the plateau to gain the foot of the northeastern ridge that was to lead us to the summit of our peak. The snow was in bad condition, and we sank in it over the boot tops. In places it was in that most tantalizing of conditions with a frozen crust that let one foot through, while the other foot held on the surface. While we were crossing the plateau, a vivid streak of lightning, or an unusually brilliant meteor, flashed athwart the northern sky, and a weird effect was produced by the moon, which, with a great halo around it, was dipping westward over the snowy peak of Mount Haast. For a few moments the moon, with half its halo, seemed to rest on the very apex of the mountain. We crossed the rest of the plateau in the shadow of the high peaks of the main divide, behind which the moon had now sunk, and, presently, in the dim, uncertain light we came up against the debris of a great avalanche that had fallen from the slopes of Mount Tasman. A mass of broken ice and snow was piled in confusion to a height of 15 or 20 feet, and we had to make a detour to avoid the obstruction. At about a quarter past 2 A.M. we commenced to ascend the long snow slope leading to the Zurbriggenarte; and in the dusk before the dawn we reached a bergschrund that might have given us a good deal of trouble to cross. Graham led carefully through the broken ice, and, peering into the dull grey light, thought he saw a bridge over which we might crawl in safety. We made a traverse to the right and climbed round under the overhanging wall of ice that formed the upper lip of the schrund, and which, had it fallen, would have crushed us out of existence. At this hour of the morning, however, it was perfectly safe, and Graham, disappearing round a huge block that towered above, crossed a frail snowbridge and gained the upper lip of the schrund. Turner followed, and I paid out the rope as he, too, gradually disappeared from view round the corner, Graham driving the handle of his axe deep in the snow, while Fyfe and I, below, took a firm stand and kept the rope taut. In a few minutes we were all safely across, and congratulating ourselves upon having so easily overcome the first serious obstacle of the climb.

We were now fairly on to the long 3000-feet snow slope that leads up to the rocks of the Zurbriggenarete. This slope was found in fairly good order. In places we could kick steps, but in other places the steps had to be chipped with the ice axes. As we slowly climbed upwards, the slope got steeper and steeper. Indeed, the angle was just about as steep as it is possible for snow to hold. After about half-an-hour's climbing we were startled by a magnificent avalanche that fell with thundering roar from high up on the broken ice slopes of Mount Tasman. It crashed on to the great plateau 2000 feet below, sending ice blocks to a great distance, and throwing up a cloud of snow like some huge breaker that sends its spray high in air above a rock-bound coast.

It was cold work standing in the steps in the chilly dawn with the ice chips from the leader's axe swishing about us. Presently the sun rose gloriously over the eastern ranges, and we were reveling in its generous warmth on the slope where, before, we had been half frozen. But the combination of sun and slope became almost more intolerable than the slope without the sun. Three thousand feet of such work is apt to become a shade monotonous even to the keenest disciple of snowcraft. This particular wall is so long and so steep that the climber must give his attention almost continually to the matter in hand. He has little time to admire the view. The steps must be cleaned out, and the rope must be held taut. Each man must keep his distance. Otherwise, a slip might be fatal. But it is monotonous work climbing slowly, hour after hour, in zigzags, with your face to the white wall. You have time to review your past life for years and years, and to think of the future for years ahead. With the dead uniformity of it all, and the never-ceasing glare in the stagnant atmosphere, there comes a monition of impending drowsiness. This you fight with an effort of the will, and some pretence at enlarging the steps that the leader has made, but which are, already, large enough in all conscience. While I was standing in the steps at a spot about halfway up the slope, I felt a strange tug on the rope, and thought it must have caught in some obstruction or have been struck by a falling block of ice; but, on looking round, I could see nothing to account for it. Some hours afterwards, while we were resting on the warm rocks above, Fyfe smilingly asked me if I had felt the pull, and then the rascal, still smiling, informed me that it was the result of a moment of actual somnolence on his part. For a second his brain had become dulled and his feet had come to a sudden stop on this never-ending ladder of ice. As the rope was taut, and I had a firm footing, the danger was nil; but it would never do for the leader to be so taken, and the leader on that particular slope has enough to do to keep him very wide awake.

Hour after hour went by, and we began to get very tired of the endless snow slope, so traversed to the right to gain the rocks. We found them difficult, with few holds for hands or feet, and so coated with snow and ice that progress was almost impossible. Reluctantly we had to traverse back to the snow slope. It was 6.40 A.M. before we reached the rocks on the main arête. A halt was called on a narrow ledge of snow. There we had a drink and some bread and marmalade, and took a number of photographs.

A bank of cloud loomed above the eastern mountains, but the sun was clear in the blue above, and as there was, at last, every prospect of fine weather, our spirits rose proportionately to the elevation gained. From this point a beautiful snow ridge rose in a gentle curve to a series of rocky crags. There was just room for our feet on this narrow ridge. On the right a steep couloir led down to the Linda Glacier, and on the left the mountain fell away in very steep slopes, for over three thousand feet, to the Grand Plateau. At the end of the snow ridge we had some fine climbing up a shoulder of rock. This was scaled without incident, except that of a falling stone which Turner dislodged, but which, fortunately, went past without hitting either Fyfe or myself. Then we climbed along another narrow snow arête, which, though steeper than the first one, was somewhat shorter. On gaining the rocks at the head of this ridge at 9 A.M., we halted for an early lunch. We replenished the wine bottle and the water bottle with the drippings of snow that we melted on a slab of warm stone.

We had now gained an altitude of between 10,000 and 11,000 feet, and the views were magnificently grand. Tasman, the second highest mountain in New Zealand, with his wonderful slopes of snow and ice, and a magnificent snow cornice, was quite close to us on the north. Then came Mount Lendenfeld, and the jagged, pinnacled ridge of Haast, which, from this point of view, seemed to bid defiance to the mountaineer. Farther along, on the main divide, rose the square top of Mount Haidinger, from which the magnificent schrunds and broken ice of the Haast Glacier fell away towards the Tasman Valley. Beyond that, the rocky peak of De la Beche, and the beautifully pure snows of the Minarets cleft the blue, leading the eye in turn to the gleaming masses of Elie de Beaumont and the Hochstetter Dome at the head of the Great Tasman Glacier. Across the valley Malte Brun towered grandly above all the other rock peaks of the range, and still farther away, towards the northeast, was the finest view of all, range succeeding range, and mountain succeeding mountain for more than a hundred miles, or as far as the eye could reach. In the distance, to the north of the main range, we looked down on a sea of clouds upon which the sun was shining, the higher peaks piercing the billows of mist and looking like pointed islands. We could plainly trace our steps along the snow arêtes that we had climbed, and across the plateau thousands of feet below. Lower still were the great schrunds and toppling pinnacles of the Hochstetter Ice Fall, and below that the magnificent sweep of the Great Tasman Glacier. Eastward a few fleecy cumulus clouds sailed over the foothills, and beyond were the plains of Canterbury and the distant sea.

An hour passed all too quickly amidst scenes of such magnificence and grandeur; but there was still a long climb ahead, and, in high spirits, we started to cut steps up another very sharp snow ridge with a drop of four thousand feet on one side. Balancing on this narrow ridge and gazing down those tremendous slopes was quite an exhilarating performance. This ridge brought us to the last rocks, which were steep and afforded some fine climbing. At the top of these rocks we found Zurbriggen's matchbox under a few pieces of splintered rock, and left a card in it. Fyfe led up to a shoulder below the final ice cap, still cutting steps, and then the order on the rope was reversed and Graham went to the front. This shoulder turned us to the left, and soon we gained the final snow arête that rose steeply almost to the summit. The last bit of the ice cap afforded easy climbing, and at one o'clock on Wednesday afternoon we stepped on to the topmost pinnacle of Aorangi thirteen hours and forty-five minutes from the time we left our bivouac. The view was again magnificent, almost indescribable. We looked across the island from sea to sea, and in addition to the views northward, eastward, and westward, we now beheld a glorious Alpine panorama stretching to the south as far as the eye could reach. The giant Tasman and all the lesser mountains were dwarfed, and the whole country was spread out like a map in relief at our feet. Hector, the third highest mountain in New Zealand, seemed a pimple; St. David's Dome had become a low peak; but Elie de Beaumont, near the head of the Tasman, still looked a grand mountain, the effect of distance seeming to make it the more imposing.

Through rents in the clouds to the westward, patches of sea appeared like dark lagoons. I stepped out of the rope to secure the first photograph that had ever been taken of the summit of Mount Cook ; then we congratulated each other, and while Graham got the provisions out of the rucksacks, Fyfe employed himself in taking in the view and coolly cutting up his tobacco for a smoke.

Fyfe had intended to take the pulses of the party, and I to make some careful notes of the surrounding mountains; but we did not do so. Professor Tyndall in his famous description of the ascent of the Weisshorn says that he opened his notebook to make a few observations, but he soon relinquished the attempt. There was something incongruous, if not profane, in allowing the scientific faculty to interfere where silent worship was a "reasonable service." Thus felt we as we gazed around at the marvelous panorama. Then thoughts of the descent began to obtrude themselves. We had climbed Mount Cook from the Tasman side. A more serious problem now presented itself. Could we descend on the Hooker side, and so make the first crossing of Aorangi?

William Hanford Edwards on Officiating Football (1916)

No other phrase will do to describe William "Big Bill" Edwards than *"larger than life."* Featured on the cover of the October 4, 1926, Time magazine as the new "Tsar" of football, Edwards, who had then accepted the presidency of the Professional Football League, pledged to make professional football a "clean, red-blooded sport ... [a] great character builder." The author of the Time magazine cover story devised the following analogy to explain Edwards's stature, "He is to football what Will H. Hays is to the cinema, Judge Landis to professional baseball." Hyperbole or no, Edwards's legend almost rivaled that of "the Father of American Football," Walter Camp. In his college days, Edwards had been a 250-pound plus All-American halfback for Princeton, a coach for two years at Princeton and Annapolis, and an occasional, and favorite "whistle" at Ivy League football games after his coaching days were over. Known in his youth as the "Peter Pan of Princeton" and said to be the biggest, fastest man to ever grace the Princeton gridiron, Edwards received national adulation and a Carnegie medal for tackling the would-be assassin of New York mayor William G. Gaynor.

In the following excerpt from his memoir Football Days, Edwards recalls an underestimated but nonetheless invaluable sporting "I" and eye—the "I" of the football referee. In characteristic good humor, he refers to all three of his calling cards: his desire for clean play, his occasional profanity, and his elephantine stature. The passage is also notable for its irony, as the player that Referee Edwards sends to the sidelines turns out to be Vic Kennard, one of football's first "specialists" and the Harvard player who was brought in for a single play to kick the winning field goal (field goals were worth four points in those days) that beat Yale 4–0 in 1908.

From "Umpire and Referee"

In my experience as an official I recall the fact that I began officiating as a referee, and had been engaged and notified in the regular way to referee the Penn-Harvard game on Franklin Field in 1905. When I arrived at the field, McClung was the other official. He had never umpired but had always acted as a referee. In my opinion a man should be either referee or umpire. Each position requires a different kind of experience, and I do not believe officials can successfully interchange these positions. Those who have officiated can appreciate the predicament I was in, especially just at that time when there was so much talk of football reform, by means of changing the rules, changing the style of the game, stopping mass plays. However, I consented; for appreciating that McClung was sincere in his statement that he would do nothing but referee, I was forced to accept the umpire's task.

It was a game full of intense rivalry. The desire to win was carrying the men beyond the bounds of an ordinarily spirited contest, and the umpire's job proved a most severe task. It was in this game that either four or five men were disqualified.

I continued several years after this in the capacity of umpire. One unfortunate experience as umpire as a result of a penalty inflicted upon Wauseka, an Indian player who had tackled too vigorously a Penn player and a policeman was called upon the field. It was the quickest way to keep the game from getting out of hand.

Washington and Jefferson played the Indians at Pittsburgh some years ago. I acted as umpire. The game was played in a driving rainstorm and a muddier field I never saw. The players, as well as the officials, were covered with mud. In fact, my sweater was saturated, the players having used it as a sort of towel to dry their hands. A kicked ball had been fumbled on the goal line and there was a battle royal on the part of the players to get the coveted ball. The stockings and jerseys of the players were so covered with mud that you could not tell them apart. As I was forcing my way down into the mass of players I heard a man shouting for dear life: "I'm an Indian! I'm an Indian! It's my ball!"

When I finally got hold of the fellow with the ball I could not for the life of me tell whether he was an Indian or not. However, I held up the decision until some one got a bucket and sponge and the player's face was mopped off, whereupon I saw that he was an Indian all right. He had scored a touchdown for his team.

An official in the game is subject to all sorts of criticisms and abuse. Sometimes they are humorous and others have a sting which is not readily forgotten.

I admit, on the account of my size, there were times in a game when I would get in a player's way; sometimes in the spectators' way. During a Yale-Harvard game, in which I was acting as an official, the play came close to the sideline, and I had taken my position directly between the players and the spectators, when some kind friend from the bleachers yelled out: "Get off the field! How do you expect us to see the game?"

I shall never forget one poor little fellow who had recovered a fumbled ball, while on top of him was a wriggling mass of players trying to get the ball. As I slowly, but surely, forced my way down through the pile of players I finally landed on top of him. I shall never forget he grunted and yelled, "Six of seven of you fellows get off of me."

It was in the same game that some man from the bleachers called out as I was running up the field: "Here comes the Beef Trust."

There was a coach of a southern college who tried to put over a new one on me, when I caught him coaching from the sidelines in a game with Pennsylvania on Franklin Field. I first warned him, and when he persisted in the offense, I put him behind the ropes, on a bench, besides imposing the regular penalty. It was not long after this, that I discovered he had left the bench. I found him again on the sideline, wearing a heavy ulster and change of hat to disguise himself, but this quick-change artist promptly got the gate.

I knew a player who had an opportunity to get back at an official, but there was no rule to meet the situation. A penalty had been imposed, because the player had used improper language. A heated argument followed, and I am afraid the umpire was guilty of a like offense, when the player exclaimed:

"Well! Well! Why don't you penalize yourself?"

He surely was right. I should have been penalized.

One sometimes unconsciously fails to deal out a kindness for a courtesy done. That was my experience in a Harvard-Yale game at Cambridge one year. On the morning before the game, while I was at the Hotel Touraine, I was making an earnest effort to get, what seemed almost impossible, a seat for a friend of mine. I had finally purchased one for ten dollars, and so made known the fact to two or three of my friends in the corridor. About this time a tall, athletic chap, who had heard that I wanted an extra ticket, volunteered to get me one at the regular price, which he succeeded in doing. I had no difficulty in returning my speculator's ticket. I thanked the fellow cordially for getting me the ticket. I did not see him again until late that afternoon when the game was nearly over. Some rough work in one of the scrimmages compelled me to withdraw one of the Harvard players from the game. As I walked with him to the sidelines, I glanced at his face, only to recognize my friend — the ticket producer. The umpire's task then became harder than ever, as I gave him a seat on the sideline. That player was Vic Kennard.

Bernard Darwin on Golf (1919)

Bernard Darwin, grandson of famed British naturalist Charles Darwin, enjoyed a dual reputation as a distinguished amateur golfer and a celebrated sports journalist during and after the Golden Age. A one-time captain of the golf team at Cambridge University, Darwin, like Bobby Jones, worked as a lawyer when he wasn't writing golf or playing it. Unlike Jones, Darwin made his reputation primarily with pen rather than putter, becoming the first to cover golf on a daily basis for such publications as The Times *of London and* Country Life. *His sportswriting has since achieved classic status, especially his chapter on Robert Tyre Jones from* Golf Between the Wars *entitled, "The Immortal Bobby." Like American golf writer O. B. Keeler,*

Darwin coauthored books with the best golfers of his day, as he did with Bobby Jones in Golf Is My Game *(1960)* and George Duncan in Present-Day Golf *(1921)*. In all, Darwin penned more than two dozen books on his favorite sport.

In the essay that follows, "Confessions of a Practicer," Darwin characteristically understates his abilities as a golfer, which have been consistently overshadowed by his acumen as a writer. In actuality, Darwin succeeded at the highest levels of the game, advancing to the semifinals in the 1909 and 1921 British Amateur and captaining Britain's first Walker Cup team. The tale of Darwin's ad-hoc captaincy is perhaps more illustrative of the participatory sportswriting principle than any other. As the story goes, Darwin the reporter was covering the Cup as a Times *correspondent when captain Robert Harris fell ill, and Darwin the golfer was asked to step in. Rusty as his game may have been, he somehow managed to beat the American captain in singles play.*

The World Golf Hall of Fame, where he is a member, describes Darwin as "the first golf writer to transcribe facts and figures into a branch of literary journalism ... with style, wit and ability."

"Confessions of a Practicer"

At a certain pleasant house where I have spent year after year a winter golfing holiday, there is an ancient Scottish retainer. He is now, alas! past work, but for many successive winters he used to greet me with a hardy annual joke: "We've put you in the big room, Mr. Darwin, so that you can play golf when you have a mind to it." I had just once, after a day of peculiarly gross errors on the green, taken a putter to bed with me and practiced against the legs of the chairs, and I was never afterwards allowed to forget it. It is the sort of reputation that one can never lose, and, indeed, I am afraid I have deserved it during most of my golfing life. It has probably done more harm than good, given more pain than pleasure, but the habit is almost impossible to break, and I must still confess myself an inveterate and almost unrepentant indoor practicer.

In my own rooms at Cambridge I wore two holes through the carpet by means of my stance, to the great distress of my bedmaker, so that I had to get a piece of linoleum to cover up the eyesore and so propitiate her. I have putted, till my back ached, over the floor of a verandah at a small hole between two slabs of slate. I have even putted on the floorboards of a bell tent at the pole. I have played short pitches into a capacious armchair. I have tethered myself by the leg to a bedpost in order to prevent my body from swaying or my knee from bending. I have employed a strange device, blessed by Harry Vardon, whereby a string was fastened at one end to the player's cap and at the other to a piece of metal that slid up the post before his eyes; I am not sure that it did not even ring a bell. In short, if there is any folly which any reader has committed he may be sure that I, too, have committed it.

Moreover, your true practicing lunatic does not confine himself to places where he can use a real club and a real ball. If he cannot swing a club he will swing the fire irons; if there is no room even for a poker, then a paper knife; nay, he will swing away vigorously without any weapon at all. A golfer of my acquaintance was one day holding forth at some length on his subject, declaring that the proper way to practice was to take out all your clubs, without any balls, and practice swinging them one after the other. "I don't agree with you at all," said another golfer, growing perhaps a little restive under the discourse. "The proper way is to take out no clubs, but a box of balls, and practice keeping your eye on the ball." His remark had the desired effect; nevertheless, I would not utterly condemn the theories that he found so tedious. Certainly I can recall many occasions when I have swung myself into what Sam Weller called an "appleplexy" with no compensating benefits whatever, but there have been just a few when I have hit upon the secret. One in particular was at Sandwich just before the Bar versus Stock Exchange match — a very good match it was incidentally, and that is a pity that it was given up. On that Friday evening I was slicing so contemptibly and continuously that ten down with eight to play seemed to stare me in the face for the next day's match. I rushed desperately back to the Bell and swung away in my room — it may have been with an umbrella, or it may have been with a toothbrush — until the last available moment before dressing for dinner. When I had tried everything in vain and was beginning to think that I should have to miss the soup, a sudden inspiration sent my arms whirling freely away after the imaginary ball. I dashed down to dinner with hair unbrushed, but filled with a new and satisfying creed. Next day I drove, as you may say, like a printed book and defeated a doughty opponent by an agreeably large margin.

It must be admitted, however, that this comes near to being the exception that proves the rule, and these overnight inspirations more often than not prove sadly disillusioning in the morning. They have an extremely disturbing effect, so that you know no peace of mind until you have actually tested the new theory with club and ball. If the first two or three shots are successful, a blessed calm settles down upon you: the restless craving is appeased, and you are probably in for a spell of decent play — until the next breakdown; but if, which is more likely, the ball does not go as you have hoped, why then you have wearied your brain and body to no purpose and your last state is much worse than your first.

I have one particularly tragic memory of indoor practicing, not my own, but somebody else's. He was a gentleman well advanced in middle life, but of a youthful and passionate keenness. We stayed together at a hotel for a meeting, and as he had never before played in a team match, his eagerness was almost painful. He lost his match by six holes. Nobody dared to condole, and he shut himself up in his room to swing away the memory of that black disgrace. For some time those listening without heard only the recurrent swish of the club. Then came a fearful crash and he was discovered plucking himself of bits of glass amid the ruins of a chandelier. He went to bed at eight, caught the half-past six train next morning and the meeting knew him no more.

To turn for a moment from the lighter and more ridiculous aspects of the subject, there is no doubt that many a golfer who thinks that he is practicing most virtuously is really doing nothing of the sort. He takes out a caddie, half a dozen balls and a club of which he is particularly fond. The caddie goes out into the long field, the player tees his six balls in a row and slogs them merrily away and then the caddie brings them back again. This may be excellent fun or exercise, though personally I like to do my practicing in secret, but it can rarely do any good. You can scarcely grow more than confident in a club, and you can waste good shots. The only practice that is really beneficial is with a club or of a stroke of which you are not the master, and in that case you must determine to take out only the recalcitrant club or to play only that particular shot. I have sometimes gone out having solemnly vowed to struggle with nothing but half-iron shots, and then yielded to the temptation to take a favorite brassie with me as well. When twilight has at last fallen, or all my balls have been lost in the heather, I have found to my extreme mortification that I have done nothing but slash gaily with the brassie, and those confounded half-iron shots have been postponed once more. Again, even if you do harden your heart and toil away at the iron shots, there is a temptation to do so in some pleasantly open spot and at no particular mark. But a half-iron shot in the abstract is of very little use. In a real game it has to be played up to a flag, and it is the fact of there being bunkers to right and left of that flag that makes your shots so crooked. If you are in a very bad way indeed, the nice open space may be allowable for a stroke or two, but you must not pamper yourself too long. Sooner or later you must put it to the touch of the bunkers.

May H. Hosfield on Deep-sea Fishing for Barracuda (1919)

May Hosfield was a relative newcomer to deep-sea fishing when she went on the following expedition off California's Monterey Peninsula. An experienced horse trainer and mountain hiker, Hosfield learned her trade from Captain Farnsworth, her companion in the "fast and furious" angling adventure that follows. Having hooked a barracuda, Hosfield declares gamely, "There is nothing I enjoy more than a real fight from my fish." Remarkable about "Sum Fishin'" is its lack of gratuitous gender self-consciousness at a time when women in sports narratives still often made apologies or concessions to their male audience. Also distinctive is the article's wartime metaphor making, which renders sharks as "beastly Huns of the sea."

"Sum Fishin'"

We who live at Santa Catalina are undoubtedly the spoiled children of the angling world. With a twelve month season which to fish, the chance of catching nearly as many fish in December as in June, and the range of angling so wide that one may take a two hundred pound fish, two hundred pounds of fish, or two hundred fish in five hours' fishing, it is small wonder that it takes "Sum Fishin'" to make us wildly enthusiastic.

I have been out many times when the water was a frothing, seething mass of fish and bait, seen the mackerel and barracouta leap far above the surface, had my bait knocked this way and that by the leaping tuna, and stood with tense muscles and high keyed nerves while my spoon passed through a school of feeding yellowtail which was churning the water to a golden lather with its myriad of glittering fins.

I have seen bait fleeing before a school of rock bass until their glistening little bodies looked like a cloth of burnished silver being rapidly undulated above the surface of the sea. And I have passed in front of such a school in the very bay of Avalon and had the terrified fish leap into my skiff, and heard their bodies beat against the side of the boat like a rain of heavy hailstones.

One evening just after sunset I watched the mirrored surface of the sea at White's Landing break into sudden fury, and as far as eye could see in the gathering dusk, I saw the white sea bass and flying fish at battle in their game of life and death.

I have caught fish until my arms ached, my fingers stiffened, and my back felt as the ones do in the advertisements for Somebody's Liver Pills; till the nine-ounce rod weighed ninety pounds, and the smooth running mechanism of the Vom Hofe reel was harder to work than a rusty iron windlass.

But only once have I stopped, on a perfect April day, with the smooth sea and warm sun and faint wind that make Catalina the ideal angling ground, and at four o'clock in the afternoon announced that my fishing was over and that if any more fish came aboard they would have to accomplish the feat by leaping into the fish tank unaided because I had helped all of them to attain such an end that I intended to.

It was just afternoon when one of the fishermen passed the word along the pier that the barracouta were "up" off Pebble Beach. News of that sort travels rapidly at Catalina and within half an hour the boatmen's bay was deserted and the thirty or more launches of the fishing fleet spread over the sea from Jew Fish Point to Avalon.

For a little while all was quiet and the boats circled about trolling, each in the spot its owner considered most favorable. Presently a few splashes of white broke the blue water. Then, just off Pebble Beach, a long black ripple was seen, advancing rapidly.

"Bait," said the Captain, laconically. "They'll open up in a minute now."

Scarcely had he finished speaking when the level wave of bait was shot by a thousand flashing bombs of living fish. Spray and anchovies went three and four feet in the air as the feeding fish leaped clear and high above the water.

From all directions the launches were coming, full speed ahead. We, being very close, were in the school almost immediately. As we approached we saw that the feeding fish were big mackerel, instead of the barracouta we were expecting.

Then, for a space, we were too busy to note much of anything. Three times my bait was taken before the line was a quarter out. Fifteen fish lay in the fish tank within almost the same number of minutes. Some were the little fellows that make most delicious eating — around a pound or two in weight — while others were the big ones that put up such a gallant fight and often weighed six pounds and over. Then came a lull in the biting, and we had opportunity to watch the natural feeding and actions of the fish and bait.

The waters about Catalina are so crystal clear that every movement of the fish, every marking even, can be noted twenty and thirty feet below the surface, out in the open sea and without artificial aids. With the assistance of the glass in the bottoms of the boats used to view the submarine gardens and the life which inhabits them, the surface glitter is eliminated and the shade diffused until fish can be watched swimming and feeding one hundred feet below the boat as clearly as in the tanks of an aquarium.

Knowing this, we leaned over the coaming and watched the mackerel. The water was literally alive with them. Swimming with incredible rapidity, they darted after the frightened anchovies, snapped them up with dexterous speed, and flashed by the launch like subaqueous rockets.

A few of the wiser anchovies rose to the surface and sought the shelter of the boat. Poor little tired creatures! They gathered about the hospitable hull as timid children hide behind their mothers' skirts. I leaned over and trailed my hand in the water. Twice they swam through my fingers, seeming in no wise disturbed by the contact, and several I actually lifted from the sea. It seemed almost kinder to bring them aboard and let them die once and for all, instead of allowing them to remain to suffer a thousand deaths in their efforts to escape from the hungry mackerel.

Then we were recalled to our fishing by the seizure of our baits. Again the angling was fast and furious. For several miles to sea and all along the coast the leaping fish frothed the water, and the boats gathered a rapid harvest. The Captain was circling close inshore.

A vicious strike almost lifted me from my seat. Many sharks were among the fish, and I concluded I had had a bite from one of these unwelcome pests when the Captain remarked, "Well, why didn't you hook him? It was a yellowtail. Be ready for another. They are just ahead."

Sure enough, a great circle, probably a thousand feet in diameter, was filled with their glistening amber tails and the water was swirling and boiling like some giant's cauldron. We worked them for some time. The Captain had a strike, but his hook straightened and he lost his fish. My bait was guiltless of attention. Then they went down as suddenly as they had risen.

We trolled about for a quarter of an hour. Far to sea we saw the flash and splash of leaping fish. Gradually we worked off shore. Suddenly, not fifty feet ahead, I saw a barracouta rise clear, turn an end over end flip in midair, and go back into the water with a tremendous splash. Before I could call out my news, a dozen broke water, and our cry of "Barracouta!" was simultaneous.

We both hooked almost immediately. During the fights the boat was surrounded by a busy school, and again and again spray dashed over us as the great fish leaped clear within three feet of our gunwale.

For several miles in each direction the boats and fish and bait were repeating the drama in which we were taking part. I shall never forget the sight. The barracouta — all about three feet long, slender, iridescent, and marvelously supple — stood on their tails and fell straight backwards into the sea, leaped clear and turned somersaults three feet in the air, shot out and in perfect rainbow dives, head in the water before the tail was clear — the long glistening body a symmetrical arch between — dashed up and up in a straight, skyward leap and then dropped forward from the height and sent the spray flying as their twelve pounds of weight hit the water.

The anchovies, utterly terrified by the peril from which there was so little escape, foolishly followed the principle of "safety in numbers" and milled themselves into balls twenty feet across and five or six feet deep.

We circled one and with a dip net lifted enough fresh bait aboard to catch all the yellowtail on the coast. Then the Captain threw out the clutch, and handed me a stoutly woven handline baited with a live anchovy.

"I'm going to give you some real action here," he said. "And if you don't have to fight harder than you have ever fought with rod and reel, and have better sport too, I'll eat your entire catch!"

I took the line wonderingly. To connect sport with handlining was a new one on me. Nevertheless I was willing to be shown, so I began paying out the cord. Less than fifteen feet had gone overboard when I left my seat with great precipitancy and only staved off an unpremeditated bath by falling to my knees on the floor and bracing my whole weight against the coaming.

My arms were being tossed about like flails, and I felt as if my head would flip loose at an instant. I had no idea what had happened, but I adhered to the first principle of handline fishing and "hung on."

Presently I realized that the Captain was shouting with laughter. I struggled to my feet, was almost jerked overboard again, and then felt the line go slack. Thankful to be delivered from such a bolt of lightening, I hauled in. Half the short line was aboard when my arms started from their sockets and a barracouta rose through the packed ball of anchovies, and made faces at me as he stood there on his tail. I opened my mouth for the air that my nose was not able to supply rapidly enough, and had it filled with very salt water as the fish jerked and fell back into the sea.

The Captain was still laughing.

Water generally cools one, but this acted with opposite effect. I braced my knees against the coaming and exerted every ounce of strength on the line. The fish came up. Then I leaned forward to grasp the sinker at the beginning of the leader, missed it, and in some inexplicable fashion found myself on the opposite side of the boat with the fish doing a cake walk a little more than an arm's length away.

If I had been a man I would, no doubt, have begun to systematically curse that fish, root, stock, and branch. As it was I said "Darn" with all the vindictiveness of my nature, and jerked the fish down to the water.

"Bring him in. Bring him in," called the Captain.

I started around the stern of the boat. The fish was agreeable for half the distance. Then he headed for China. I consider long ocean voyages in war time dangerous, so set myself to persuading him that the California coast was quite pleasant enough.

I don't know how long we argued the matter over the stern. I was nearly ready to concede the wisdom of his plan when he turned straight to the Captain. A second later the leader was safe in those strong hands, and I dropped back on my seat and mopped most of the surplus water from my face with my sleeve. It was not time for the niceties of life and scented handkerchiefs.

"Well, how did you like it?" the Captain grinned at me. I happened to notice that his line was overboard. Suddenly it began to move, and before I could answer his question, I saw the grin disappear as he shot to the boat side and went through a portion at least of the maneuvers I had just concluded.

It was my turn to laugh.

By the time his fish was safely in the tank I had recovered my wind.

There is nothing I enjoy more than a real fight from my fish, and I had certainly had one on that handline. Like Oliver Twist, I asked for more.

I had it. And plenty. Sometimes the fish got away after a couple of quick dashes. Other times I brought them to the Captain's hand and they gave an unexpected twist and shook free. Again and again I clung to the stern, the chairs, the coaming — anything I could get braced against. Spray kept me pleasantly cool, and made the floor a gliddering danger. One fishtank overflowed and the second came into use.

Between bites we watched the fish.

So close to the boat that we leaned over the coaming and dipped our hands into them at will, milled the anchovies. Packed in such a solid mass that their individual progress was scarcely perceptible, they slowly shouldered each other along and by the combined efforts of their countless numbers gave the body a swirling motion. Apparently realizing that the boat would give them a modicum of shelter, they crowded against her whenever possible, and I took delight in thrusting my hand and arm into their mass and feeling the smooth friction of their little bodies as they pressed against it in passing.

Presently this became too dangerous. Four or five six-foot sharks had been lazily swimming about and cutting into the bait whenever it left the boat's side. They grew bolder and bolder, and at last I started back with horrified haste as one rose under my hand, and thrust its blunt nose through the packed anchovies not a foot from my face.

Soon the other sharks followed the example of the first and we were forced to watch the saddening spectacle of these beastly Huns of the sea gorging themselves so hoggishly that the crushed and mangled bait dripped from mouths too full to hold it. I longed for a gun as must those who stood empty-handed in Belgium and watched the work of the sharks of Germany.

One feels quite differently in watching fish feeding upon bait. Time and again a half dozen big barracouta rushed the school, shot skyward through its midst, and sent showers of the little fish flying by the force of the impact. But this seemed fair enough. The barracouta caught two or three at a rush, took a good deal of violent exercise in so doing, and then darted about after the anchovies they had scattered at their leap and sometimes caught them and sometimes not.

They took a chance. They caught no more of the bait, in proportion, than we caught of them. While the sharks merely wallowed into the school, guzzled as much and more, than they could hold, irreparably maimed countless anchovies with their cruel teeth, and then leisurely sank below the boat and rolled malicious, piggish eyes in disdain at our fury.

The Captain grew more and more restless. Then he drew his line aboard, threw down his bait, and reached for the gaff hook. I knew what was coming and cannily retired to the other side of the boat, where I had not long to wait. A terrible thumping and pounding against the hull told me the strong hook had gone home. I turned to watch the struggle just in time to receive a young wave of spray from the thrashing tail. Then quiet reigned. When I had finished wiping my eyes I saw the Captain wringing the front of his dripping shirt and smiling.

"That one won't monkey around here for a while anyway," he said. We had drifted a little way from the bait, so I ceased fishing for a while and watched the life below me. The barracouta were evidently getting well filled for they swam about lazily, their bodies the color of dull gold in the diffused light. They paid no attention to the sharks and the sharks returned the compliment.

My hook was still baited. Occasionally one approached it cautiously, made a half-hearted snap and then slowly proceeded. Others struck the leader with nose or body and gave startled swirls and shot off out of my ken. Their tiny fins fluttered in the water like the wings of a moth, but it was quite evident that their main propelling power lay in their long snake-like bodies that shoved them forward in sinuous undulations.

It was curious to watch them after taking the hooked bait. They snapped it so quickly that I could scarcely either see or feel the movement. For a second or two they continued their slow swimming. Then the line tightened, and as the hook went home, they rushed surfaceward with express-train speed.

Generally the rush took them entirely clear of the water and the leader thrashed about perilously as they twisted and pivoted in midair. Sometimes they turned just under the surface and attempted to depart for realms unknown. Again they headed for the milling anchovies and those long suffering little creatures were thrashed about like chaff. But whatever they did, they did it in a hurry — after that first tiny pause.

It delighted me to have them get away. Sport ceases to be sport and descends to mere slaughter when the chances are not somewhere near equal. At least half of my battles ended in the victory of the fish, and they seemed to take particular delight in flinging the hook free with such strength that I often had a busy time dodging it as it came whanging aboard.

Of course I am well aware that handline fishing is "beyond the pale" with the great majority of anglers. And rightly, too, under most circumstances. To land a fish on a handline while trolling is about as hazardous as shooting the chickens in one's backyard.

But to "still fish" for barracouta or fish of like size and over, with less than fifty feet of line out, and the fish biting directly under the boat, is far from a "sure thing." To my mind it is not the weight or variety of tackle one uses, but the fairness of the fight to both fish and fisher, that constitutes real sport.

One can fight a fish on three-six for an hour and "ease" it up to the gaff with it scarcely realizing what is happening to it, or — most probably — lose it halfway and send it off to perish a miserable death from starvation and the constant worry of the hook in its mouth or throat. Or one can have a rapid, vivid battle of fifteen minutes of hard brain and muscle work on heavy tackle and bring a still fighting but outgeneraled antagonist to the boat either to be released to entire freedom, or quickly and humanely dispatched and later used for food for a war-starved world.

Occasionally one may go still farther, and, for the novelty of the thing, try the short, quick fight of the handline as herein described and get an entirely new thrill from the fishing game. Most of the fish can be landed inside of three minutes. That is, those that are landed at all. One loses two-thirds of them. But it is the busiest minutes the ordinary angler ever experienced and I, for one, have never had to do half the alert thinking when assisted by the perfected drags, and appreciable leverage of rod and reel as when relying solely on my bare hands and quick wits to outgame the bundle of fighting fury on the end of my short line.

Many, many times I was the one who was outgeneraled and my fish freed themselves with continually surprising ease. A sudden shoot to the surface, a violent shake of the body, and my hook was flung twenty feet away. A quick run under the boat with a sudden reverse movement to gain a bit of slack, and the line came in empty. A rush straight for me, far too fast for any hands to keep a taut line, and again I had lost out. A dive bottomwards that started my arms from their sockets, followed by a couple of quick jerks, and another catch was free, free and unharmed and untired; vitality left to dart off and elude the sharks with undiminished quickness. A slight tear in the cartilaginous side of the mouth but no yards of trailing line to drag and catch on every bit of kelp or wreckage, or vicious hook to torture out life in slow death.

Yes, I maintain that handline fishing may be real sport under proper conditions.

After each struggle I was less anxious for the next. The Captain was still amusing himself with the sharks as the recurrent thumpings and spray showers mixed with occasional bits of subdued profanity testified. I wiped the salt rime from the crystal of my watch and saw that it was five minutes to four. Far too early to stop fishing. Why the afternoon had scarcely commenced! I looked at my hands. In spite of the many weeks of steady fishing that had passed, they were sore. I felt my arms. Pretty tired. I looked at my clothes. Pretty wet. And at the fishtank. Pretty full.

Another boat drew up by our school of anchovies.

"Oh, look at the bait!" its occupants called, and the boatman hurriedly produced a dip net. He scooped several buckets full aboard, and we watched the silvery spray of scales as the fish thrashed about in the unwelcome air.

My unbaited hook trailed idly in the water.

"What's the matter? Out of bait?" queried the Captain.

"No, but out of the mood of fishing. I'm tired. Let's call it a day and go in," I suggested.

He smiled broadly. "Do you mean to say you've got enough fishing for once?"

"I guess I have. I never expected to, but I've actually caught my fill."

Without a word he threw in the clutch and headed toward Avalon. Dreamily the green beauty of the Island slid past us. Sea gulls, too full for further feeding, covered the rocks at Pebble Beach. At sea, the boats flashed white and then showed gray as they turned the sunned or shaded side toward us. A few were following our example and trolling slowly shoreward.

At the dock we counted our catch. Seventy-eight barracouta with a total weight of eight hundred and twelve pounds. "Sum Fishin'!"

Zane Grey on Fishing for Bonefish (1919)

Among an elite group of sportsman-writers that included Jack London and Ernest Hemingway, Zane Grey was by far the most prolific, authoring over 90 books, most of them westerns. While Grey is better known for the Wild West fictions that were eventually made into movies by Paramount, his body of nonfiction sportswriting nevertheless impresses. An example is his overlooked 1919 offering of participatory angling encounters, Tales of Fishes. *Grey, one of the first millionaire authors, was an accomplished athlete who attended the University of Pennsylvania on a baseball scholarship before eventually playing minor league ball in Wheeling, West Virginia. He would devote much of his later life to deep-sea fishing in New Zealand, from where he wrote many articles on fishing for major periodicals of the day, and where he set several fishing world records.*

"THE BONEFISH"

In my experience as a fisherman the greatest pleasure has been the certainty of something new to learn, to feel, to anticipate, to thrill over. An old proverb tells us that if you wish to bring back the wealth of the Indias you must go out with its equivalent. Surely the longer a man fishes the wealthier he becomes in experience, in reminiscence, in love of nature, if he goes out with the harvest of a quiet eye, free from the plague of himself.

As a boy, fishing was a passion with me, but not more for the conquest of golden sunfish and speckled chubs and horny catfish than for the haunting sound of the waterfall and the color and loneliness of the cliffs. As a man, and a writer who is forever learning, fishing is still a passion, stronger with all the years, but tempered by an understanding of the nature of primitive man, hidden in all of us, and by a keen reluctance to deal pain to any creature. The sea and the river and the mountain have almost taught me not to kill except for the urgent needs of life; and the time will come when I shall have grown up to that. When I read a naturalist or a biologist I am always ashamed of what I have called a sport. Yet one of the truths of evolution is that not to practice strife, not to use violence, not to fish or hunt — that is to say, not to fight — is to retrograde as a natural man. Spiritual and intellectual growth is attained at the expense of the physical.

Always, then, when I am fishing I feel that the fish are incidental, and that the reward of effort and endurance, the incalculable and intangible knowledge emanate from the swelling and the infinite sea or from the shaded and murmuring stream. Thus I assuage my conscience and justify the fun, the joy, the excitement, and the violence.

Five years ago I had never heard of a bonefish. The first man who ever spoke to me about this species said to me, very quietly with serious intentness: "Have you had any experience with bonefish?" I said no, and asked him what kind that was. His reply was enigmatical. "Well, don't go after bonefish unless you can give up all other fishing." I remember I laughed. But I never forgot that remark, and now it comes back to me clear in its significance. That fisherman read me as well as I misunderstood him.

Later that season I listened to talk of inexperienced bonefishermen telling what they done and heard. To me it was absurd. So much fishing talk seems ridiculous, anyway. And the expert fishermen, whoever they were, received the expressive titles: "Bonefish Bugs and Bonefish Nuts!" Again I heard arguments about the tackle rigged for these mysterious fish and these arguments fixed my vague impression. By and by some bonefishermen came to Long Key, and the first sight of a bonefish made me curious. I think it weighed five pounds — a fair-sized specimen. Even to my prejudiced eye that fish showed class. So I began to question the bonefishermen.

At once I found this type of angler to be remarkably reticent as to experience and method. Moreover, the tackle used was amazing to me. Stiff rods and heavy lines for little fish! I gathered another impression, and it was that bonefish were related to dynamite and chain lightning. Everybody who would listen to my questions had different things to say. Not two men agreed on the tackle or bait or ground or anything. I enlisted the interest of my brother R. C., and we decided that, just to satisfy curiosity, to go out and catch some bonefish. The complacent, smug conceit of fishermen! I can see now how funny ours was. Fortunately it is now past tense. If I am ever conceited again, I hope no one will read my stories.

My brother and I could not bring ourselves to try for bonefish with heavy tackle. It was preposterous. Three — four — five pound fish! We had seen no larger. Bass tackle was certainly heavy enough for us. So in the innocence of our hearts and the assurance of our vanity, we sallied forth to catch bonefish.

That was four years ago. Did we have good luck? No! Luck has nothing to do with bonefishing. What happened? For one solid month each winter of those four years we had devoted ourselves to bonefishing with light tackle. We stuck to our colors. The space of this whole volume would not be half enough to tell our experience — the amaze, the difficulty, the perseverance, the defeat, the wonder, and at last the achievement. The season of 1918 we hooked about fifty bonefish on three-six tackles — that is, three-ounce tips and six-thread lines — and we landed fourteen of them. I caught nine and R. C. caught five. R. C.'s eight-pond fish justified our contention and crowned our efforts.

To date, in all my experience, I consider this bonefish achievement the most thrilling, fascinating, difficult, and instructive. That is a broad statement and I hope I can prove it. I am prepared to state that I feel almost certain, if I spent another month bonefishing, I would become obsessed and perhaps lose my enthusiasm for other kinds of fish.

Why?

There is a multiplicity of reasons. My reasons range from the exceedingly graceful beauty of a bonefish to the fact that he is the best food fish I ever ate. That is a wide range. He is the wisest, shyest, wariest, strangest fish I ever studied; and I am not excepting the great *Xiphias gladius*— the broadbill swordfish. As for the speed of the bonefish, I claim no salmon, no barracuda, no other fish celebrated for its swiftness of motion, is in his class. A bonefish is so incredibly fast that it was a long time before I could believe the evidence of my own eyes. You see him: he is there perfectly still in the clear, shallow water, a creature of fish shape, pale green and silver, but crystal-like, a phantom shape, staring at you with strange black eyes; then he is gone. Vanished! Absolutely without your seeing a movement, even a faint streak! By peering keenly you may discern a little swirl in the water. As for the strength of the bonefish, I actually hesitate to give my impressions. No one will ever believe how powerful a bonefish is until he has tried to stop the rush and heard the line snap. As for his cunning, it is utterly baffling. As for his biting, it is almost imperceptible. As for his tactics, they are beyond conjecture.

I want to append here a few passages from my notebooks, in the hope that a bare, bald statement of fact will help my argument.

First experience on a bonefish shoal. This wide area of coral mud was dry at low tide. When we arrived the tide was rising. Water scarcely a foot deep, very clear. Bottom white, with patches of brown grass. We saw bonefish everywhere and expected great sport. But no matter where we stopped we could not get any bites. Schools of bonefish swam up to the boat, only to dart away. Everywhere we saw thin white tails sticking out, as they swam along, feeding with noses in the mud. When we drew in our baits we invariably found them half gone, and it was our assumption that the blue crabs did this.

At sunset the wind quieted. It grew very still and beautiful. The water was rosy. here and there we saw swirls and tails standing out, and we heard heavy thumps of plunging fish. But we could not get any bites.

When we returned to camp we were told that the half of our soldier crab baits had been sucked off by bonefish. Did not believe that.

Tide bothered us again this morning. It seems exceedingly difficult to tell one night one night before what the tide is going to do the next morning. At ten o'clock we walked to the same place we were yesterday. It was a bright, warm day, with just enough breeze to ruffle the water and make fishing pleasant, and we certainly expected to have good luck. But we fished for about three hours without any sign of a fish. This was discouraging and we could not account for it.

So we moved. About half a mile down the beach I thought I caught a glimpse of a bonefish. It was a likely-looking contrast to the white marl all around. Here I made a long cast and sat down to wait. My brother lagged behind. Presently I spied two bonefish nosing along not ten feet from the shore. They saw me, so I made no attempt to drag the bait near them, but I called to my brother and told him to try to get a bait ahead of them. This was a little after flood tide. It struck me then that these singular fish feed up the beach with one tide and down with another.

Just when my brother reached me, I got a nibble. I called to him and then stood up, ready to strike. I caught a glimpse of the fish. He looked big and dark. He had his nose down, fooling with my bait. When I struck him he felt heavy. I put on the click of the reel, and when the bonefish started off he pulled the rod down hard, taking the line fast. He made one swirl on the surface and then started up shore. He seemed exceedingly swift. I ran along the beach until presently the line slackened and I felt the hook had torn out. This was disappointment. I could not figure that I had done anything wrong, but I decided in the future to use a smaller and sharper hook. We went on down the bench, seeing several bonefish on the way, and finally we ran into a big school of them. They were right along shore, but when they saw us we could not induce them to bite.

Every day we learn something. It is necessary to keep out of sight of these fish. After they bite, everything depends upon the skillful hooking of the fish. Probably it will require a good deal of skill to land them after you have hooked them, but we have had little experience at that so far. When these fish are along the shore they certainly are feeding, and presumably they are feeding on crabs of some sort. Bonefish appear to be game worthy of any fisherman's best efforts.

It was a still, hot day, without any clouds. We went up the beach to a point opposite an old construction camp. Today when we expected the tide to be doing one thing, it was doing another. Ebb and flow and flood tide have become as difficult as Sanskrit synonyms for me. My brother took an easy and comfortable chair and sat up the beach, and I, like an ambitious fisherman, laboriously and adventurously waded out one hundred and fifty feet to an old platform that had been erected there. I climbed upon this, and found it a very precarious place to sit. Come to think about it, there is something very remarkable about the places a fisherman will pick out to sit down on. This place was a two-by-four plank full of nails, and I cheerfully availed myself of it, and, casting my bait out as far as I could, I calmly sat down to wait for a bonefish. It has become a settled conviction in my mind that you have to wait for bonefish. But all at once I got a hard bite. It quite excited me. I jerked and pulled the bait away from the fish and he followed it and took it again. I saw this fish and several others in the white patch of ground where there were not any weeds. But in my excitement I did not have out a long enough line, and when I jerked the fish turned over and got away. This was all right, but the next two hours sitting in the sun on that seat with a nail sticking into me were not altogether pleasurable. When I thought I had endured it as long as I could, I saw a flock of seven bonefish swimming past me, and one of them was a whopper. The sight revived me. I hardly breathed while that bunch of fish swam right for my bait, and for all I could see they did not know it was there. I waited another long time. The sun was hot — there was no breeze — the heat was reflected from the water. I could have stood all this well enough, but I could not stand the nails. So I climbed down off my perch, having forgotten that all this time the tide had been rising. And as I could not climb back, I had to get wet, to the infinite amusement of my brother. After that I fished from the shore.

Presently my brother shouted, and I looked up to see him pulling on a fish. There was a big splash in the water and then I saw his line running out. The fish was heading straight for the framework on which I had been seated, and I knew if he ever did get there, he would break the line. All of a sudden I saw the fish he had hooked. And he reached the framework all right.

I had one more strike this day, but did not hook the fish. It seems this bonefishing takes infinite patience. For all we can tell, these fish come swimming along with the rising tide close in to shore and they are exceedingly shy and wary. My brother now has caught two small bonefish and each of them gave a good strong bite, at once starting off with the bait. We had been under the impression that it was almost impossible to feel the bonefish bite. It will take work to learn this game.

Ernest Hemingway on Rainbow Trout Fishing (1920)

> *Ernest Hemingway's reputation as a sportsman extraordinaire is well-established, even mythic. In the short introduction to his anthology* By-line Ernest Hemingway, *scholar William White points out that "Hemingway's literary apprenticeship was served in journalism," a statement with which Hemingway would no doubt agree, as he considered his early journalism somewhat too facile. This short article, "The Best Rainbow Trout Fishing," from the* Star Weekly *represents one of over 150 Papa Bear wrote for the* Toronto Daily Star *and* Star Weekly *between 1920 and 1924. Hemingway also covered tuna fishing and bullfighting, among other sports, during this period, though this piece, while making minimal use of "I," is notable for the way in which Hemingway integrates his own well-practiced sporting expertise. In part, Hemingway's purpose in the feature that follows is to tell it like it is—as he puts it: "Magazine writers and magazine covers to the contrary, the brook or speckled trout does not leap out of the water after he has been hooked."*

"The Best Rainbow Trout Fishing"

Rainbow trout fishing is as different from brook fishing as prize fighting is from boxing. The rainbow is called *Salmo iridescens* by those mysterious people who name the fish we catch and has recently been introduced into Canadian waters. At present the best rainbow trout fishing in the world is in the rapids of the Canadian Soo.

There the rainbow have been taken as large as fourteen pounds from canoes that are guided through the rapids and halted at the pools by Ojibway and Chippewa boatmen. It is a wild and never-frazzling sport and the odds are in favor of the big trout who tear off thirty or forty yards of line at a rush and then will sulk at the base of a big rock and refuse to be stirred into action by the pumping of a stout fly rod aided by a fluent monologue of Ojibwayan profanity. Sometimes it takes two hours to land a really big rainbow under those circumstances.

The Soo afford great fishing. But it is a wild nightmare kind of fishing that is second only in strenuousness to angling for tuna off Catalina Island. Most of the trout too take a spinner and refuse a fly and to the 99 percent pure fly fisherman, there are no one hundred percenters, that is a big drawback.

Of course the rainbow trout of the Soo will take a fly but it is rough handling them in that tremendous volume of water on the light tackle a fly fisherman loves. It is dangerous wading in the spots that can be waded, too, for a misstep will take the angler over his head in the rapids. A canoe is a necessity to fish the very best water.

Altogether it is a rough, tough, mauling game, lacking in the meditative qualities of the Izaak Walton school of angling. What would make a fitting Valhalla for the good fisherman when he does would be a regular trout river with plenty of rainbow trout in it jumping crazy for the fly.

There is such a one not forty miles from the Soo called the — well, called a river. It is about as wide as a river should be and a little deeper than a river ought to be and to get the proper picture you want to imagine in rapid succession the following fade-ins:

A high pine covered bluff that rises steep up out of the shadows. A short sand slope down to the river and a quick elbow turn with a little flood wood jammed in the bend and then a pool.

A pool where the moselle-colored water sweeps into a dark swirl and expanse that is blue-brown with depth and fifty feet across.

There is the setting.

The action is supplied by two figures that slog into the picture up the trail along the riverbank with loads on their backs that would tire a pack horse. These loads are pitched over the heads into the patch of ferns by the edge of the deep pool. That is incorrect. Really the figures lurch a little forward and the tump line loosens and the pack slumps into the ground. Men don't pitch loads at the end of an eight-mile hike.

One of the figures looks up and notes the bluff is flattened on top and that there is a good place to put a tent. The other is lying on his back and looking straight up into the air. The first reaches over and picks up a grasshopper that is stiff with the fall of the evening dew and tosses him into the pool.

The hopper floats spraddle-legged on the water of the pool an instant, an eddy catches him and then there is a yard-long flash of flame, and a trout as long as your forearm has shot into the air and the hopper has disappeared.

"Did you see that?" gasped the man who had tossed in the grasshopper.

It was a useless question, for the other, who a moment before would have served as a model for a study entitled "Utter Fatigue," was jerking his fly rod out of the case and holding a leader in his mouth.

We decided on a McGinty and a Royal Coachman for the flies and at the second cast there was a swirl like the explosion of a depth bomb, the line went taut and the rainbow shot two feet out of the water. He tore down the pool and the line went out until the core of the reel showed. He jumped and each time he shot into the air we lowered the tip and prayed. Finally, he jumped and the line went slack and Jacques reeled in. We thought he was gone and then he jumped right under our faces. He had shot upstream towards us so fast it looked as though he were off.

When I finally netted him and rushed him up the bank and could feel his huge strength in the tremendous muscular jerks he made when I held him flat against the bank, it was almost dark. He measured twenty-six inches and weighted nine pounds and seven ounces.

That is rainbow trout fishing.

The rainbow takes the fly more willingly than he does bait. The McGinty, a fly that looks like a yellow jacket, is the best. It should be tied on a number eight or ten hook.

The smaller flies get more strikes but are too small to hold the really big fish. The rainbow trout will live in the same streams with brook trout but they are found in different kinds of places. Brook trout will be forced into the shady holes under the bank and where alders hang over the banks, and the rainbow will dominate the clear pools and the fast shallows.

Magazine writers and magazine covers to the contrary, the brook or speckled trout does not leap out of the water after he has been hooked. Given plenty of line he will fight a deep rushing fight. Of course, if you hold the fish too tight he will be forced by the rush of the current to flop on top of the water.

But the rainbow always leaps on a slack or tight line. His leaps are not mere flops, either, but actual jumps out of and parallel with the water from a foot to five feet. A five-foot jump by any fish sounds improbable but it is true.

If you don't believe it, tie into one in fast water and try and force him. Maybe if he is a five-pounder he will throw me down and only jump four feet eleven inches.

Bill Tilden on the Psychology of Tennis (1921)

William Tatem Tilden II, or "Big Bill" for short, achieved a larger than life personality equaling that of on- and off-field legends Babe Ruth, Jack

Dempsey, and Helen Wills. *The world number one for seven years running and the victor in seven U.S. singles titles, Tilden was a rarity in tennis — a late bloomer who didn't break into the singles winner's circle in a major until he had reached his late 20s. Even with a belated start, Tilden achieved unprecedented dominance, winning every major title he contested for six straight years, and earning, in 1950, the title "greatest tennis player of the first half of the Twentieth Century" from the Associated Press.*

The stylish, cerebral, hard-hitting Tilden popularized the game on center court and in the pages of his two seminal tennis books, The Art of Lawn Tennis *and* Match Play and the Spin of the Ball. *In retirement, he continued to write — penning, producing, and performing money-losing Broadway shows that earned him a reputation as a frustrated writer. Tilden, who died penniless, invested much of his own fortune in his literary and dramatic endeavors while refusing to turn professional until 1930. In his article "Tilden Brought Theatrics to Tennis," ESPN.com's Ron Borges, citing the $50,000 offer Big Bill once turned down from promoter Charles C. "Cash and Carry" Pyle, recounts an emblematic exchange between Pyle ("Mr. Tilden, I think you're a damn fool") and Tilden ("Mr. Pyle, I think you're right."). In the excerpt below, from the Art of Lawn Tennis,* Tilden makes the famous claim, *"The tennis star of today owes his public as much as the actor owes the audience"— a bit of wisdom gleaned from both the theatrical and athletic stage.*

FROM "THE PSYCHOLOGY OF MATCH PLAY" AND "THE PSYCHOLOGY OF FITNESS"

The first and most important point in match play is to know how to lose. Lose cheerfully, generously, and like a sportsman. This is the first great law of tennis, and the second is like unto it — to win modestly, cheerfully, generously, and like a sportsman.

The object of match play is to win, but no credit goes to a man who does not win fairly and squarely. A victory is a defeat if it is other than fair. Yet again I say to win is the object, and to do so, one should play to the last ounce of his strength, the last gasp of his breath, and the last scrap of his nerve. If you do so and lose, the better man won. If you do not, you have robbed your opponent of his right of beating your best. Be fair to both him and yourself.

"The Play's the thing," and in match play a good defeat is far more creditable than a hollow victory. Play tennis for the game's sake. Play it for the men you meet, the friends you make, and the pleasure you may give to the public by the hard-working yet sporting game that is owed them by their presence at the match.

Many tennis players feel they owe the public nothing, and are granting a favor by playing. It is my belief that when the public so honors a player that they attend matches, that player is in duty bound to give of his best, freely, willingly, and cheerfully, for only by so doing can he repay the honor paid him. The tennis star of today owes his public as much as the actor owes the audience, and only by meeting his obligations can tennis be retained in public favor. The players get their reward in the personal popularity they gain by their conscientious work.

Any player who really enjoys a match for the game's sake will always be a fine sportsman, for there is no amusement to a match that does not give your opponent his every right.* A player who plays for the joy of the game wins the crowd the first time he steps on the court. All the world loves an optimist.

The more tennis I play, the more I appreciate my sense of humor. I seldom play a match when I do not get a smile out of some remark from the gallery, while I know that the gallery always enjoys at least one hearty laugh at my expense. I do not begrudge it them, for I know how very peculiar tennis players in general, and myself in particular, appear when struggling vainly to reach a shot hopelessly out of reach.

Two delightful elderly ladies were witnessing Charles S. Garland and myself struggle against Mavrogordato and Riseley at the Edgbaston tournament in England in 1920. One turned to the other and said: "Those are the Americans!"

"Oh," said the second lady resignedly, "I thought so. The tall one [meaning me] looks rather queer."

During the Davis Cup match against the French at Eastbourne, I went on the court against Laurentz in my blue "woolly" sweater. The day was cold, and I played the match 4–1 in Laurentz' favor, still wearing it. I started to remove it at the beginning of the sixth game, when the gallery burst into loud applause, out of which floated a sweet feminine voice: "Good! Now maybe the poor boy will be able to play!"

For the first time I realized just what the gallery thought of my efforts to play tennis, and also of the handicap of the famous "blue-bearskin" as they termed it.

My favorite expression during my Davis Cup trip happened to be "Peach" for any particularly good shot by my opponent. The gallery at the Championship, quick to appreciate any mannerism of a player, and to, know him by it, enjoyed the remark on many occasions as the ball went floating by me. In

---

*The running-in of a portion of a separate, noncontiguous chapter, "Chapter VIII: The Psychology of Fitness" is here indicated by the insertion of a line space preceding the run–in material. The sentence here noted represents the first sentence of the sixteenth paragraph of the run–in chapter.

my match with Kingscote in the final set, the court was very slippery owing to the heavy drizzle that had been falling throughout the match. At 3–2 in my favor, I essayed a journey to the net, only to have Kingscote pass me cross court to my backhand. I turned and started rapidly for the shot murmuring "Peach" as I went. Suddenly my feet went out and I rolled over on the ground, sliding some distance, mainly on my face. I arose, dripping, just in time to hear, sotto voce, in the gallery at my side: "A little bit crushed, that Peach." The sense of humor of the speaker was delightful. The whole sideline howled with joy, and the joke was on me.

I am always the goat for the gallery in these little jokes, because it is seldom I can refrain from saying something loud enough to be heard.

I remember an incident that caused great joy to a large gallery in Philadelphia during a match between two prominent local players. One of the men had been charging the net and volleying consistently off the frame of his racquet, giving a wonderful display of that remarkable shot known the world over as "the mahogany volley." His luck was phenomenal, for all his mishit volleys won him points. Finally, at the end of a bitterly contested deuce game in the last set, he again won the deciding point with a volley off the wood, just as a small insect flew in his eye.

He called to his opponent: "Just a moment, I have a fly in my eye."

The disgusted opponent looked up and muttered: "Fly? Huh! I'll bet it's a splinter!"

There was a certain young player who was notoriously lax in his eyesight on decisions. He could never see one against himself. He became noted in his own locality. He and another boy were playing a team of brothers who were quite famous in the tennis world. One of these brothers had a very severe service that the local Captain Kidd could not handle at all. So each time the visiting player served close to the line, the boy would swing at it, miss it, and call "Fault!" There was no umpire available and there was no question of the older team losing, so they let it go for some time. Finally a service fully three feet in was casually called out by the youngster. This proved too much for the server, who hailed his brother at the net with the query: "What was wrong that time?"

"I don't know," came the reply; "unless he called a foot fault on you!"

The assurance of some young players is remarkable. They know far more about the game of other men than the men themselves. I once traveled to a tournament with a boy who casually seated himself beside me in the train and, seeing my tennis bag, opened the conversation on tennis and tennis players. He finally turned his attention to various people I knew well, and suddenly burst out with: "Tilden is a chop stroke player. I know him well." I let him talk for about ten minutes, learning things about my game that I never knew before. Finally I asked his name, which he told me. In reply he asked mine. The last view I had of him for some time was a hasty retreat through the door of the car for air.

Lawrence S. Clark on "Autobumming" (1922)

Published several years before a numbered U.S. highway system was overlaid on the nation's roadways, this little known account by roadster-adventurer Lawrence S. Clark confirms the Lincoln Highway Association's 1916 description of cross-country road travel as "something of a sporting proposition." Though there were a couple hundred national "auto trails" in place by the time of Clark's 2000-mile postwar "road rally," most were poorly marked and some were unpaved. The term "fliverist" enjoyed something of a vogue during the 1920s, as evidenced by the 1926 Moving Picture World review of the W.C. Fields comedy So's Your Old Man, of which reviewer Epes W. Sargeant wrote, "It is a wise fliverist who knows his own Ford." By 1920, when a long-distance auto trip had ceased to be a rarity, as Clark confirms in this article, the "sport" became how cheaply and/or how quickly you could "Ford" around the country. In the Golden Age, the Midwest was something of a hotspot for auto racing and automobiles in general, as Henry Ford-backed racing pioneer Barney Oldfield, the first man to reach 60 miles per hour on a mile racetrack in 1903, hailed from Ohio, and the first Indianapolis 500, financed by Indiana-born racer-entrepreneur Carl Fisher, was held in the nation's Heartland in 1911.

From "Six Weeks in a Ford"

Autobumming, fliveristing, motor caravanning, call it what you will. It's the greatest sport on earth.

A few years ago, and a very few at that, anyone would have hesitated a long time and planned for months before even considering a trip of 500 miles. Now the average motorist considers a trip of less than 1,000 miles a mere pleasure jaunt, and even cross-country journeys do not hold the terrors in store for the tourist they formerly did.

Last year there were thousands of parties on the roads all over the country seeking — and finding — recreation, education, and health. Last winter many toured the Southern states, proverbial American gypsies, traveling from city to city, working here and there, all their belongings strapped on their cars. This summer, according to all indications, the roads literally will be crowded with tourists from every state in the national seeking enjoyment, on business, or combining the two.

Why is the automobile travel so popular? Perhaps the answer lies in the fact that the auto tourist is a freelance, at liberty to go and come as pleasure dictates. Maybe it is a reaction back to the primitive, a desire to live in the open, close to nature, away from the hustle, bustle, and stage-like sham of city life. Perhaps it is a hangover of the war, recalling a desire of service men to an outside life after a brief taste again of the cities. In my opinion it is all of these, with the additional reason that it furnishes a maximum of enjoyment for a minimum outlay.

Last summer my brother and I were fortunate enough to combine business and pleasure in an extensive auto trip through ten Middle Western states, going completely across nine of them. We traveled nearly five thousand miles in exactly six weeks in our Ford touring car. Our total expenses for the trip, including gasoline, oil, repairs, food, and lodging amounted to $242.50.

We "did" Yellowstone and Rocky Mountain National Park, stopped for a day at the proposed Roosevelt National Park in the midst of the North Dakota Badlands and near the ranches where the famous President spent some of his young manhood. We visited the Pike's Peak region, and investigated the mysteries of Denver, Kansas City, and Chicago before returning home to Minneapolis.

Our budget of expenditures, prepared before starting, and based on a trip of 4500 miles lasting five weeks, called for $300. We actually traveled nearly five thousand miles and were on the road for six weeks.

The budget allowed for these items:

276 gals gasoline at 26 cents	$69
5 gals. lubricating oil at $1.25	$6
Car and tire repairs, etc.	$25
Food (for two)	$80
Hotel Expense	$50
Incidentals (for two)	$70
Total:	**$300**

Although we carried our camp outfit with us, we put in the item of "Hotel expense" in order to be on the safe side, thinking that perhaps we should not care to be nomads during the entire journey. However, on the whole trip we camped out every night we were on the road.

We kept fairly accurate record of expenses, always putting down in the "little black book" any gasoline and oil purchases, but sometimes forgetting accounting theory when purchasing groceries, or while "blowing" ourselves at a public dance hall or bath house. "Food" and "incidentals" cover a multitude of sins and their accuracy is not guaranteed. But the summary of the expenditures prepared after the trip was over shows we spend our money as follows:

236 gals. gasoline at (average) 24.156 cents	$57.01
12 gals. lubricating oil at (average) $1.14	$13.76
Differential oil	$1.28
Cost of tire repairs	$6.45
Cost of car repairs	$6.00
Food	$95.00
Incidentals	$35.50
Entrance Fee, Yellowstone National Park	$7.50
Tent, camp bed, equipment, etc.	$20.00
Total	**$242.50**

On a basis of 5,000 miles of travel, that figures out exactly 4.85 cents per mile of travel. Can anyone compare that for economy with other forms of sightseeing?

It was interesting to note the constantly changing prices of gasoline as we went along. I have charted the different prices we paid as shown herewith. The highest price was 40 cents per gallon in Yellowstone National Park (where it is well worth it), and the lowest 16.7 in Kansas City. At Casper, Wyoming, where the gasoline is piped directly from the refinery across the street to the filling station, we were charged 25 cents per gallon for the mobile fluid. And when we reached Denver, we found that the same gasoline shipped by rail some 300 miles was selling for 23 cents!

For the entire trip, including many mountain roads, we averaged about 19 miles for each gallon of gas, at a cost per mile of 1.321 cent. Our oil mileage was about 90 miles to a quart, a cost per mile of 0.317 cent. This was for an ordinary Ford touring car, with no gas-saver attachments of any kind driven by two ordinary, dub drivers, over all kind of good, bad, and indifferent roads.

Tire and car repairs were far less expensive than we figured. How the total bill for these two items, including two new inner tubes that we bought, came to only $12.45, we cannot yet understand. I did all the tinkering with the engine, and repaired the numerous punctures myself, and by the time the trip was over, thought seriously of seeking a job as a "flivver pedicure," so expert had I become in doctoring the "inners" of the car.

But consider for a moment the fact that from the time we left Pueblo, Colorado, until sometime after we reached Minneapolis, an unbroken stretch more than 2,000 miles through Kansas and Missouri in hot, dry weather, and also in rainstorms through mud, across Illinois sand, and Wisconsin wet clay, I made no adjustment to the motor of the car, and touched it only to add a pint of oil now and then. We consider it not a bad record.

Like most other persons, traveling in Fords, we found the car had a tendency to overheat on mountain roads. We remedied this to some extent by removing the sides of the hood of the machine and fastening to the top pieces by coil springs to the hooks that hold the sides down. This contrivance allowed the air free passage all around the engine and aided in keeping it cool, even on long uphill grinds in low gear.

Our camp equipment consisted of a "Ford Autobed" an ingenious contrivance with which we made a bed on the top of the seatbacks of the car, using the seat cushions as bed springs, and a set of wooden slats to cover the other vacant spaces.* It was a very comfortable resting place, although the car had to be parked on level ground to assure a sound sleep, as we discovered one night in the mountains. We couldn't rollout because of the top bows and side curtains, but we could be uncomfortably rolling down to one side unless the ground was fairly level.

We also carried a lightweight auto tent, which fitted over one side of the car and served as a dressing room, a kitchen in case of rain, or a storage place for our luggage if we wanted to go "stepping," or on a short side trip without baggage.

Three woolen army blankets apiece comprised our bedding. We kept them rolled in small canvas sacks about the size about the size of 98-pound flour sacks. On very cold nights we would sleep together, with three blankets over and three under us, but usually we rolled up separately, each in his own blankets.

Many tourists we met had portable gasoline stoves. We, however, depended upon the old faithful campfire. Of course, some foresight was necessary — gathering of dry wood before a rainstorm, and keeping some dry tinder always with you — but we had no trouble in getting a good fire every time we wanted one. In some places in the Dakota Badlands and the Wyoming desert places, we found wood a might scarce article, but we always managed to scrape enough together to boil our coffee, or to stew our stew.

The clothes we wore were about the smallest item in the incidental expenditures. Secondhand army breeches, picked up at about a dollar a pair, a stout pair of army shoes, woolen shirts, and wrap leggings complete the outfit. We each had short sheepskin coats which felt warm and nice in the mountains and evenings, even though only the middle of August. We carried no "dude" clothes, but went wherever we desired in our khaki.

We had lots of company. Tourists everywhere; men and women, and children wore khaki, looked like hoboes; were dirty, dusty, and the men often unshaved, but everywhere everybody was happy, cheerful, healthy, and all declared themselves to be having the time of their lives.

In practically every town of any size in the West we found a tourist camp.

*Preceding the sentence here noted, ten contiguous paragraphs — in which the author describes the food consumed en route — have been excised for concision as emphasized by the insertion of an extra line space. The sentence here noted marks the return to the core narrative on page 164.

Wandering autoists are furnished with free wood, good water, tables and benches, fireplaces, writing paper and, in some of the more progressive places, hot and cold shower baths, gas stoves, a laundry, and even dance floors with phonographs and a plentiful supply of the latest — for that part of the country — dance records. All this is given free of charge for the use of the tourists.

Farther south, however, and as one came east, especially after crossing the Missouri River, the tourist camps became an almost forgotten institution. Here and there you would find a camp, maintained by someone who has been farther west and who has been impressed favorably with the camps out there, but these are exceptions in Missouri and Illinois rather than the rule as in Kansas, Colorado, Montana, and Wyoming.

In all of our travels we used road maps and guides picked up along the way. Of course, we had a general idea of where we were going and about how we were going and about how were going to get there before we left home, but for the details of the roads, conditions, detours, etc. we waited until we were on the ground, and found this to be the more satisfactory method.

We did not get off a trailed road for any length of time during the entire journey and did not get lost once — although sometimes in crossing Montana plateaus and Wyoming deserts the trail marks became so far separated that we would nearly give up hope, only to find a black arrow on yellow (Yellowstone Trail marker) or a black "H" on a yellow stone (Yellowstone Highway marker) a little beyond the spot where we thought the end of the world should be located!

Going west we followed the National Parks Highway to Yellowstone Trail for several hundred miles to Montana; from the park, the Yellowstone Highway, a part of the National Park to Park Highway, led us through Wyoming down to Estes Park and Rocky Mountain National Park. The Pike's Peak Ocean to Ocean Highway was our road from there, through Denver to Colorado Springs.

We went to Pueblo on the National Old Trails Highway and then crossed eastern Colorado and most of Kansas on the Kansas-Colorado boulevard (which is a misnomer), getting on the New Santa Fe Trail before entering Kansas City. We took the Cannon Ball trail across Missouri, ferried the Missouri River, followed the trail through the southeast corner of Iowa, and across Illinois to Chicago. Wisconsin and Minnesota both have efficient state highway systems with plainly marked roads, so the trip home to Minneapolis from Chicago was made without difficulty in spite of a heavy rainstorm during those three days on the road.

When touring, everybody knows everybody else. Always willing to lend a helping hand, always cheerful in his self-imposed sacrifice of some of the modern conveniences, and always willing to sit around a blazing campfire, puffing on his pipe, and tell stories about the road over which he has just come that make the tenderfoot quake with fear of it. The American tourist, normally a cultured person, turned gypsy for a while, is following in the footsteps of his forefathers in exploring his native country. Only the "forty-niners" of today cross the continent in comfort, on air cushions propelled by explosions, in their automobile prairie schooners.

Henry Ford on Auto Racing (1922)

Thought of primarily as an industrialist, Detroit-born Henry Ford had little choice but to race his four-cylinder, eighty-horsepower "999" car prior to finding speed junkie Barney Oldfield as his test driver. The passage that follows, adapted from Ford's autobiography My Life and Work, *describes in first person the tycoon's early experiences behind the wheel. Though not a journalist or writer per se, Ford's recollections show the importance of sport racing to the growth of the American automobile industry and anticipate a future consumer marketing formula that all but required, à la Arnold Palmer and Pennzoil motor oil, the use of the pitched product by a celebrity or businessman-inventor. In the last paragraph, Ford describes his own hands-on racing of the Model B on the ice at Lake St. Clair, where Ford, forty years old at the time, reportedly reached speeds of over ninety miles per hour and set a land speed record. Ford's backing was also instrumental in the establishment of the Indianapolis 500.*

From "What I Learned about Business" and "Starting the Real Business"

But in the beginning there was hardly anyone who sensed that the automobile could be a large factor in industry. The most optimistic hoped only for a development akin to that of the bicycle. When it was found that an automobile really could go and several makers started to put out cars, the immediate query was as to which would go fastest. It was a curious but natural development — that racing idea. I never thought anything of racing, but the public refused to consider the automobile in any light other than as a fast toy. Therefore later we had to race. The industry was held back by this initial racing slant, for the attention of the makers was diverted to making fast rather than good cars. It was a business for speculators.

A group of men of speculative turn of mind organized, as soon as I left the electric company, the Detroit Automobile Company to exploit my car. I was the chief engineer and held a small amount of the stock. For three years we continued making cars more or less on the model of my first car. We sold very few of them; I could get no support at all toward making better cars to be sold to the public at large. The whole thought was to make to order and to get the largest price possible for each car. The main idea seemed to be to get the money. And being without authority other than my engineering position gave me, I found that the new company was not a vehicle for realizing my ideas but merely a moneymaking concern — that did not make much money. In March 1902 I resigned, determined never again to put myself under orders. The Detroit Automobile Company later became the Cadillac Company under the ownership of the Lelands, who came in subsequently.

I rented a shop — a one-story brick shed — at 81 Park Place to continue my experiments and to find out what business really was. I thought that it must be something different from what it had proved to be in my first adventure.

The year from 1902 until the formation of the Ford Motor Company was practically one of investigation. In my little one-room brick shop I worked on the development of a four-cylinder motor and on the outside I tried to find out what business really was and whether it needed to be quite so selfish a scramble for money as it seemed to be from my first short experience. From the period of the first car, which I have described, until the formation of my present company, I built in all about twenty-five cars, of which nineteen or twenty were built with the Detroit Automobile Company. The automobile had passed from the initial stage where the fact that it could run at all was enough, to the stage where it had to show speed. Alexander Winton of Cleveland, the founder of the Winton car, was then the track champion of the country and willing to meet all comers. I designed a two-cylinder enclosed engine of a more compact type than I had before used, fitted it into a skeleton chassis, found that I could make speed, and arranged a race with Winton. We met on the Grosse Point track at Detroit. I beat him. That was my first race, and it brought advertising of the only kind that people cared to read. The public thought nothing of a car unless it made speed — unless it beat other racing cars. My ambition to build the fastest car in the world led me to plan a four cylinder motor. But of that more later.

These ideas were forming with me during this year of experimenting.* Most of the experimenting went into the building of racing cars. The idea in

---

*The running-in of a portion of a separate, contiguous chapter, "Chapter III: Starting the Real Business" is here indicated by the insertion of a line space preceding the run-in material. The sentence here noted represents the first sentence of the sixth paragraph of the run-in chapter. Between the conclusion of the previous excerpt in Chapter II and the beginning of Chapter III as here run-in, fifteen contiguous paragraphs — in which the author details early Ford advertising campaigns — have been excised for concision as emphasized by the insertion of an extra line space.

those days was that a first-class car ought to be a racer. I never really thought much of racing, but following the bicycle idea, the manufacturers had the notion that winning a race on a track told the public something about the merits of an automobile — although I can hardly imagine any test that would tell less.

But, as the others were doing it, I, too, had to do it. In 1903, with Tom Cooper, I built two cars solely for speed. They were quite alike. One we named the "999" and the other the "Arrow." If an automobile were going to be known for speed, then I was going to make an automobile that would be known wherever speed was known. These were. I put in four great big cylinders giving 80 H.P. — which up to that time had been unheard of. The roar of those cylinders alone was enough to half kill a man. There was only one seat. One life to a car was enough. I tried out the cars. Cooper tried out the cars. We let them out at full speed. I cannot quite describe the sensation. Going over Niagara Falls would have been but a pastime after a ride in one of them. I did not want to take the responsibility of racing the "999" which we put up first, neither did Cooper. Cooper said he knew a man who lived on speed, that nothing could go too fast for him. He wired to Salt Lake City and on came a professional bicycle rider named Barney Oldfield. He had never driven a motor car, but he liked the idea of trying it. He said he would try anything once.

It took us only a week to teach him how to drive. The man did not know what fear was. All that he had to learn was how to control the monster. Controlling the fastest car of today was nothing as compared to controlling that car. The steering wheel had not yet been thought of. All the previous cars that I had built simply had tillers. On this one I put a two-handed tiller, for holding the car in line required all the strength of a strong man. The race for which we were working was at three miles on the Grosse Point track. We kept our cars as a dark horse. We left the predictions to the others. The tracks then were not scientifically banked. It was not known how much speed a motor car could develop. No one knew better than Oldfield what the turns meant, and as he took his seat, while I was cranking the car for the start, he remarked cheerily: "Well, this chariot may kill me, but they will say afterward that I was going like hell when she took me over the bank."

And he did go.... He never dared to look around. He did not shut off on the curves. He simply let that car go — and go it did. He was about half a mile ahead of the next man at the end of the race!

The "999" did what it was intended to do: It advertised the fact that I could build a fast motorcar. A week after the race I formed the Ford Motor Company. I was vice president, designer, master mechanic, superintendent, and general manager.

That "Model B"—the first four-cylinder car for general road use—had to be advertised.* Winning a race or making a record was then the best kind of advertising. So I fixed up the "Arrow," the twin of the old "999"—in fact practically remade it—and a week before the New York Automobile show I drove it myself over a surveyed mile straightaway on the ice. I shall never forget that race. The ice seemed smooth enough, so smooth that if I had called off the trial we should have secured an immense amount of the wrong kind of advertising, but instead of being smooth, that ice was seamed with fissures which I knew were going to mean trouble the moment I got up speed. But there was nothing to do but go through with the trial, and I let the old "Arrow" out. At every fissure the car leaped into the air. I never knew how it was coming down. When I wasn't in the air, I was skidding, but somehow I stayed top side up and on the course, making a record that went all over the world!

Lewis R. Freeman on Playing Semipro Baseball in Montana (1922)

Lewis Freeman, introduced previously in this volume, published book-length sports participations as well as articles. Down the Yellowstone, *one of several volumes Freeman released, includes several additional sport adventures peripheral to his ambitious float down the Yellowstone River, including a historically valuable description of Freeman's recruitment to play baseball in the Montana bush leagues.*

From "Calamity Jane"

Before that week was over I had one foot in a newspaper editorial sanctum and the other on the initial sack of a semiprofessional baseball team. As both footings seemed certain to develop into stepping-stones to the realization of the most cherished of my childhood's ambitions (I had never cared much about being President), the river voyage to the Gulf went into complete discard—or rather into a twenty-year postponement. I became an editor as a direct consequence of making good on the ball team; I ceased to be an editor as a direct consequence of betraying a sacred trust laid upon me by

---

*Preceding the sentence here noted, eight contiguous paragraphs—in which the author details early advertising campaigns—have been excised for concision as emphasized by the insertion of an extra line space. The sentence here noted marks the return to the core racing narrative on page 57.

the ball team. This was something of the way of it: Livingston had high hopes of copping the championship of the Montana bush league, which, at the time of my arrival, was just budding into life with the willows and cottonwood along the river. For this laudable purpose a fearful and wonderful aggregation had been chivvied together from the ends of baseballdom, numbering on its roster about as many names that had once been famous in diamond history as those that were destined to become so. Of the team as finally selected three or four of us were known to the police, and at least two of us came into town on brake beams. One of us was trying to forget the dope habit, and another — our catcher and greatest star — had just been graduated from a rum-cure institute.

All of us were guaranteed jobs — sinecural in character of course. Paddy Ryan, one of the pitchers, and two or three others were barkeepers. There was also one night-watchman, one electrician, and one compositor. I was rather a problem to the management until the editor of the *Enterprise* was sent to the same institute recently evacuated by our bibulous catcher. Then I was put in his place — I mean that of the editor. I don't seem to recall much of my editorial duties or achievements, save that one important reform I endeavored to institute — that of getting a roll of pink paper and publishing the *Enterprise* as a straight sporting sheet — somehow fell through.

They tried me out at center in the opening game against Billings, and after the second — at Bozeman — I became a permanency at first base, my old corner at Stanford. Besides holding down the initial bag, I was told off for the unofficial duty of guarding the only partially rum-cured catcher — seeing that he was kept from even inhaling the fumes of the seductive red-eye, a single seance with which meant his inevitable downfall for the season.

I played fairly promising ball right along through that season, and but for the final disaster which overtook me in my unofficial capacity as Kiley's keeper might have gone on to the fulfillment of my life ambition. Up to the final and deciding series with Butte, I kept my thirsty ward under an unrelaxing rein, with the result that he played the greatest baseball of his career. Then a gang of Copper City sports, who had been betting heavily on the series, contrived to lure Riley away for a quarter of an hour while I was taking a bath. He was in the clouds by the time I located him, and rapidly going out of control into a spinning nosedive. He crashed soon after, and when I left him just as the dawn was breaking through the red smoke above the copper smelters, he was as busy chasing mauve mice and purple cockroaches as the substitute we put in his place that afternoon was with passed balls. To cap the climax — in endeavoring to extend a bunt into a two-bagger, or some equally futile stunt — I strained an old "Charley Horse" and went out of the game in the second inning. We lost the game, series and championship, and

I, incidentally, ceased to be a rising semipro ball player and a somewhat less rising country editor.

I have failed to mention that I did have one more fling at the Yellowstone that summer. Lamartine remodelled his skiff as we had planned, and one Sunday when Livingston had a game on at Big Timber we decided to make the run down by river. Pushing off at daybreak we arrived under the big bluff of Big Timber a good hour or two before noon. I find this run thus celebrated in an ancient clipping from the Livingston *Post*, contemporary of the *Enterprise*:

> Mr. L. R. Freeman, Mr. Armstrong, and Sydney Lamartine made the trip from this city to Big Timber last Sunday in a flat-bottomed boat. The river course between this city and Big Timber is fully 50 miles, and the gentlemen made the trip without mishap in six hours. Several times the boat had narrow escapes from being turned over, but each time the skill of the boatmen prevented any trouble. Quite a crowd assembled on the Springdale bridge and watched the crew shoot the little craft through the boiling riffle at that point, cheering them lustily for the skill they displayed in swinging their boat into the most advantageous places. The trip is a hazardous one, but full of keen enjoyment and spice and zest. The time made is without doubt the fastest river boating ever done on the Yellowstone, and it is extremely doubtful if the record has been duplicated on any other stream. Mr. Freeman, who has had considerable experience in boating in Alaska, says that he never has seen a small boat make such splendid time.

I don't remember a lot about that undeniably speedy run save that we stopped for nothing but dumping water out of the boat. Last summer, with a number of seasons of swift-water experience to help, I took rather more than nine hours to cover the same stretch. I suppose it was because the river and I were twenty years older. Age is a great slower down, at least where a man is concerned. I do seem to recall now that I stopped a number of times on this last run to see which was the smoother channel. Doubtless the old Yellowstone was just as fast as ever.

Fred H. Harris on Ski Jumping (1922)

In the following article, aptly billed by Outing *magazine as "The Founder of the Dartmouth Outing Club Tells How He Learned the Norwegian Art," Dartmouth ski enthusiast Fred H. Harris does just that. The excerpt focuses on Harris's first, daring attempts at a ski jump. In a piece of Dartmouth College history entitled "Founding of the Outing Club," Harris, class of 1911, writes, "Many a time when up against some problem in Freshman Math, which seemed to me almost impossible of solution, I would slap on the old skis, go out for a three hours trip, brush out the mental cobwebs in that clear, frosty air, and find on return that the solution of my problem was comparatively easy." One year after the publication of this charmingly-written piece, Harris was named president of the newly formed Eastern United States Ski Association. Harris's contributions to skiing in the region are more recently documented in* New England Skiing *by E. John B. Allen. A ski jump in Brattleboro, Vermont, also now bears Harris's name. Significantly, Harris also appears in the American Olympic Association's list of active members in the* Olympic Official Report Lake Placid 1932, *demonstrating his lifelong involvement in the sport.*

From "How I Learned to Ski"

When my father gave me for a Christmas present a pair of skis somewhat on the Norwegian model, I showed some great disappointment and asked if I couldn't have the money instead to buy lumber and to make some myself. In the old shop at the back of the house, I began to make skis for all the neighbors. Altogether, I made about thirty pairs. Later on, I had to go back on my own teachings.

The possibilities of skiing were so alluring that I began to study the technical and scientific aspects. I found that my amateur theories were all wrong, and I had to unlearn everything and begin over again. I had learned when sliding downhill to keep my legs wide apart, crouch way down, and lean back on a long hickory pole to prevent falling backwards. Old photos of me sliding downhill look exactly like the pictures of the old witch riding a broomstick. This "three point suspension" theory looked reasonable, but the cramped position would almost tire me out on a long slide. I now discovered that the right way was to keep my feet close together, stand erect, and depend in no way on a pole or poles for support or balance. Gradually all my old theories were supplanted. This shows the necessity of starting right.

When I went to Dartmouth, I took my skis with me. I had them all decorated with brass trimmings and my old gunboats aroused much admiration. I had about the only pair of skis in town, and, on my cross-country trips, I rarely ever saw a ski track save my own. Old residents of Hanover tell me how astonished they were to see me for the first time climb uphill without taking off my skis. The idea then was that skis were only good for sliding downhill and that they should be carried uphill on one's back.

It was not until I went to Canada that I really began to learn anything about skiing as it should be done. It was at this time also that I first became acquainted with a real ski jump.

Of course whenever skiing is mentioned, one thinks of ski jumping. My first experience on a big ski jump was at the time of a ski jumping competition held by the Montreal Ski Club during one of the Montreal Winter Carnivals. On the way up on the train, I had talked of little else but skiing and had mentioned to my father that I thought I would like to try a big jump once.

On the trolley on the way out to the competition, I asked the man seated next to me, who was wearing the badge of the Montreal Ski Club, it if were possible for a stranger to try the club's big jump. He was very affable and courteous, and, on arriving at the hill, he introduced me to the secretary of the club.

The secretary urged me to go into the competition; but one look at the hill made me decline with thanks, as I did not care to show my inexperience before such a throng of spectators as then gathering. The sight of the jumpers shooting off into space over the eight-foot high takeoff which was made of blocks of ice caused my eyes to bulge out of my head. I knew then and there that I did not want to go on exhibition in any such performance as that. The spills on some of the practice jumps confirmed me in my opinion.

It was very spectacular scene and there was much life and excitement. The spectators crowded against the ropes and flags which lined the course, and as far as I could see, there was a black line of newcomers crowding toward the hill. The boxes of honor near the jump were filled with royalty, government officials, and the judges. The whole thing made a great impression on me.

Soon the competition started, and one after another the jumpers shot down the long hill, across a wooden trestle spanning a road, out on to the takeoff, and launched themselves into the air. I gasped at some of the spills when it seemed as if the jumper would never pick himself up alive and I marveled at the skill and "form" of better jumpers. I believe the longest jump that day was ninety feet. It seemed a terrific leap to me.

After the jumping was over and the crowd began to disperse, I inadvertently remarked to my father, "I have a good mind to go up and try that jump once." He didn't say much, but his attitude seemed to say, "You have done a lot of talking and it's about time that you gave us a rest or else come across with the goods." (I afterwards found he didn't want me to try it at all.) The hill looked worse every time I glanced at it, but feeling that I would never hear the last of it I didn't make good, I climbed to the top of the hill and put on my pair of homemade skis which I brought with me. I have since thought how those expert Montrealers must have smiled to see me with my homemade outfit.

There were several other jumpers at the start and I watched them go one by one. I scarcely noticed when happened to them as I was so concerned over my own impending fate. The last man went down, and then I knew it was up to me. If the hill had looked bad from below, it was appalling from above. It seemed to me if I went over that jump I couldn't help but land on the rooftops of the city so far below. I confess that it was one of the hardest things I ever did to force myself down that hill.

I didn't dare to look at the jump when I started. I looked at a point about twenty feet down and let the skis carry me away. By that time I was committed. The speed increased, the scenery flew by, and the tears began to stream out of my eyes. I could see the jump coming nearer every instant, and it looked like a precipice. I knew nothing about the correct way of making the spring from the takeoff and my form was the worst possible.

I attempted to spring, but I doubt if I was more than half erect when I shot off the jump, homemade skis and all. It seemed to me as if I would never land. Finally my skis touched the snow. I had only gone seventy feet, but it seemed a long distance to me. Things began to happen right away. I lost my balance and fell back on to my hands. Somehow, I was able to get up on my skis and rushed on down the hill.

What to do was the next question. I knew nothing about making a telemark swing, and instead of making a curve and stopping I shot over a sidewalk, banged across a trolley track, and finally came to a stop after going several hundred yards down a street. I was surprised to find myself none the worse for my experience. My father said he had never seen such an expression on any human countenance as there was on my face when I went off the jump.

I have purposefully described the vicissitudes and hard knocks I encountered in learning to ski simply to emphasize that they are not necessary.* I am convinced that with proper outfit and good instruction, the beginner can learn in two weeks what it took me four years to learn.

Skiing is not difficult if one starts right. It is nearly useless to start with incorrect or incomplete outfit. It is surprising how quickly people pick up skiing if they understand the fundamentals and if they have the benefit of proper coaching.

I was asked one winter by the management of the Woodstock Inn, Woodstock, Vermont, to run a two days' winter carnival. The manager wanted a large ski jump built. It seems strange but the requirements of an ideal ski

---

*Preceding the sentence here noted, four contiguous paragraphs — in which the author strays from ski jumping — have been excised for concision as emphasized by the insertion of an extra line space. The sentence here noted marks the return to the core narrative.

jumping hill are so exacting that very few suitable hills can be found. For this reason, the length of the jumps in the Eastern United States has not been as great as in the West.

We found a good hill, fortunately, and with the aid of carpenters I built a jumping platform. We drew in tons of snow with a pair of horses to make the course smooth below the jump. The tournament scheduled for February twenty-second was open to all, and the Dartmouth ski jumpers were invited to compete. I had been out of college for several years and was not then competing actively in tournaments. All of the jumpers coming were friends of mine, and I had no desire to compete against them. My interest was wholly to have the carnival go off as smoothly as possible.

Some of my friends began to jolly me about my being a "has-been," and one day I overheard a conversation between two strangers to the effect that I had "gone by." This stirred me up a little and gave me a new zest for the situation. I resolved to find out if I was entirely out of it, and from then until the time of the tournament, I spent every spare minute practicing on the jump.

On the day of the jumping contest, I could not enter as I had to act as judge. The favorite from Dartmouth ran true to form and won the event with three splendid jumps averaging a little over ninety feet each. These jumps set up a new Eastern United States record. After the contest, the winner asked permission to try to break his own record. On successive jumps, he made ninety-four, ninety-five, and ninety-six and a half feet. The crowd went wild with enthusiasm. On a last magnificent attempt, my friend jumped ninety-nine feet and the crowd cried, "Give him an even hundred!"

This jumper announced that he was through, and I then asked permission to try the jump. The officials said I might but their attitude seemed to say plainly. "Yes; but we doubt if there's much use of your trying."

On my first jump I made but eighty-eight feet, and I could feel that although tolerant and friendly, the officials wondered if it was best to hold open the event long enough for me to try another jump. I didn't know but what they were right, but wasn't quite satisfied, so I told them I would like to try once more to jump. Two of my friends were acting as markers that day and on the way up I said to them, "I'd like to jump ninety feet before I die." They said "Go to it. We are with you. We will stand at the ninety-foot mark and see if you can come down with us."

On the way to the top, I figured that on the first jump I had not sprung with all my might from takeoff, that I had not had the maximum speed possible, and that I had timed my jump a little too soon. I resolved to correct all three of these things if possible.

I remember the sun was just setting behind the horizon when I prepared to start. Mount Killington stood out sharply against the horizon thirty miles away. A beautiful pink tint covered the snow. The course was as fast as ice.

To gain more speed I took a running start and gave a shove before dropping my poles at the edge of the drop. The approach to the jump was very steep and I felt as if I were falling through space. It seemed as if I had no more than crouched down before the takeoff was coming right into my face. I waited until at the very edge of the takeoff and then I jumped with every once of strength I had.

The usual interval between the spring and the landing went by and still I was in the air. I tried to reach the ground with my feet but it was not there. I saw my friends, the markers, go by and still I had not landed. I could see the comparatively level ground below the jump coming up and into my face too fast for comfort. Finally I touched the snow. Fortunately, I held my stance and shot down the hill. I returned to hear the distance. I hoped I had gone a little over ninety feet. I gasped when the markers yelled down. "One hundred feet, six inches!"

Ernest Hemingway on Lugeing (1922)

This second piece from the inimitable Papa Bear and the The Toronto Star-Weekly *avoids the presumed bias of the first person altogether by translating Hemingway's hands-on knowledge into the second person "you." While Hemingway's trademark bravado bubbles up in such statements as "steering a luge takes about as long to learn as riding a bicycle," the author takes care to offer this participatory caveat: "That is all there is to steering, but there is a great deal more to keeping your nerve."*

"The Swiss Luge"

Chamby Sur Montreux, Switzerland — The luge is the Swiss flivver. It is also the Swiss canoe, the Swiss horse and buggy, the Swiss pram and the Swiss combination of riding horse and taxi. Luge is pronounced *looge,* and is a short, stout sled of hickory built on the pattern of little girls' sleds in Canada.

You realize the omnipotence of the luge when on a bright Sunday you see all of Switzerland, from old grandmothers to street children, coasting solemnly down the steep mountain roads, sitting on these little elevated pancakes with the same tense expression on all their faces. They steer with their feet stuck straight out in front and come down a twelve mile run at a speed of from twelve to thirty miles an hour.

Swiss railroads run special trains for lugeurs between Montreux, at the edge of Lake Geneva, and the top of Col du Sonloup, a mountain 4,000 feet above sea level. Twelve trains a day are packed on Sunday, with families and their sleds. They put up their lunch, buy an all-day ticket, good for any number of rides on the winding, climbing, Bernese Oberland railway, and then spend the day sliding gloriously down the long, icy mountain road.

Steering a luge takes about as long to learn as riding a bicycle. You get on the sled, lean far back and the luge commences to move down the icy road. If it starts to sheer off to the right you drop your left leg and if it goes too far to the left you let your right foot drag. Your feet are sticking straight out before you. That is all there is to steering, but there is a great deal more to keeping your nerve.

You go down a long, steep stretch of road flanked by a six hundred foot drop-off on the left and bordered by a line of trees on the right. The sled goes fast from the start and soon it is rushing faster than anything you have ever felt. You are sitting absolutely unsupported, only ten inches above the ice, and the road is feeding past you like a movie film. The sled you are sitting on is only just large enough to make a seat and is rushing at motor car speed towards a sharp curve. If you lean your body away from the curve and drop the right foot, the luge will swing around the curve in a slither of ice and drop shooting down the next slope. If you upset on a turn, you are hurled into a snow bank or go shooting down the road, lugeing along on various plane surfaces of your anatomy.

Additional hazards are provided for the lugeurs by hay sleds and wood sleds. These have long, curved-up runners, and are used to haul the hay down from the mountain meadows where it was cut and cured in the summer, or to bring down great loads of firewood and faggots cut in the forests. They are big, slow-moving sledges and are pulled by their drivers, who haul them by the long curved-up runners and pull themselves up in front of their loads to coast down the steepest slopes.

Because there are so many lugeurs, the men with the hay and wood sleds get tired of pulling their loads to one side when they hear a lugeur come shooting down, shouting for the right of way. A lugeur at thirty miles an hour, with no brakes but his feet, has the option of hitting the sleds ahead of him or shooting off the road. It is considered a very bad omen to hit a wood sled.

There is a British colony at Bellaria, near Vevey, in the canton of Vaud, on Lake Geneva. The two apartment buildings they live in are at the foot of the mountains and the British are nearly all quite rapid lugeurs. They can leave Bellaria, where there will be no snow and a mild, spring-like breeze, and in half an hour by the train be up in the mountain where there are fast, frozen roads and thirty inches of snow on the level. Yet the air is so dry and crisp and the sun shines so dry and crisp and the sun shines so brightly that while the Bellarians are waiting for a train at Chamby, halfway up the mountain to Sonloup, they have tea out of doors in the afternoon in perfect comfort, clad in nothing heavier than sports clothes.

The road from Chamby to Montreux is very step and fairly dangerous for lugeing. It is, however, one of the favorite runs of the Britons from Bellaria, who take it nightly on their way home to their comfortable apartment buildings just above the lake. This makes some very interesting pictures, as the road is only used by the most daring lugeurs.

One wonderful sight is to see the ex-military governor of Khartoum seated on a sled that looks about the size of a postage stamp, his feet stuck straight out at the sides, his hands in back of him, charging a smother of ice dust down the steep, high-walled road with his muffler straight out behind him in the wind and a cherubic smile on his face while all the street urchins of Montreux spread against the walls and cheer him wildly as he passes.

It is easy to understand how the British have such a great Empire after you have seen them luge.

Ring Lardner on Sport and Play (1922)

A minor exception is here gladly made for Ring Lardner, who, while not often an athletic participant in the games he covered, so deeply felt and knew sport that his absence from any volume dedicated to first-person Golden Age sportswriting would be conspicuous. The essay that follows, reprinted from Civilization in the United States: An Inquiry by Thirty Americans *edited by Harold E. Stearns, finds the iconoclastic Lardner taking the average American fan to task both for his tendency toward hero worship and for his justification of popular sports on the grounds that they provide needed exercise. Written just three years after the Chicago Black Sox scandal deeply and forever disillusioned Lardner, who covered the team for the* Chicago Tribune, *"Sport and Play" fairly drips with sour-grapes cynicism, revealing an affinity for the jaundiced style of H. L. Mencken and Lardner's friend F. Scott Fitzgerald. Lardner, like Paul Gallico, achieved notoriety as a writer of sports fiction and also, like Gallico, largely abandoned sports journalism for imaginative writing. In the wake of the Black Sox debacle, Lardner left Chicago for Great Neck, New York, which he refers to in the piece below, and there became close friends with the F. Scott and Zelda Fitzgerald.*

"Sport and Play"

Bartlett does not tell us who pulled the one about all work and no play, but it probably was the man who said that the longest way round was the shortest way home. There is as much sense in one remark as in the other.

Give me an even start with George M. Cohan, who lives in Great Neck, where I also live, without his suspecting it — give us an even start in the Pennsylvania Station and route me on a Long Island train through Flushing and Bayside while he travels via San Francisco and Yokohama, and I shall undertake to beat him home, even in a blizzard. So much for "the longest way round." Now for the other. If it were your ambition to spend an evening with a dull boy, whom would you choose, H. G. Wells, whose output indicates that he doesn't even take time off to sleep, or the man that closes his desk at two o'clock every afternoon and goes to the ballgame?

You may argue that watching ballgames is not play. It is the American idea of play, which amounts to the same thing, and seventy-five percent of the three hundred thousand citizens who do it daily, in season, will tell you seriously that is all the recreation they get; moreover, that deprived of it, their brain would crack under the strain of "business," that, on account of it, they are able to do more work in the forenoon, and do it better, than would be possible in two or three full days of close sticking on the job. If you believe them, inveterate baseball fans can, in a single morning, dictate as many as four or five twenty-word letters to customers or salesmen, and finish as fresh as a daisy; whereas the non-fan, the grind, is logy and torpid by the time he reaches the second "in reply to same."

But if you won't concede, in the face of the fans' own statement, that it is recreation to look on at baseball or any other sport, then let me ask you to invite to your home some evening, not a mere spectator, but an active participant in any of our popular games — say a champion or near-champion golfer, or a first string pitcher on a big league baseball club. The golfer, let us say, sells insurance half the year and golfs the rest. The pitcher plays eight months of the year and loafs the other four. Bar conversation about their specialty and you won't find two duller boys than those outside the motion picture studios.

No, brothers, the bright minds of this or any other country are owned by the men who leave off work only to eat or go to bed. The doodles are the boys who divide their time fifty-fifty between work and play, or who play all the time and don't even pretend to work. Proper exercise undoubtedly promotes good health, but the theory that good health and an active brain are inseparable can be shot full of holes by the mention of two names — Stanislaus Zbyzsko and Robert Louis Stevenson.

It is silly, then, to propound that sport is of mental benefit. Its true, basic function is the cultivation of bodily vigor, with a view to longevity. And longevity, despite the fact that we profess belief in a postmortem existence that makes this one look sick, is a thing we poignantly desire. Bonehead and wise guy, believer and skeptic — all of us want to postpone as long as possible the promised joyride to the Great Beyond. If to participate in sport helps us to do that, then there is good reason to participate in sport.

Well, how many "grown-ups" (normal human beings of twenty-two and under need not be considered; they get all the exercise they require, and then some) in this country, a country that boasts champions in nearly every branch of athletics, derive from play the physical benefit there is in it? What percentage take an active part in what the sporting editors call "the five major sports" — baseball, football, boxing, horse racing, and golf? Let us take them one by one and figure it out, beginning with "the national pastime."

Baseball. Twenty or twenty-one play. Three hundred to forty thousand look on. The latter are, for two hours, "out in the open air," and this, when the air is not so open as to give them pneumonia and when they don't catch something as bad or worse in the streetcar or subway train that takes them and brings them back, is a physical benefit. Moreover, the habitual attendant at ballgames is not likely to die of brain fever. But otherwise, the only ones whose health is appreciably promoted are the twenty or twenty-one who play. And they are not doing it for their health.

Football. Thirty play. Thirty thousand look on. One or two of the thirty may be killed or suffer a broken bone, but the general health of the other twenty-nine or twenty-eight is improved by the exercise. As for the thirty thousand, all they get is the open air — usually a little too much of it — and, unless they are hardened to the present-day cheerleader, a slight feeling of nausea.

Boxing. Eight to ten play. Five thousand to sixty thousand look on. Those of the participants who are masters of defense may profit physically by the training, though the rigorous methods sometimes employed to make an unnatural weight are certainly inimical to health. The ones not expert in defensive boxing, the ones who succeed in the game through their ability to "take punishment" (a trait that usually goes with a low mentality) die, as a rule, before reaching old age, as a result of the "gameness" that made them "successful." There is a limit to the number of punches one can "take" and retain one's health. The five or sixty thousand cannot boast that they even get the air. All but a few of the shows are given indoors, in an atmosphere as fresh and clean as that of the Gopher Prairie day-coach.

Horse Racing. Fifty horses and twenty-five jockeys play. Ten thousand people look on. I can't speak for the horses, but if a jockey wants to remain a jockey, he must, as a rule, eat a great deal less than his little stomach craves, and I don't know of any doctor who prescribes constant underfeeding as conducive to good health in a growing boy.

Racing fans, of course, are out for financial, not physical, gain. They, like the jockeys, are likely to starve to death while still young.

Golf. Here is a pastime in which the players far outnumber the lookers-on. It is a game, if it is a game, that not only takes you out in the open air, but makes you walk, and walking, the doctors say, is all the exercise you need, if you walk five miles or more a day. Golf, then, is really beneficial, and it costs you about $25.00 a week the year round.

So much for our "five major sports." We look on at four of them, and if we can support the family, and pay taxes and insurance, on $1250 a year less than we earn, we take part in the fifth.

The minor sports, as the editor will tell you, are tennis, boating, polo, track athletics, trapshooting, archery, hockey, soccer, and so on. Not to mention games like poker, bridge, bowling, billiards, and pool (now officially known as "pocket billiards" because the Ladies' Guild thought "pool" must have something to do with betting), which we may dismiss as being of doubtful physical benefit, since they are all played indoors and in a fog of Camel smoke.

Of the outdoor "minors," tennis is unquestionably the most popular. And it is one whale of a game — if you can stand it. But what percentage of grown-ups play it? I have no statistics at hand, and must guess. The number of adult persons with whom I am acquainted, intimately or casually, is possibly two thousand. I can think of ten who play as many as five sets of tennis a year.

How many of the two thousand play polo or have ever played polo? One. How many are trapshooters? Two. How many have boats? Six or seven. How many run footraces or jump? None. How many are archers? None. How many play hockey, soccer, lacrosse? None.

If I felt like indulging in a game of cricket, which God forbid, whom should I call up and invite to join me?

Now, how many of my two thousand acquaintances are occasional or habitual spectators at baseball games, football games, boxing matches, or horse races? All but three or four. The people I know (I do not include ballplayers, boxers, and wrestlers, who make their living from sport) are average people; they are the people you know. And the overwhelming majority of them don't play.

Why not? If regular participation in a more or less interesting outdoor game is going to lengthen our lives, why don't we participate? Is it because we haven't time? It takes just as much time to look on, and we do that. Is it because we can't afford it? We can play tennis for as little as it costs to go to the ballgame and infinitely less than it costs to go to the races.

We don't play because (1) we lack imagination, and because (2) we are a nation of hero-worshippers.

When we were kids, the nurse and the minister taught us that, if we weren't good, our next stop would be hell. But, to us, there was no chance of the train's starting for seventy years. And we couldn't visualize an infernal excursion that far off. It was too vague to be scary. We kept right on swiping the old man's cigars and giggling in the choir. If they had said that misdemeanors such as those would spell death and eternal fire, not when we were old, but tomorrow, most of us would have respected father's property rights and sat through the service with a sour pan. If the family doctor were to tell us now that unless we got outdoors and exercised every afternoon this week, we should die next Tuesday before lunch, you can bet we should get outdoors and exercise every afternoon this week. But when he tells us that, without healthful outdoor sport, we shall die in 1945 instead of 1949, why, it doesn't mean anything. It's a chimera, a myth, like the next war.

But hero-worship is the national disease that does most to keep the grandstands full and the playgrounds empty. To hell with those four extra years of life, if they are going to cut in on our afternoon at the Polo Grounds, where in blissful asininity, we may feast our eyes on the swarthy Champion of Swat, shouting now and then in an excess of anile idolatry, "Come on, you Babe. Come on, You Baby Doll!" And if an hour of tennis is going to make us late at the Garden, perhaps keep us out of our ringside seats, so close to Dempsey's corner that (O bounteous God!) a drop of the divine perspiration may splash our undeserving snout—Hang up, liver! You're on a busy wire!

Albert Soiland on Transpacific Yacht Racing (1924)

Albert Soiland's intimate 1924 recounting of sailing the Pacific from Los Angeles to Honolulu, reprinted here from his book The Viking Goes to Sea, *remains one of the purest participatory sportswriting accounts of its era. The race, run to this day as the TransPacific or TransPac, was, then as now, a dangerous venture, and Soiland's first paragraph describes a difficult parting from his wife. The founding commodore of the Newport Harbor Yacht Club, Dr. Soiland was also a pioneering radiologist, making his the epitome of the Golden Age amateur spirit. As an avid historian and organizer of the race up and through the 1930s, Soiland documented the first female to captain a sailboat in the TransPac, writing, "Due to the exigencies of Captain McNutt's strenuous obligations, he was prevented from securing sufficient time off to make the race, and in order not to disappoint the Race Committee, his charming and splendid sailing wife volunteered to skipper the boat."*

Under Mrs. McNutt's captaincy, Soiland duly noted, the McNutt team won the race.

FROM *THE VIKING GOES TO SEA*

The outstanding feature of the regatta held at UI Santa Barbara during the month of July was the Honolulu Race, and to a casual observer even, it was apparent that interest in local events of the regatta was secondary to this big feature. All were keyed up and impatiently awaiting the last day of the week, which would see the gallant craft on their way across the broad expanse of the Pacific. Saturday, July 21st, broke out with a fresh, westerly breeze. The participants, owners and crews, were busily engaged getting aboard provisions, water and supplies. The day before, Mrs. Soiland and I had visited Santa Barbara provision dealers and had selected enough food material, it appeared, to suffice for a cruise around the world, and when arranged for delivery, I doubted whether the little vessel could accommodate such a formidable array of boxes, cans, cartons, crates, and packages, and on top of this, Mrs. Soiland, with her wonderful thoughtfulness, had surreptitiously placed onboard many delicacies which the cook later served at unexpected moments, much to our delight and enjoyment. The food was finally stored away, but the water problem was more difficult. The tank capacity being small, we proceeded to fill five gallon tins with water and stow them away wherever we could find space. This made the supply ample.

At twelve noon, everything was snugly belayed. Our wives came on board for the last good-byes: wishing us Godspeed and luck. With thirty minutes to spare before the starting gun, we cast off to shake out our sails, get the crew warmed up, in order to show the natives how to get over the line first. Right here, I must stop to call the roll, and introduce the crew. Meet the lanky first mate, C. W. Bradbury, otherwise "Brad," the Beau Brummell of the ship. In private life a respectable merchant with seagoing proclivities. He was the deadly enemy of dirt and disorder, and also had an enormous aptitude for work and grub—a fine combination. The second mate, Staff Commodore Claude Putnam, of the Newport Harbor Yacht Club, our artist "Put," official scribe and keeper of the social log. An artist by profession and a Bohemian by choice. His good nature and light profanity, uttered in generous quantities, had an invigorating effect on the ship's ensemble. Otto Wildey, prominent builder of city blocks and Staff Commodore of the California Yacht Club, was bos'n and starboard watch. In addition, Otto was leader of the ship's barbershop quartet, and we nearly ruined our singing voices trying to keep step with him to the tune of "Down on the Little Pee Dee," during the graveyard watches. Beecher Hungerford, cultured orchardist from the sunny southland, known as "Beech," the bos'n's mate and chief of the port watch, completed the roll of Corinthians. Beech had much to do, but little to say, and he did both very well. Alexander McDermott shipped as assistant sailing master, and "A. B." (which is French for "able-bodied seaman") Mac had spent many years at sea in ships, but on none so small as the *Viking*. On the trip over, he was willing and agreeable, and assisted in every way he could in the navigation and sailing of the yacht. Last, but by no means least, came Bill Bahrt, the genial cook, but more of him later. I almost forgot, with becoming modesty, to mention "me — himself" the skipper, Albert Soiland, M. D., physician and surgeon in ordinary, to His Majesty, the American Public; weekend devotee to the king of outdoor sports, yachting, and at the present writing, admiral of the fleet of organized Pacific Coast yachtsmen. We were now out, looking over the other Honolulu racers, all jockeying for the start. The *Mariner* had just swung into the channel. She was very graceful and her canvas fitted wonderfully well. The black *Idalia* looked like a dangerous contender. She was slender, rakish looking, and slipped thru the water without effort. The trim *Diablo* was outside also, and looked like a real racer. We, on the little *Viking*, were beginning to feel foolish and somewhat apprehensive as to our ability to even make a showing against such a galaxy of stars, but we gritted our teeth and said, "On with the dance." It was now just five minutes before the starting gun, and the ketch *Spindrift* had joined the skirmishers, but the big *Poinsettia* was still serenely at anchor. Just then, as I called an order to bout ship for the line, the main peak bridle broke, and our gaff suddenly developed alarming symptoms. It was exasperating, after having persistently gone over every part of the ship and rigging and finding no flaws, to have such a foolish accident spoil our grandstand getaway over the line. However, Mac made a hurried coupling of the parted bridle, and succeeded also in mashing his finger badly, but we got the peak up high enough to blow us over the starting line in third place. The *Diablo* was first, the *Mariner* second, then the *Viking*, *Idalia*, and *Spindrift* in order named. Just as we went over, the *Poinsettia* was crawling up with her canvas half set, and was the last to get the starter's okay.

The sendoff was one never to be forgotten. The whole city of Santa Barbara was alive with action. Bells rang, whistles shrieked, the multitude onshore shouted farewell, waving hats and handkerchiefs. Every craft on the bay joined in an escorting procession, and followed us out to sea. Those who came by and gave us a real parting salute, were the power yacht, *Lady Luck*, with Commodore Shirley Meserve of the Newport Harbor Yacht Club aboard, carrying as passengers Mrs. Meserve, Mrs. Smith, Mrs. Fenton, Mrs. Soiland, Mrs. Putnam and Mrs. Briggs, and then the power yacht, *Mandarin*, with Vice Commodore Herbert Cornish of the California Yacht Club and Rear Commodore Warmington with their wives and guests. They saluted us so vigorously with the ship's cannon that they blew off a piece of their teakwood rail.

With such a royal sendoff, we felt that we had at least the good wishes of many true friends, and we started in on our long race with renewed hopes.

Shortly after leaving Santa Barbara, the *Idalia* bore up under our lee, and in spite of warnings shouted, her bowsprit threatened our rail, so that we were compelled to luff several times to avoid collision. The man at *Idalia's* wheel evidently did not know the rules of the road, but he finally wore away and gave us sea room.

The afternoon was beautiful, a fresh westerly wind, smooth seas, and every yacht in the race making fine time. It was interesting to watch the early maneuvers, the *Mariner*, *Poinsettia*, and *Idalia* started tacking up the coast to clear the west end of Santa Cruz Island. The *Spindrift* and *Diablo* with easy sheets ran for the west end of Anacapa Island. I decided to make a shortcut out to sea by skirting the east end of Santa Cruz, which proved to be poor judgment, for after making a record run across the Santa Barbara channel, we slid into a flat spot at 5 P.M., right off Smugglers' Cave, and there we lay. There was a rattling good breeze all around us, but we were simply chained in a small circle of dead calm, not over a city block in length. We were now all glum, for to leeward we could see the *Spindrift* and *Diablo* making good weather for the open sea. We knew that the three big fellows had already made the west end of Santa Cruz and were now perhaps squared away for Honolulu. It was discouraging, and we sat in the cockpit and swore softly at one another, the blame falling directly upon my shoulders for having laid out such a bum course. As time wore on, we were cheered perceptibly by Bill, the cook, announcing supper, and as the sea was smooth, he served us a rattling good mess. After supper, I set the first watch, but as there was nothing to do except to whistle for wind, everyone sat in the cockpit and discussed our chances in the race. Just before dusk, a large yawl drifted into our calm circle, and all were much surprised to learn it was the *Poinsettia*, scratch boat in the race. They had started a reach to windward, but put into the lee of the island to make repairs to some of their sails. All night long we drifted about one another, but made no progress on our course. Towards morning, a light breeze blowing high caught the tall topsail of the *Poinsettia*, and she was soon hull down on her way. The poor little *Viking* did not reach high enough to get the wind, and she lay still becalmed with every other yacht merrily on its way. It was a blue Sunday morning that dawned on July 22nd, as nothing is so demoralizing as to slat around in a groundswell with no wind, everything onboard banging and bumping, with the crew full of sour balls. During the forenoon, little catspaws from the north gave us steerage way, and by eight bells, 23½ hours out, we had only covered forty-four nautical miles from Santa Barbara, latitude 33° 53' N., longitude 119° 54' W. There was no sun, and we took our position from shore bearings. One advantage obtained from drifting about was that I was enabled to check up our compass by making cross bearings on the islands, and thereby working out a satisfactory deviation chart.

By one o'clock, the wind began to freshen briskly from the northwest, and with a westerly swell running, setting our course S.S.W., we were off with the open sea before us, making nine knots. During the afternoon, the wind increased to half a gale, the sea rose, and we were rail down, a little wet, but happy to be on our way. Just before dusk, we made out a sail to leeward, bound northeast, and as she came up under our lee, were astonished to see it was the *Poinsettia*, full and by, homeward bound, with everything set but the topsail. We were at a loss to account for the *Poinsettia's* withdrawing from the race, and went down to our supper full of surmises. Down below, we found the galley upset, and Bill, the cook, bemoaning that he could not keep the fire going on account of too much sea and pounding forward. So we had sandwiches and cold tea.

The first watch kept all sail set and we were bowling along right merrily, but the little ship shivered from truck to keel, caused by the impact with the big head seas. By midnight, she was down to the house and laboring so hard that all hands were called to lower the mainsail. It was now blowing almost a gale from the northwest, so I ordered the jib down, after which she made better weather of it, running with foresail and forestay sail only. It was a miserable night. Everybody wet and cold, but not a murmur of complaint, and determined to sail the little craft to her destination in the shortest possible time. We were steering southwest by west and plowing along at a good gait.

By daylight, Monday, July 23rd, the ocean was a seething mass of white topped breakers with a misty sky and a howling gale, not a sail nor living thing in sight. It was impossible to use a camera, although I did want to try to convey to my friends just how a small boat looks when at play with Neptune's forces apparently bent on her destruction. In the first place, views made at close quarters are never good, and secondly, it was impossible to stand on any elevated part of the vessel without being washed overboard. Anyway, we were too busy with the problem of keeping our little yacht right side up and by the course. The watch on deck had to hang on for dear life, and the ones below were all parked on the leeside, it being impossible to stay in the weather bunks. The poor cook was a sorry sight. All night long, he had been dodging dishes and pans, and appeared sadly in need of repairs. Once during the night, when he was trying to get a wink of sleep by lying flat upon the galley floor with his head parked on a sail cover in the forepeak, his body wedged under the galley stove, and his legs extended into the main cabin, a sudden lurch of the vessel tore the fastenings off the icebox doors, and all the contents, including ice, milk, butter, eggs, tomatoes, a side of bacon, two hams, and other sundries, plastered themselves all over poor Bill's countenance. This was the only time I ever heard Bill cuss in Danish, but after he scraped this potpourri omelette out of his eyes and ears and off his manly bosom, he set to work bravely and made as much restitution as possible. By some hook or crook, he managed to get enough heat out of the stove to give us all a cup of hot coffee, which braced us up wonderfully.

By nine o'clock, the wind had fallen a little, so we set the mainsail with double reef, and the yacht worked ahead in grand style. At eight bells noon, with no sun, we charted out our position by dead reckoning, latitude 33° 07' N., longitude 121° 47' west, course W. S. W. For lunch, Bill worked up a little hot soup for us, served in iron cups, as most of the ship's fancy china had already been broken. We had to drink the soup, for no spoons could be used, as it required all our agility and resourcefulness to maintain a respectable perpendicular position in order to steer the soup into our stomachs thru the proper channel. It seems now incredible that a thing made of wood, like our little boat, could stand so much up and down, lateral, end to end, and sidewinding motions without breaking all to pieces and casting us into the cold, dark sea. The wind held all day, and we were carrying double reefed mainsail, foresail, and forestay sail close hauled. At four o'clock, we took our mileage from the log, and had made good 172, course W. S. W. The sea was now running a little easier, and Bill, the cook, set to work to get us a little real food, our first warm meal in two days. Brad, the first mate, had already built into the table some dish racks fastened with ship's clamps, so we made out pretty well. Hot soup, beans, roast beef, potatoes, cake and coffee. We had been taking plenty of water over the weather side, so everything on deck was wet and cold. The night watches were all dolled up in sweaters and slickers, but not a mother's son of them complained about being cold, or attempted in any way to shirk his unpleasant duties. Quite frequently, a big comber would crash into the little ship and shake her like a leaf on a tree. She would creak and tremble in every plank, but would emerge triumphantly from the onslaught, and slide gracefully into the oncoming seas.

The crew was now thoroughly familiar with its duties, and sea legs were being rapidly developed. We no longer stumbled awkwardly over boxes, water kegs, ropes and gears, but found our stations with becoming agility. Two little packages, neatly wrapped and labeled for the skipper, were discovered in the main locker. One said, "Open on third day out," and the other, "Open on fourth day out." This being the third day, the first package was duly opened. It proved to be that classic of sea stories, *Sailing Around the World Alone*, by Captain Slocum, and was presented by our well known fellow club member, Paulsen Visel. A letter was enclosed, wishing us all sorts of good luck, also an original poem calculated to banish all gloom from forepeak to after scupper. The ship's company perked up a bit. Otto Wildey, the chief bos'n, started to sing, "Ain't we got fun." Put, the artist, made the first entry in his social log, and Beech broke the silence by a three-word sentence, "Damn cold night."

On deck, Tuesday morning, July 24th, chilly air, lumpy sea, but taking no green water over the topsides. No sun, and a grey, empty horizon. We shook out the reefs in the main, set the jib, and plowed along at an angle of forty degrees. After a good warm breakfast, we opened the second package, presented to the ship by Mrs. Putnam. It proved to be a bewitching damsel with lines and curves unadorned, and comparable only with Mack Sennett's most ravishing bathing beauty. Each one onboard wanted this maiden for his very own, and Brad wanted to eat her alive, but, as she was built out of soap, he desisted. Finally, by unanimous consent, she was accorded a prominent place in the ship's boudoir, where all could pay her due homage daily.

Gertrude Ederle on Swimming the English Channel (1926)

Named one of the top 100 sportswomen of the twentieth century by CNN and Sports Illustrated, *Gertrude Ederle is the largely forgotten heroine who was the first woman to swim across the English Channel. At twenty, armed with a contract from both the* New York Daily News *and* Chicago Tribune *for the exclusive rights to her personal story and after competing against several other women then in training to beat her to the milestone, Ederle set off to swim the 21-mile English Channel between Gris-Nez, France, and Kingsdown on the English coast. She completed the 35-mile journey (rough seas forced her into a circuitous route) in just over fourteen and a half hours, smashing the existing men's record by over two hours.*

The journalistic competition for Ederle's story was fierce, so much so that she swam between two tugboats, one occupied by Ederle's family (her father "Pop" and her sister Margaret), her trainer (Thomas Burgess), and favored Daily News *writer Julie Harpman. The other tug was commissioned by rival journalists with whom Harpman refused to share a boat. Onboard the tug, Ederle's family played upbeat music throughout to keep the swimmer's spirits buoyed, so that Ederle's recollections of the record-setting swim were forever accompanied in memory by the song "Let Me Call You Sweetheart." In the* Chicago Tribune *article below, Ederle tells her own journalistic story just hours after completing an exhausting, shark-threatened, sea-battered swim that further aggravated a childhood hearing problem. She would become partially deaf within two years of her historic triumph. When* she returned to her native New York City, she was given a tickertape parade attended by a reported two million well-wishers and offered a contract to play herself in the film Swim Girl, Swim. While the Channel crossing represented the apogee of Ederle's fame, her greatest sanctioned athletic feat may well have been the gold medal she won in the 4 × 100-meter relay and the two bronzes earned in the 100 and 400 freestyle in the 1924 Paris Olympics. In writing a remembrance for the Boston Globe on the occasion of Ederle's death in late 2003 Polly Anderson of the Associated Press wrote, "In a roaring decade in which Americans cheered daredevils, few were as celebrated as Ms. Ederle."

"GERTRUDE TELLS OWN STORY OF HOW SHE CONQUERED CHANNEL"

By Gertrude Ederle

DOVER, England, August 7—[2. A.M.]—Here it is several hours since I have accomplished the ambition of my life as a swimmer and I am rather at a loss for words to tell what I have been able to do or how I did it.

I am more than a little dazed by my success and by the abuse I took from the roughest sea I ever encountered for any considerable length of time. At that, I was sure all the time I would make the crossing today, whatever the conditions.

Suffered from Cramps

Probably not more than a quarter of an hour after I took off from Gris Nez I experienced rather severe cramps in my stomach but as my trainer was then cautioning me to take it easy and save up for the tougher stages of the swim, I saw no occasion to mention that fact, for I then would have had to put back, no doubt, and after the seizure passed, make a fresh start.

Likely it was the peach I ate for breakfast dessert. Trainer Burgess did not entirely approve of it anyway, but I felt like eating it.

Just a Long Hard Swim

But, anyhow, the discomfort soon wore off as I continued to swim slowly for a time. And after that it was all just a good, long hard swim. I never dreamed that they were worrying about me along about the eleventh hour, as they tell me they were, until someone—I don't know who—called to me loudly to board the tug.

At first I thought somebody was kidding me, and then I was angry, but I could not make out who had shouted the order and as I knew it was not Pop or Burgess, I dismissed it from my mind.

"The Worst Is Over"

It was more heartening to me every time one of my swimmer friends came alongside me to keep me company, but I think the sweetest words I ever heard were those from Pop and Burgess and Margaret and Julie Harpman when, after we had gone past the nasty Goodwin Shoals, they suddenly burst forth with the assurances that I could not miss then — that the worst of it was over.

The seas were vicious and icy, but the nearness of the shore and the pelting rain seemed to flatten out the water a bit for short intervals, and I knew I was making good time. At no time did I feel weak physically while I was in the water. It was great news when Burgess instructed me to spurt across the tide toward the beach that proved to be toward Walmer castle Deal, from Kingsdown.

Spurts to Shore

"It won't be long now," I told myself — and it wasn't.

I experienced an intoxicating feeling of elation as I swam underwater through the heavy surf and found a footing in the beach sand. I can't fully describe that sensation. My head swam a bit — it had been so long since I stood erect. But I was not groggy nor particularly fatigued.

I wanted sleep, not food; rest and quiet, not congratulations; I judge we had been on the boat traveling to Dover fifteen or twenty minutes before a good old-fashioned tired feeling overcame me — the reaction from the excitement and exertion, I guess.

I'm pretty tired and good and ready for bed right now and I won't try to dictate more of this jumbled up excuse for what they say ought to be an "impression story," but I want to say the stupid delay in landing here at Dover, because all of us lacked our passports, and the order to be on hand at the passport office at 10 this morning, seemed to contribute more to my weariness than any amount of swimming could ever do.

Bobby Jones on Golfing the Majors (1927)

Robert Tyre Jones Jr., the quintessential amateur sportsman of the Golden Age, was also a gifted writer and an unusually self-reflective athlete. Holding university degrees in engineering, literature, and law from Georgia Tech, Harvard, and Emory respectively, Jones had both the ability and the inclination to document his unprecedented feel for the game, as the five major books he authored or coauthored demonstrate.

Cowritten with his friend and Atlanta Journal *sportswriter O. B. Keeler, the short passage that follows from* Down the Fairway *might be summarized as "Bobby Jones on patience" as, in it, he offers a firsthand account of a single year, 1926, that began with a resounding defeat at the hands of Walter Hagen and ended in British and U.S. Open wins. Jones, who battled a fierce on-course temper in his early life, initially thought to skip the British Open after a bruising defeat in the British Amateur, but decided to enter with something to prove to the British fans, who remembered his quitting the 1921 British Open in the middle of his third round. Despite what he called his "most inglorious failure" in golf, Jones was one the most admired athletes of his day, a man Grantland Rice named, along with Ruth and Dempsey, as one of the "three leading worldwide names in sport." Robert Tyre Jones Jr. retired at the age of twenty-eight after winning golf's Grand Slam and receiving a tickertape parade said to rival Lindberg's. In his "retirement," Jones would go on to found Augusta National Golf Club, home to The Masters.*

From "The Biggest Year"

Golf is a very queer game. I started the year 1926 with one glorious licking and closed it with another. And it was the biggest golf year I'll ever have. Walter Hagen gave me the first drubbing, and of all the workmanlike washings-up I have experienced, this was far and away the most complete. He was national professional champion; I was national amateur champion; we liked to play against each other; and a match was arranged for the late winter season in Florida; a 72-hole affair, the first half at the Whitfield Estates Country Club at Sarasota, where I was spending the winter, and the second half a week later at Walter's course at Pasadena. Walter was simply too good for me. My irons were rather seriously out of line, it is true, but no excuses are to be offered when the other fellow, on two really great courses — I regard the Whitfield Estates course as one of the best in America — is never over par on any round, and is four strokes better than par at the finish on the sixty-first green, where the match ended with me sinking a forty-five foot putt for a birdie 3 in the effort to go a little farther, and Walter sinking a forty-footer for a half, to chop my head off. Walter played the most invincible match golf in those two days I had ever seen, let alone confronted. And I may add that I can get along very comfortably if I never confront any more like it. He beat me 12–11.

That match did me a lot of good, I think. I had been playing very good golf all winter, and in a series of seven fourball matches with Tommy Armour as a partner, against pairs of the best professionals in the country, Tommy and I had not lost a match. I fancied I was in for a good season, and then this drubbing came along and showed up glaringly the defect in my iron play which had started troubling me at Skokie, in the open championship of 1922. I set to work on that department, and I think it was Jimmy Donaldson, who was with Armour at Sarasota, who gave me the correct line — too much right hand in the stroke. I worked on the irons whenever I had a chance up to the British invasion. And the irons served me fairly well the rest of the year.... Whenever I could get the feel that I was pulling the club down and through the stroke with my left arm — indeed, as if I were hitting the shot with the left hand — it seemed impossible to get much off line. Curious thing. The older school of professionals always insisted the golf stroke was a left-hand stroke, you know.

The United States Golf Association named Watts Gunn and me on the international team of eight members to play at St. Andrews, Scotland, for the Walker Cup; an event played every two years, alternately in this country and Great Britain. We also were to play as individuals in the British Amateur championship at Muirfield, Scotland; and four of us — Watts, Roland MacKenzie, George Von Elm and I — were to stay over and play in the British Open championship at St. Anne's-on-the-Sea, England.

And here's another odd quirk of fate, if it may be dignified by that name. I was getting awfully homesick — leaving my wife and little daughter (a year old), and the rest of my family; and I really wanted to get back a few weeks in advance of the United States Open championship; and when I started in the British Amateur championship May 24, I already had booked my passage home on the *Aquitania*, with the members of the team who were sailing two days after the Walker Cup match, which followed close after the British amateur. I had decided to play in the British Open, which was only a couple of weeks before our own open championship at the Scioto Country Club, Columbus.

I went fairly well in the opening rounds of the British Amateur — they start the entire field playing 18-hole matches in the event, you know, and keep on day after day, two matches a day, until only two are left, who play a 36-hole match in the finals. I don't like 18-hole matches. I may be all wrong, but I can't like them. Too much can happen in one round, over which neither golfer has any jurisdiction. But no matter — they are coming into fashion in this country, too; and the last national amateur at Baltusrol, where they played two 18-hole matches to start with, saw the two ultimate finalists, George Von Elm and myself, almost knocked off in Round I. George had to got to the nineteenth hole with Ellsworth Augustus, and I go the eighteenth with Dicky Jones.

Anyway, I got to the top of my game by the fifth round and shot my head off against Robert Harris, 1925 British Amateur champion. I won nine of the twelve holes the match lasted, defeating him 8–6. And next morning a youngster named Andrew Jamieson, about my age, gave me a tidy lacing, 4–3, in fifteen holes on which he never was above par, and was twice below it, granting that the first hole is a par 5, on the measurement. I wasn't shooting par golf, but I wasn't so bad, at that. He just beat me.

Now, that was the sixth round, and everybody that morning was openly expecting me to breeze on through to the finals (the eighth round in British championships) and there meet Jess Sweetser, who, after a severe match with Francis Ouimet, another of our team, was going steadily along and seemed certain to win through the upper bracket.

I felt pretty blue when Jamieson stopped me. And more than ever I wanted to go home. But here's the working of fate. If I'd been fortunate enough to go on through and win the British Amateur, I'd certainly have sailed for home a week later, on the *Aquitania*.

Then I got to thinking that if I went home now it would look somewhat as if I were sulking over failing to win the British Amateur championship — the Lord knows I was disappointed, because I'd love to win it. But truly I wasn't sore. And I didn't want people to think so. Moreover, I remembered that I hadn't behaved very well on my first visit, five years earlier. And I thought I'd like to stay over and show people I really could shoot some golf, at times. I hadn't showed any golf yet, except that twelve-hole burst against Robert Harris. And so I thought I'd stay on for the British Open, and try my best to show them a little good golf. I had little enough hope of winning the British Open. No amateur had won it since 1897, when Harold Hilton's name went on the beautiful old trophy, five years before I was born. But I thought maybe I could make a decent showing, and anyway I was determined, no matter where I finished, that I'd not pick up this time.... The British are a wonderful sporting people, and I wanted them to think kindly of me and to believe I could shoot a little golf.

Amelia Earhart on Flying the Atlantic (1928)

Amelia Earhart's fascinating book 20 Hrs. 40 Min. *documents the first flight by a woman across the Atlantic, though the Newfoundland-to-Wales, 21-hour marathon was not a solo. In fact, Earhart, pulled in as a substitute when Amy Phipps Guest declared the flight too dangerous, did not do any flying, but did sit at the instrument panel occasionally as the passage* that follows makes mention. Specifically, Earhart's duty was keeping the flight log for pilot Wilmer Stultz and copilot/mechanic Louis Gordon, which she did faithfully and with great humor and insight. Aiming for Ireland but running out of gas, the pilots brought the Friendship *down in what they thought was the English countryside but turned out to be the rocky, fogged-in coast of Wales.* Upon her arrival, Earhart was dubbed "Lady Lindy" by the press after Charles Lindbergh who had soloed the Atlantic one year earlier.

Earhart's fragmented, documentary prose is unusually poetic, even jolly, demonstrating both her pluck as a sportswoman and some of the bravado that would eventually contribute to her tragically unsuccessful circumnavigation of 1937. Though not always thought of as a "sportswoman," Earhart and her publisher-husband George Putnam were determined both that she set distance and speed records and that she tell her story in popular prose. Shortly after becoming the first woman to solo across the Atlantic in 1928, Earhart participated in the Santa Monica-to-Cleveland Air Derby, placing third and cementing her reputation as a sportswoman-aviator par excellence.

From "Across"

Logbook: 140 m.p.h. now. Wonderful time. Temp. 52. The heater from the cockpit warms the cabin, too.

Bill says radio is cuckoo. He is calling now.

There is so much to write. I wonder whether ol' diary will hold out.

I see clouds coming. They lie on the horizon like a long shoreline.

I have just uncurled from lying on Major Woolley's suit for half an hour. I came off this morn with such a headache that I could hardly see. I thought if I put it to sleep it might get lost in the billows of fog we were flying over.

There is nothing to see but churned mist, very white in the afternoon sun. I can't see an end to it. 3600 ft. temp. 52, 45 degrees outside. I have eaten an orange, one of the originals. At T. our infrequent oranges came from Spain, undernourished little bloods.

Very "original" those oranges, almost historic! They were purchased in Boston in the dark ages of the *Friendship's* takeoffs. In the three unsuccessful efforts during that fortnight of disappointments, they went out to the ship with us each morning and came back again to the hotel. But sturdy oranges they proved to be, and nearly a month later were still in good form when they finally found a place on our mid-Atlantic menu.

On the transatlantic flight three oranges, appropriately from California, comprised my bill-of-fare with the exception of probably a dozen malted milk tablets. The sandwiches and the coffee I left to the boys. Somehow I wasn't hungry and, curiously, at the end of the trip there still wasn't any particular desire for food.

Logbook: 4:15. Bill has just opened the motor to climb over this fog. We are 3800 and climbing.

Creatures of fog rear their heads above the surroundings. And what a wallop we get as we go through them.

Bill has just picked up XHY British Ship *Rexmore*, which gives us bearing. 48 no. 39 west 20:45 GMT. The fog is growing patchy and great holes of ocean can be seen. XHY will inform NY of our position.

As I look out of the window I see a true rainbow — I mean the famous circle. It is of course moving at our speed and is on our right, sun being to port a trifle. I have heard of color circles in Hawaii.

The sun is sinking behind a limitless sea of fog and we have a bright rainbow, a fainter ring and, if I am not seeing things, a third suggestion on the edge. The middle is predominately yellow with a round grey shadow in the center. Is it caused from us or our props?

This is not an unknown phenomenon. Subsequently, I learned the rainbows were caused by our propellers.

Logbook: I do believe we are getting out of fog. Marvelous shapes in white stand out, some trailing shimmer veils. The clouds look like icebergs in the distance. It seemed almost impossible to believe that one couldn't bounce forever on the packed fog we are leaving. The highest peaks of the fog mountains, (oh, we didn't get it out) are tinted pink, with the setting sun. The hollows are grey and shadowy. Bill just got the time. O.K. sez he. 10:20 London time my watch. Pemmican is being passed or just has been. What stuff!

The pink vastness reminds me of the Mojave Desert: Also: *J'ai mire dans ma prunel Petite minute eblouie La grande lumiere eternele.*

(Bill gets position. We are out 1096 miles at 10:30 London time) — and having done so he is content to die. I wish I had that poem here.

One of the greatest sights is the sun splashing to oblivion behind the fog, but showing pink glows through apertures in the fog. I wish the sun would linger longer. We shall soon be grey-sheathed.

We are sinking in the fog.

4000 ft.

The light of the exhausts is beginning to show as pink as the last glow of the sky. Endless foggies. The view is too vast and lovely for words. I think I am happy — said admission of scant intellectual equipment.

I am getting housemaid's knee kneeling here at the table gulping beauty.

I was kneeling beside the chart table, which was in front of the window on the port side. Through it I looked northward. It was at this time that I took several photographs.

On the starboard side of the plane was another window. The table itself, a folding device, was Bill's chart table on which he made his calculations. Close by was the radio. Even though one could stand up in the cabin, the height of the table was such that to see out of the window one had to lean on the table or kneel beside it. There was nothing to sit on, as sitting equipment had been jettisoned to save weight.

Logbook: The sea for a space. Hooray. Slim has just hung a flashlight up for illuminating the compass. This light makes the radium impossible to see. Soon it will be dark enough without the flash.

The faint light of the radium instruments is almost impossible to see in dawn or twilight, when it is neither dark enough for the contrast of the radium to show nor light enough to see the numerals themselves.

Logbook: It is about 10. I write without light. Readable?

Have you ever tried to write in the dark? I remember sitting up in bed at school composing themes after lights. During those night hours on the *Friendship* the log was written with the help of my good left thumb. I would not turn on the electric light in the after cabin lest it blind Bill at the controls. And so I penciled my way across the page of the diary thankful for that early training with those better-late-than-never-themes. The thumb of my left hand was used to mark the starting point of one line. The problem of this kind of blind stenography is knowing where to start the next line. It didn't always work. Too often lines piled up one on the other and legibility suffered.

Logbook: The sea was only a respite. Fog has followed us since. We are above it now. A night of stars. North the horizon is clear cut. To the south is a smudge.
The exhausts send out glowing meteors.
How marvelous is a machine and the mind that made it. I am thoroughly occidental in this worship.
Bill sits up alone. Every muscle and nerve alert. Many hours to go. Marvelous also. I've driven all day and all night and know what staying alert means.
We have to climb to get over the fog and roughness.
Bill gives her all she has. 5000 ft. Golly how we climb. A mountain of fog. The north star on our wing tip.
My watch says 3:15. I can see dawn to the left and still a sea of fog. We are 6000 ft. high and more. Can't read dial.

Slim and I exchange places for a while. All the dragons and sea serpents and monstrosities are silhouetted against the dawn.

9000 ft. to get over them.

The two outboard motors picked up some water a while ago. Much fuss.

At least 10,000 ft. 13 hours 15 minutes on the way.

I lose this book in Major Woolley's pockets. There are too many.

Big enough, that suit to lose myself in. Size 40, and fur lined. It is returned now, appropriately autographed. The Major has threatened to stuff and place it in a museum.

Logbook: Still climbing. I wish the sun would climb up and melt these homogeneous teddy bears.

Beside these grotesques in the fog, which we all remarked, there were recurrent mountains and valleys and countless landscapes amazingly realistic. Actually when land itself did appear we could not be sure that it was not an illusion too. It really took some moments to become convinced that it was reality.

Logbook: Slim has just changed bats in the flashlight hanging over the compass.

The compass was hung rather low, so far from Bill's eye that it was difficult to read its illuminated face. So Slim arranged a flashlight focused on it.

Logbook: We are going down. Probably Bill is going through. Fog is lower here, too. Haven't hit it yet, but soon will so far as I can see from back window.... Everything shut out.

Instrument flying. Slow descent, first. Going down fast. It takes a lot to make my ears hurt. 5000 now. Awfully wet. Water dripping in window. Port motor coughing. Sounds as if all motors were cutting. Bill opens her wide to try to clear. Sounds rotten on the right.

3000 ft. Ears not so painful. Fog awful.

Motors better, but not so good.

It is getting lighter and lighter as day dawns. We are not seeing it dawn, however. I wish I knew radio. I could help a lot.

We are over* stratum now. At 3000. Bill comes back to radio to find it on the blink.

---

*Earhart's original note here read "That is the way it is written in the logbook. So far no one can make out the word before stratum. Can you?—A.E."

We are running between the clouds still, but they are coming together. Many clouds all about ... shouldn't bother. Port motor coughing a bit. Sounds like water. We are going to go into, under or over a storm. I don't like to, with one motor acting the way it is.

How grey it is before; and behind, the mass of soggy cloud we came through, is pink with dawn. Dawn "the rosy fingered," as *The Odyssey* has it.

Himmel! The sea! We are 3000. Patchy clouds. We have been jazzing from 1000 to 5000 where we now are, to get out of the clouds. At present there are sights of blue and sunshine, but everlasting clouds always in the offing. The radio is dead.

The sea for a while. Clouds ahead. We ought to be coming somewhat in the range of our destination if we are on the course. Port motor off again. 3000 ft. 7 o'clock London.

Can't use radio at all. Coming down now in a rather clear spot. 2500 ft. Everything sliding forward.

8:50. 2 Boats!!!!

Trans steamer.

Try to get bearing. Radio won't. One hr's gas. Mess. All craft cutting our course. Why?

So the log ends.

Its last page records that we had but one hour's supply of gas left; that the time for reaching Ireland had passed; that the course of the vessel sighted perplexed us; that our radio was useless.

Where were we? Should we keep faith with our course and continue?

"Mess" epitomized the blackness of the moment. Were we beaten?

We all favored sticking to the course. We had to. With faith lost in that, it was hopeless to carry on. Besides, when last we checked it, before the radio went dead, the plane had been holding true.

We circled the *America*, although having no idea of her identity at the time. With the radio crippled, in an effort to get our position, Bill scibbled a note. The note and an orange to weight it, I tied in a bag with an absurd piece of silver cord. As we circled the *America*, the bag was dropped through the hatch. But the combination of our speed, the movement of the vessel, the wind and the lightness of the missile was too much for our marksmanship. We tried another shot, using our remaining orange. No luck.

Should we seek safety and try to come down beside the steamer? Perhaps one reason the attempt was never attempted was the roughness of the sea which not only made a landing difficult but a takeoff impossible.

Bill leaped to the radio with the hope of at least receiving a message. At some moment in the excitement, before I closed the hatch which opens in the bottom of the fuselage I lay flat and took a photograph. This, I am told, is the first one made of a vessel at sea from a plane in transatlantic flight.

Then we turned back to the original course, retracing the twelve-mile detour made to circle the steamer. In a way we were pooling all our chances and placing everything in a final wager on our original judgment.

Quaintly, it was this moment of lowest ebb that Slim chose to breakfast. Nonchalantly he hauled forth a sandwich.

We could see only a few miles of water, which melted into the greyness on all sides. The ceiling was so low we could fly at an altitude of only 500 feet. As we moved, our miniature world of visibility, bounded by its walls of mist, moved with us. Half an hour later into it suddenly swam a fishing vessel. In a matter of minutes a fleet of small craft, probably fishing vessels, were almost below us. Happily their course paralleled ours. Although the gasoline in the tanks was vanishing fast, we began to feel land — some land — must be near. It might not be Ireland, but any land would do just then.

Bill, of course, was at the controls. Slim, gnawing a sandwich, sat beside him, when out of the mists there grew a blue shadow, in appearance no more solid than hundred of other nebulous "landscapes" we had sighted before. For while Slim studied it, then turned and called Bill's attention to it.

It was land!

I think Slim yelled. I know the sandwich went flying out the window. Bill permitted himself a smile.

Soon several islands came into view, and then a coastline. From it we could not determine our position, the visibility was so poor. For some time we cruised along the edge of what we thought was typical English countryside.

With the gas remaining, we worked along as far as safety allowed. Bill decided to land. After circling a factory town he picked out the likeliest looking stretch and brought the *Friendship* down in it. The only thing to tie to was a buoy some distance away and to it we taxied.

Helen Wills on Wimbledon Tennis (1928)

In the one-of-a-kind chapter that follows, penned by Golden Age tennis darling Helen Wills in her book Tennis, *the author achieves the perfect compound vision of the participant-writer—first as player, second as observer. Wills's role as observer was fated rather than chosen, as an emer-*

gency appendectomy forced her to withdraw in the third round of the 1926 Wimbledon. Though a professional for most of her career, Helen Wills, better known by her married name Helen Wills Moody, is included here not only because she writes as an observer as well as a player but because the victories she describes in the first half of her essay occurred prior to 1927 when she was still an amateur.

    Wills is remembered as one of the elite athletes of the Golden Age of Sport for her winning of 19 of 22 majors and an incredible 158 straight matches at the peak of her career. In 1950, the AP voted Wills the number one women's tennis star of the first half century and Frenchwoman, Suzanne Lenglen, Wills's archrival, as number two. Known for her methodical, emotionless on-court demeanor, Wills was famously nicknamed "Little Miss Poker Face" by Grantland Rice. For her part, Wills, who claimed all she ever thought about in competition was getting the ball over the net, is quoted by Inside Tennis writer Paul Fein as saying, "I know I would hate life if I were deprived of trying, hunting, working for some objective within which there lies the beauty of perfection." In the same Inside Tennis April 2005 cover story, "Who Is the Greatest Female Player Ever?" Wills comes in third behind only Steffi Graf and Martina Navratilova.

From "An Outline of My Tennis Days"

There are two ways of seeing Wimbledon — as a spectator and as a player. In 1924 I had had the player's experience at Wimbledon; in 1926 I saw the place through the eyes of a spectator, and was impressed with the different angle from which one saw the event.

    I went each afternoon, for the two weeks of the tournament, and can well understand why many tennis enthusiasts buy their tickets for the entire two weeks. It became quite fascinating, the watching of the games, the following of the different players throughout their matches. The crowd at Wimbledon is a very knowing one, when it comes to tennis, and appreciates the fine points of the game.

    You go out in the early afternoon — (the best matches never start before two o'clock) — and watch tennis until teatime; then you go out to one of the tea pavilions and have tea and cakes, and perhaps strawberries and cream. The match must be a good one, and close, to be able to compete with tea for the spectator's favor at this hour of the day. After tea, back again for the remaining matches.

    It is not only a part of the audience who follow this routine. There are thousands of people. In order to avoid having to wait in line for tea, many among the onlookers bring little baskets with sandwiches, cakes, and hot tea in thermos bottles, and open them in the grandstand while watching the games.

    The tickets for Wimbledon are usually all sold months in advance, and it is practically impossible to obtain seats at the last minute, unless one happens to know one of the competitors or one of the officers of the club. Many people come, buying tickets for the day that enable them to watch the matches on the outside courts, but which do not enable them to see the center court games. It is arranged by the committee that all of the best players in the tournament have one or two of their preliminary matches on the outer courts so that those who have not been fortunate enough to obtain seats for the center court, can look on. Also, there are a limited number of reserved seats along side of the center court which are sold daily, and behind these there is a narrow space for standing room.

On the last days of the tournament, and also when there are exciting matches, queues wait to purchase these daily tickets, from as early as five or six in the morning, outside the gates.

The most important matches are always played on the center court. Court number one, which adjoins it, has a little grandstand of its own, and here the next and most interesting matches are held. The outside courts, of which there are fifteen or twenty, are filled during the earlier rounds, and there is a constantly moving crowd of onlookers who move from one court to another, watching the games. Then, as play goes on, all attention is drawn to the center court, where the last survivors of the tournament compete. Indeed, during a final match, the outside grounds of the All England Club have a completely deserted look. If it were not for the parked motors cars, looking like shiny black beetles in the fields, you would not suspect that any one was about.

But within the enclosure of the center court there are row upon row of spectators absorbed in the game that is being unrolled before them. At times, during an intense rally, there is a silence when only the sound of ball upon racquet is heard; then, at the finish of the rally, applause breaks forth, deafeningly. I think that the sound of so many hands clapping is like rain falling. It is at Wimbledon. Listen when you go there.

The arrival of the King and Queen is always an event of interest, and a crowd gathers about the door when their motor stops. There is a special entrance for them, and for those who have the privilege of sitting in the royal box. The box is directly at the end of the court, and has in the first row comfortable chairs. Here sit, at various times, the King and Queen, and at various times the Duke and Duchess of York, the King of Spain, Lord Balfour, and others. When the King and Queen enter the box, it is customary for the audience to rise from its seats, and to wait until the royal spectators have taken their chairs. I have seen the players on the court turn, and stand facing the royal box until the King and Queen were seated, but as they always enter unexpectedly, frequently the players are so engrossed in the game that they are not aware of anything else that is happening.

In 1926, the King and Queen came frequently to the tennis, and the Duke of York participated in the men's doubles.

The Queen enjoyed seeing Mlle. Lenglen play and came one day to the tennis on an afternoon when there was an unusually good array of events scheduled.

The time came for Mlle. Lenglen's appearance on the court, and the spectators were looking forward to her entrance.

But no one came out on the court. It lay empty for fifteen minutes or more. The onlookers began to stir restlessly in their seats, for this had never happened at Wimbledon before. But no Suzanne. Then a men's match was put on. It is no easy matter to patch up the center court schedule, if some player fails to appear, because it is practically impossible to locate in the grandstand, upon short notice, the participants of the following match.

Finally, overcome with curiosity, I left my seat and wandered back into the women's locker room, trying to pretend that I was not at all interested in finding out what had happened! I heard a number of explanations: that Mlle. Lenglen had been at lunch until late and that the committee had failed to let her know the hour of her match, that she had become ill, that she had arrived and then decided not to play, because of a falling out with someone. I never did discover why she did not play, and why she kept the Queen and the audience waiting. I think that the real reason was known alone to the committee of the All England Club. It was never made public.

However, even with Suzanne gone, there were many interesting matches. Especially so was that between Mrs. Kathleen McKane Godfree and Senorita Lili de Alvarez. It was the Spanish girl's first experience at Wimbledon. I had played against her twice upon the Riviera and had found her game unusually fast. She adapted herself to the grass surface, and played excellent tennis against Mrs. Godfree in the finals. They had a three-set match, which Mrs. Godfree won because she was a trifle more steady, and because she is a little more suited to match play. She has an ideal temperament for tournament competition, in that she is always calm, and in that she can play up from a bad score. Senorita de Alvarez is more spectacular to watch, more dashing, perhaps, upon the court, but is not as imperturbable, by nature, as the Englishwoman, and I think that it was because of this that Mrs. Godfree won the title.

When the tournament was finished I realized that I had enjoyed being an onlooker almost as much as being a competitor — almost! There is a view obtained of the tennis at Wimbledon by the spectators that the player does not get, and vice versa. The player arrives for his match, goes out upon the court, comes in immediately to change, and by the time he gets out again, no matter how quickly he changes, some of the most interesting matches may be finished. The onlooker, on the other hand, does not see the interesting sidelights of tennis playing, get to know the players, or know the real reasons for various things that happen in the tennis world. In knowing the individual players, their natures, and how they react under varying conditions, it is quite frequently possible to predict the outcome of matches.

Sometimes it is interesting to sit in the women's locker room, during the height of a large tournament, and watch the contestants coming and going, to hear the conversations, and to listen to the comments on various players and matches. It is here that the very heart of a tournament is centered. After the match there are some who cover their defeat with a smile, others who explain why they were not able to win. A few are equally nonchalant upon victory or defeat, but these are rare. As the door swings open and two players come in from their match, words are not necessary to tell which is the winner, which the loser. Almost always one can see it written upon their faces more plainly than in words. While tennis is a sport, yet, at the moment, to one who loves the game, the match is tremendously important. If it were not so, players would not bother to gather together to compete in tournaments. The one who enjoys best her game plays with all her heart.

After Wimbledon was over, I returned to New York, with the hope that I might play in the American tournaments. I had a few uneasy practice games at Forest Hills, the first after my operation, and found that my strokes were all rather feeble. I was sure they would improve, however, and entered two tournaments. I finally realized, unwillingly, that match play was a physical impossibility, and returned to California, where I again entered the university at Berkeley, and did not have a racket in my hand for a number of months. Eight months elapsed before I could really enjoy my game again.

My enthusiasm could not die, however, where tennis was concerned, and in the spring I began to play again.

Feeling fit, upon the court, I tried out my game in a small tournament at Pasadena, in southern California. Tournament play is the test for endurance. Curiously enough, match play seems to take more strength than regular, everyday play. It must be because the player is, perhaps even unknowingly, under a certain amount of strain. Not that it is a harmful sort of strain, but it is a natural one under the circumstances. One tries hard to make his shots come off as well as possible, to make the most of the openings in the play itself, to concentrate continuously upon the game. Although one tries to do this to a certain extent in an everyday match, the atmosphere of competitive tennis is bound to stimulate the play and to make it more intense. Hence, it is more strenuous.

Having had to be on the sidelines at Wimbledon the year before, made me very eager to take part in the 1927 tournament. I was not invited by the Tennis Association to represent it, but was advised by them, instead, to remain at home. But my heart was set upon playing that June at Wimbledon, and so I set out for England with my mother. She has been on the sidelines for every tournament match that I have ever played, away from home, and I am sure that I could not play if she were not there.

I wanted to take part in some of the English tournaments before Wimbledon, as I had never done so before. I had a week of practice on the grass, for it takes about that long to become accustomed to the new surface. I enjoyed my preliminary tournaments tremendously. They were held outside London at smaller clubs, and had a more informal atmosphere than the great Wimbledon. It was interesting to see the typical English tennis club and to see why tennis has become such a nationally popular game as it is in England.

One of the clubs where I played had been in the same spot for years. Its turf was old and excellent. I met many of the members, and found that even the older ones had played tennis there together as children. Adjoining the courts was a wide green cricket field. The club, with its tennis and cricket, had grown to be part of the members' lives. It was, to many, the setting of happy memories. The clubhouse itself was very small, and a quite casual sort of place, but there was a wide veranda where tea could be served in the afternoon.

The week before the championship tournament, the higher ranking players tried out the courts at Wimbledon. Most of the better players are members of the All England Club. I, because I was a visiting player, had been given a guest card, so that I could practice on the courts. Of course, no one could play on the center court, for it was sacred to the championship games. It had been tended, watered, rolled, and cared for, until it resembled velvet. No clover dared show its head here! The outside courts were in good condition, and it was upon them that we had our practice games.

I must describe the club's setting. It lies in a little depression, with low wooded hills rising on three sides. The trees are large and very green. On the fourth side, across the main road, is a small golf course at the edge of a little lake. The golf club is not connected with the tennis club, however, but it is pleasing to the eye, and its soft green fairways increase the beauty of the surroundings. On a sunny day the All England Club is a charming place for tennis.

The outside grass courts, of which there are fifteen or twenty, have tall hedges of yew growing between them, so that the players have a perfect background, dark green, against which to follow the flight of the ball. Beyond the grass courts are seven or eight dark red "En Tout Cas" courts which can be used immediately after rain.

The clubhouse itself, the locker rooms, the offices, the lounges, and the tearooms, form a part of the center court grandstand, which is so tall and large that there is sufficient room for the entire clubhouse to be built beneath it, and to form its outside walls. The first day of the championship games at the All England Club brings out an enormous crowd of spectators, and, of course, all the contestants. Monday is the opening day. My first match was on Tuesday, when I met Gweneth Sterry, a young and attractive English player of about twenty-two, with blue eyes and rosy cheeks. Her mother was a champion at Wimbledon when she was a girl, and had taught her daughter tennis so that she might play there, too. Gweneth played with spirit the day we met. This, coupled with the fact that her serves were severe, made the match a three-set affair, which I finally managed to win.

The weather seemed to be against all tennis during the two weeks of this season's Wimbledon. The preceding June the sun had shone every day upon the players. But there was nothing this June but rain and overcast skies during the whole period, with the exception of the one afternoon when Tilden played [Henri Jean] Cochet. The matches were held off by showers daily. Nothing is more tiring for a player than to be ready for his match and then to sit waiting for hours. It is far more tiring than the match itself and can rob one of all one's enthusiasm. The spectators sat dejectedly but patiently in the stands, watching the huge tarpaulin that covered the center court to keep it dry. The patience of an English tennis crowd is remarkable. If there is a chance of the play's continuing, no one leaves for home. The enormous canvas covering that keeps the rain from the center court is quite an unusual thing. At the first sign of a sudden shower, a corps of groundsmen appears and quickly and efficiently rolls the canvas over the court. If the rain is severe, the canvas is hoisted with ropes from pulleys at the end of the court, so that the water drains off to the sides. As soon as the shower is over, the canvas is rolled up promptly, and play is resumed on a dry court.

An interesting match in the ladies' singles was that between Miss Joan Fry and Miss Betty Nuthall, both young English players. Betty had defeated the American champion, Mrs. Mallory, in the round before, and it was thought that she would triumph against Joan. There was much excitement among the onlookers. It was a most attractive match between Betty and Joan, both fair-haired, both keen and enthusiastic, both so serious during the play. After a long three-set struggle, in which Betty, for a time, was nearly the winner, Joan came up from behind and finally won. Good players and good sports, they went off the court when it was over, smiling and talking to each other.

I watched the match with keen interest, because I was to play the winner. It is always interesting to watch the player whom you are going to meet in action, as well as helpful, for you can see what form she is in, and what her stronger and weaker points are.

Joan and I played on the following day, but she seemed not nearly as steady as she had been the day before, and I was fortunate enough to win. The finals, which came on the Saturday of the second week, were almost put off because of the rain, which threatened every moment. I had looked forward to meeting Senorita de Alvarez again, and now it was to take place. I had played against her twice on the Riviera, but she had improved since then, as I had discovered in watching her earlier games in the tournament. Especially was she more steady than she had been. This, coupled with speed, is a difficult combination to meet, at any time upon the court.

Lili is an interesting opponent, because of the fact that she plays swiftly, with more of a man's than a woman's speed. She is animated and full of life and her game is an unusually daring one. She frequently chooses a more difficult shot when an easier one would do. For this reason she is capable of the unexpected, and can surprise a player completely with her acutely angled swift forehand drive, and her equally sharply angled backhand. She is one who gets a great deal of pleasure from her game. If she wins, she has a gay laugh for her success. If she loses, a little shrug of her shoulders, and she quickly puts it out of her mind.

Our first set went at six games to two for me, but the score does not show how close the play was. I had to try continually to keep the balls away from her favorite strokes. She has the ability of answering a fast shot with a fast shot which makes her a difficult adversary. In the second set the game score was closer, being six to four in my favor. This set was closer than the first and was practically even until a certain rally, which was the turning point. This particular rally was a very long one. We were both at the baseline, and the ball came and went swiftly many times over the net. Then Lili advanced to the net, volleying my drive. Her volley was quite short, and in such a place that I had barely time to reach it before it bounced for a second time. From my position on the court I found a passing ball impossible to make. I tried a lob, and it barely skimmed the top of her upraised racket, and fell quickly into the backcourt out of her reach. We were both out of breath after this effort. Luckily for me, I was a little less overcome than she, and before she got back into her stroking again the next two games were passed and the match was mine. This rally was one of the most exciting to me of any that I can remember.

The dream nearest a player's heart is that of winning a title at historic Wimbledon, to have one's name inscribed on the shields that carry the names of the winners from the very first, when tennis was new. My feelings, as the last ball traveled over the net, and as I realized that the final match was mine, I cannot describe. I felt that here was a prize for all the tennis, all the games, I had ever played since I was a little girl.

Eddie Eagan on Boxing Against Jack Dempsey (1932)

Arguably the most forgotten American amateur athlete of the late Golden Age, Edward Patrick Francis "Eddie" Eagan remains the first man and only person to medal at both a summer and winter Olympic games, feats he achieved in boxing (Summer 1920) and bobsledding (Winter 1932). Showing true amateur elan, Eagan had taken up the sport of bobsledding just three weeks prior to winning gold, according to his United States Olympic Committee profile. Born to a poor Denver family, Eagan, in the following passage from his memoir Fighting for Fun, *describes fighting an exhibition match against the great Jack Dempsey in front of Eagan's hometown Denver crowd. A college student and a Denver Amateur Champion (D.A.C.) at the time he went toe-to-toe with Dempsey, Eagan was badly overmatched. As it turns out, the bout between Eagan and Dempsey proved a contest between two of the great gentleman athletes of Golden Age Sport. Eddie Eagan would go on, like Bobby Jones, to successfully practice law after his competitive days were over. He also served his country as a colonel in World War II. Though the 1932 copyright date of* Fighting for Fun *places Eagan's narrative just after the period typically thought of as the Golden Age, the events Eagan remembers fall firmly in the time period.*

"JACK DEMPSEY TEACHES ME A NEEDED LESSON"

Dempsey had done nothing really sensational at that time. He had fought some rising contenders with varying success. He had not then met such men as Bill Brennan, Fred Fulton or Carl Morris. To be billed on the Empress Vaudeville Circuit as, "The Coming World's Champion" was "bolony," according to my admirers.

Many of my pals urged me to challenge him at the theater. I demurred, but fate was to bring us together in the ring.

Denver women were raising money for the Red Cross. Someone realized the box-office value of having Dempsey meet the Denver champion in a charity exhibition. Local good Samaritans figured a boxing exhibition would draw the men, while singing and dancing acts would attract the women, so that all Denver would respond.

"Mr. Dempsey will box you a three-round exhibition," a sweet-voiced lady told me one day over the telephone. "Friday night at the Empress Theater, and as we knew you would consent, we already have put it in the papers."

The news came as a complete surprise, but I was glad to get the chance to box Dempsey. Newspaper pictures showed him to be of normal build about six feet in height. He did not weigh as much as Blossom, whom I knocked out in the D.A.C. tournament. In my ignorance I was cocky.

The few days before the bout were crowded with dreams and training. For the first time in my life I would box before women as well as men. I tingled with self-conscious anticipation. Several beautiful coeds of the university were to sell programs, and one of them was The Girl. I pictured her awe at my display of skill, speed, and punching power. Victory would have a new thrill with her looking on.

I ran five miles each morning. In the afternoon I went to a gymnasium where I boxed with some professionals. They assured me where there was dynamite in both my right and left. The big night came. I never questioned the outcome.

Everybody patted me on the back and gave me a cheerio. I waited in the wings of the stage in my togs while an uncertain soprano sang, "It's a long way to Tipperary." Some pretty girls danced. A Tommy related his war experience, in the hollow voice of one who has been gassed. A bathrobe hid my quaking knees and pounding heart. There was no fear in my system, but I quivered with excitement.

Our exhibition was the last event of the evening. Those entertainers who had finished their parts in the program were standing around in costume. They were relaxed and smiling. I was tense and thirsty. The minutes dragged endlessly.

I asked for water. Mahoney, my second, gave it to me. The boxing ring was being put in place by the stage hands.

"Here comes Jack Kearns, Dempsey's manager," Lou whispered. Kearns's hair was neatly plastered, an aroma of perfume clung to him, and he wore a diamond stickpin. With a slight swagger he strode to the center of the footlights.

"Ladies and Gentlemen, it is indeed a pleasure for Jack Dempsey and myself to be here in Denver and to contribute our services to the Red Cross," he announced. "As many of you know, Dempsey was born in this wonderful state and is unquestionably the greatest exponent in the world of the manly art of self-defense. [Jess] Willard refuses to fight him, although we will post a twenty-thousand dollar forfeit. This evening Dempsey will box an exhibition with your amateur champion."

Kearns motioned to me in the wings, and Lou pushed me out on the stage. There was loud and prolonged applause. The glare of the lights troubled me less than the hundreds of eyes upon me. I knew those eyes were looking to me to glorify the hometown title against the native son who had wandered afar.

"Otto Floto, the famous sportswriter, will referee," Kearns continued, "and now, ladies and gentlemen, let me introduce the Mauler from Manassa,

Colorado, future heavyweight champion of the world, Jack Dempsey." Kearns's voice finished in crescendo. There was a roll of drums and a blare of trumpets with the orchestra in the pit below. The curtain went up and there stood Jack Dempsey in a crouching boxing pose, with gloves already on. Kearns is a master showman. Dempsey was given applause by the spectators, but it was not as generous as that given me.

Dempsey looked much bigger in his boxing trunks than in his pictures. He was unconcerned as he watched my gloves being put on.

Otto Floto called us to the center of the ring and said, "Now, boys, a nice fast exhibition, and Jack, remember there are women out there, so don't hit hard."

Such comment provoked me. Floto knew that I had won the amateur heavyweight tournament. Why had he failed to caution me about heavy punching?

"I will shoot a stiff right across to his chin as soon as the bell rings," I planned.

We walked to opposite corners and stood regarding each other.

Just before the gong sounded, a neighborhood house fan in the gallery shrilled, "Knock him stiff as a railroad tie, Eddie."

The crowd laughed. My railroad boys in the gallery were expecting great things of me, I knew. The bell rang.

I rushed across the ring and met Dempsey as he was coming out of his corner. His chin was tucked in close to his shoulder. I shot a right to that ambushed jaw and it landed hard. Other heavyweights had been plunged into sleep with that punch. To my amazement Dempsey still stood, though a look of surprise crossed his face.

"Keep it up, Eddie" yelled the gallery.

Feinting with a left, I threw another terrific right at that knockout target—the jawbone. It landed, and Jack Dempsey's head bobbed. Then he began to weave his head, shoulders and body rhythmically.

He hummed the tune "Everybody Two-step," keeping time with his whole body. Even his feet as they scraped the resined canvas seemed to be tapping in time.

I stepped around, looking for another potshot to the point. Then something fell on my head! It felt like a rafter from the roof. I never saw it coming.

As I opened my eyes, I felt two padded gloves under my armpits, the support of the ropes at my back, and heard the distant voice of Otto Floto:

"Hold him up a little longer, Jack, and for heaven's sake go easy on your punches."

Then a shove and I was again floating around in the space. The crowd's distorted faces circled and slanted, now up, now down. The tune "Everybody

Two-step" hummed in my befuddled brain. Before me a rhythmic tiger, with a human face, was weaving and bobbing. Soft brown cushions like fairyland balloons were making circles before my eyes. Suddenly one of those cushions came toward my nose and halted lightly on it, then looping over it, fell like a bomb on the side of my neck. The lights went out. When they shone again there was a splitting feeling in my head. Once more strong arms, stout ropes, supported me.

"Be careful, Jack, I tell you, make it look like a clinch a little longer," growled Floto's voice near my ear.

Understanding broke through my clouded consciousness, I must not fall; yet I knew if even a feather touched me, a steel scaffold could not support me.

"If you hit me again, Jack, you won't be able to hold me up," I whispered, as he shoved me away still humming "Everybody Two-step." A smile flitted across Dempsey's face, and he toyed playfully with me in a clinch.

"All right, kid, but don't try any more of your funny rights," he said.

The bell was a welcome sound. Still it was only the end of the first round.

I walked towards the wrong corner, and was guided to my own by the kind hand of Otto Floto.

"Cut the next two rounds short," I heard him tell the timekeeper.

On my stool at last, I wondered how I ever would get up again.

"What's the matter, Eddie? You're not fighting right," my second complained, as he put the smelling salts close to my nose for a big whiff. "That guy must have a granite jaw. Your first punch should have dropped him."

His words seemed futile. If he ever had tried to swim up Niagara Falls he would have known the way I felt.

At the beginning of the second round, Lou helped me up. Jack came to meet me. He cuffed me around and clinched.

"Come on, you're not hurt. Hit me," he said before we broke.

I shot some feeble jabs which connected. He let me do it, and as we again clinched he said:

"Keep it up. Those kids out there expect it of you."

No more rafters feel on my head, and no more telephone poles hit me on the side of the neck, so I weathered the playful but none too gentle taps of Dempsey.

"Gee, you looked great then," said Lou, at the end of round two. He didn't know that Jack was a good actor, as well as a generous one.

The third round was a repetition of the second and I never knew a more welcome sound than the final bell. There was the usual cheering and clapping as Jack Dempsey and I shook hands.

Come over to my dressing room, kid, and I'll show you a few things," Jack said, putting his huge forearm over my shoulders and leading me offstage.

In the dressing room, he showed me his theory of fighting. "It is all rhythm," he said. "When I land, every ounce of my weight goes into the punch. The timing of it I get by humming a tune and crashing in when I see an opening."

He showed me his method of avoiding a punch by holding his jaw close to his shoulder. "Even when I do roadwork I practice arching my head so my chin comes down to my chest." He illustrated that, then went on: "Always keep your right hand pasted close to your jaw, it acts as a guard, then if you want to shoot a right cross, you're in a good position."

He showed me his favorite punch — a left hook. "I usually feint a few times with a straight jab and then I whip over the left hook." How well I knew that punch and its effects!

"In the clinches, Eddie, I rip them into the body until they can't stand it, then when they drop their arms, I nail them on the neck." I knew about that, too! His blow to the neck was not a rabbit punch delivered with the wrist, but a fair one with the knuckles.

Jack demonstrated his theory of footwork. "I never dance around a lot and waste energy, but I keep crowding and weaving in close to my opponent and landing on him when he stays still."

In parting he said, "You're a good puncher, Eddie. You know how to box and you'd be a good professional. But Otto Floto tells me you're in college. Stick to it, kid. I wish I had your chance. The professional gets darn little money and lots of punches."

Little did he foresee the million-dollar gate. Little did I dream I would attend three world-famous universities.

Yet Jack was to be my guest at Yale and Harvard, and after garnering all his wealth and ring honors, he was to repeat that he envied me the choice I made.

Arnold Eric Sevareid on Canoeing from Minnesota to the Hudson Bay (1935)

In Canoeing with Cree, *one of the most remarkable participatory accounts of any age, a young Eric Sevareid, a kid who would go on to become one of the most famous television and radio journalists of the mid century, tells of his precedent-making, 2250-mile canoe trip with classmate Walt*

Port from the Minnesota River to Canada's Hudson Bay. Like Joseph Knowles before them, the boys became media sensations, as their regular reports were published by editor George H. Adams of The Minneapolis Star. In the foreword to Canoeing with the Cree, Adams wrote, "The boys in this story ... have demonstrated that the frontiers of courage and romance, still exist, beyond which only the exceptional soul will venture. One has only to choose a setting for the drama.... If your heart seeks the unexplored, the setting does not matter. Your will life will be an adventure." Sevareid, raised along the Mouse River in North Dakota, grew up to become a war correspondent for the legendary CBS Edward R. Murrow team. At times, Sevareid seemed destined for even unintended adventure, as when, in 1943, he was forced to parachute out of a distressed airplane into the Burmese jungle along with nineteen other survivors including the diplomat John Paton Davies. A lover of the solitude offered by the outdoors, Sevareid was an unlikely television and radio journalist, described by Jim Wooten in a May 1995 Columbia Journalism Review piece as "frightened by microphones and cameras, blinded by lights, burdened with an expressionless voice, resistant to coaching and improvement."

From "We're Off!" and "The New Life"

Now the Four Way Lodge is opened, now the Hunting Winds are loose,
Now the Smokes of Spring go up to clear the brain;
Now the Young Men's hearts are troubled for the whisper of the Trues;
Now the Red Gods make their medicine again....
We must go, go, go away from here.
On the other side the world we're overdue...

It was a warm May afternoon, and my class in English literature was almost ended when I happened to turn to that page of Kipling. The sunshine was streaming in the room, shining on a bent-over head of light hair in front of me and falling in funny speckles on the book page. As the spots of light shifted back and forth over the type, it seemed as though the letters were alive and crawling in bewilderment, trying to get away.

I watched them curiously for a while, and the lines of the verse I had just read kept sounding in my brain over and over again. I heard nothing else until the teacher said, in a loud voice that made the letters suddenly stop their movement: "Tomorrow it will be *Paradise Lost.*"

That completely awakened me and I had an overwhelming sense that everything was wrong. *Paradise Lost*, indeed! As long as I remained in that suddenly confining room, I knew it was lost. Paradise was outdoors, out on the greening hills and along the lazy river.

I could see that Walt was thinking hard of something too, for he seemed to be staring at the window, looking right through the file of students who were walking from the room. In a minute it was quiet and he and I were alone.

He got up slowly, walked over by me and slumped down in the next seat. As he screwed up his fountain pen he said: "Bud, why in the world don't we get out of here this summer — go somewhere. I'd be partial to the North Pole or South Africa, myself."

So that is how it all started. Mr. Kipling made the first move, but I guess Walt Port will have to get most of the credit or the blame. It wasn't South Africa or the North Pole we headed for, but it was well on the way toward the latter. It was Hudson Bay.

Walt really had kept a plan for the trip a secret with himself all through high school, waiting until graduation to spring it.

Briefly, it was this: We would paddle a canoe up the Minnesota River from Minneapolis, our home, to Big Stone Lake, on the South Dakota line, into the Red River of the North, down that river into Canada and Lake Winnipeg, up the east shore of the lake to Norway House and, at that point, attempt a hazardous wilderness jump of five hundred miles to the bay. It would be the first time an all-water trip had ever been made from Minnesota to the North Atlantic Ocean.

Marvelous! It sounded so simple then. But the problems in the way were many, and the first was finances.

"I've an answer to that," I announced after a few moments' heavy thought. "Why not get one of the newspapers in town to finance us? We could write weekly stories for them about our progress." (I was editor of the school paper and considered myself a second Robert Louis Stevenson.)

"Bud," Walt said with admiration, "for once in your spotted career you have an idea. Do you think we can put it over?"

One newspaper did turn us down. Impossible, they told us, for two high-school kids, one nineteen (Walt) and the other seventeen (me) to make a trip like that. Grown men would fail at it. Besides, our stories probably would not be any good, anyway.

But Mr. W. C. Robertson, managing editor of the *Minneapolis Star*, thought differently. Or at least he did after we had harried him for a week.

One day he called us down to his office. "All right, boys, we'll ride with you," he announced briefly.

Stopping only long enough to thank him with a gasp, we tore out of the newspaper building for the nearest camping goods store to begin selecting our outfit. Never, never had we been so excited! People stopped to stare at the two of us, one long and lean, the other short and stocky, galloping through the streets, talking as fast as we could with both our mouths and all our hands.

Considering our inexperience, we finally selected a fairly compact and durable outfit. Our canoe was eighteen feet long, an American made cruiser model, with a wide beam and a small keel. Some canoeists argued against the use of a keel, but later on we were thankful we had one.

The *Sans Souci*, we christened her. That was Walt's idea. It means "without care." We painted on her "Minneapolis to Hudson Bay." In order to beat other buyers for the canoe, which was secondhand and on which the middle thwart was missing, we had to skip some of our final examinations.

One necessary item we deliberately neglected to secure until we were assured of the *Star's* backing was the consent of our folks, who were caused more worry the ensuing summer than the hides of Walt and me were worth. But when they saw we had everything figured out almost to the last detail, they said "yes" like good sports. Both our dads wished they could go too. It really was a wonder they let us go. Some of our teachers at school called them and insisted that we would surely get lost in the wilderness, that we would drown, or that we would be wrecked in the rapids. A college professor who was planning to go up in the north country on a scientific expedition the next spring offered to take us along if we would give up this trip, and said that we never could hear the waterfalls until it was too late. And the football coach, who wanted us to save money so we could go to college the next fall, argued with us for several hours.

But our minds were made up. I suppose people try to discourage everyone who starts a trip like ours. You just have to make up your minds you can do it and then go ahead.

The principal of the school thought it was great. He announced it at a student-council meeting and said it was "the nearest thing to the Lewis and Clark Expedition he had ever heard of."

Commencement night finally rolled around. Here were our classmates, all around us, faces shining, proud as peacocks, and there were our teachers and folks beyond the footlights. My heart tugged a little at the thought of leaving them all so soon. Would we see them again?

Walt was president of our class, by right of general admiration, although he always said it was my political maneuvering. He led the march for the diplomas and awkwardly turned the wrong way, leading the whole class off the stage at the wrong exit. I'm afraid Walt wasn't thinking of diplomas that night. He was thinking of Indians and rapids and Mounted Police.

Walt came to stay at our house the night before we set out. We sat around the fireplace for long time, talking excitedly, until finally father chased us up to bed, fearful that we would be too tired for our first day's travel. But I could not sleep much.

Early light was beginning to show the things in my room — my typewriter, my old easy chair, and my books on the desk — when I opened my eyes on that day we started out. Then I think I realized, fully and clearly for the first time, the immensity of the thing we were about to attempt. I went cold to the pit of my stomach, but just for an instant. Walt stirred, grunted and sat up, and I had other things to think about.

I suppose it was harder for our folks to say good-bye than for us. They must do all the worrying and wondering about our safety. It is always easier when you are doing the thing yourself.

It was June seventeenth. Finally we pushed off into the Mississippi, rode the fast current down a mile and turned into the channel of the Minnesota River, which empties into the Mississippi at Minneapolis.*

The New Life

We were off!† The trail stretched ahead, a twisting stream of gleaming green water. As we began to paddle against the stiff current, we could hear a bugle playing and the guns firing at Fort Snelling. Overhead several airplanes were circling—not in our honor, for our start was very inauspicious, but the unintentional salutations were timely.

At the first bend I turned and looked back. Our families were still on the dock, watching. A few more strokes of our paddles and green willows slid out and hid the dock. We were alone with the green water, the mossy banks, and the trees which bent over the edge.

Walter and I had lots of ideas about how we would work things. We decided at the start to get up every morning at five o'clock, take an hour's rest at noon and paddle until five in the evening, which would give us about ten hours of paddling a day. But there is no use in making many schedules while you are out in the woods, for things seldom happen in regular fashion.

The first day we learned a little about paddling in time with each other, using a short, powerful stroke. We made one plan at least which we did stick to. We decided that one of us would take the stern and the other the bow each noon and the next noon we would change about.

We worked out a system for getting tanned also, for it was very hot on the river, and for the first few days our faces and hands were blistered raw. We would take off our shirts for five minutes for a few days and increase the time by five minutes each day after that. Later, on Lake Winnipeg, when the days were cool and no one was about, we traveled simply in white trunks.

"Always camp by a spring of water," the woodcraft books read, and that's what we tried to do that first night. Drainage ditches and sewers confused us for a long time, but finally we found an honest-to-goodness spring of fresh

---

*The sentence following the note, which reads "We started out on the trip with the follow equipment," and the subsequent, lengthy inventory that concludes Chapter I have been omitted for the sake of concision.

† The running-in of a portion of a separate, contiguous chapter, "The New Life," is here indicated by the insertion of a subhead of the same name preceding the run-in material. The sentence here noted represents the first sentence of the run-in chapter.

water, and following book rules, we camped there, even if the spot was not very good. Later on we simply filled our water bag from some farmer's pump and camped wherever we pleased.

Walt was elected official cook that first night and his cooking, if I may call it that, resulted in shriveled chunks of ham resembling cinders. Raw prunes and tea completed the meal.

If I ever make another long trip, I will not take an army pup tent. The obstinate piece of canvas got more out of shape and more difficult to erect every night, and it was a blessing when we could discard it.

How much easier it is to sit in a chair at home and read about "the things to do when camping." Things look so easy in print, but when the tent won't go up, when the beans tip in the fire, when the water won't boil and when it suddenly begins to rain in the midst of supper, then all the directions in the world won't help and it's every man to his own method. For Walter and I, when we started out, knew practically nothing of woods life. Never before had we really traveled by canoe. So everything we learned at firsthand and many were the sears, burns, cold meals and miserable nights that accumulated before all the lessons were learned.

We draped several yards of netting over the tent entrance and blocked up the sides with our clothes — but try to keep mosquitoes out when they are determined to get in! One of the reasons we were bitten so freely was my pair of feet. They are too far from my head, and more than once I kicked out the netting.

Walt still insists he slept well the first night on the trail. I admit without shame that I did not. The ground seemed awfully hard. We used four blankets, spread between two ponchos, rubber sheets that protected us from the damp ground and which kept our blankets dry when we did not use the tent. So our arrangement amounted practically to a large sleeping bag.

Everything was damp the next morning, including our spirits, for a heavy fog had descended and soaked all our equipment. Thereafter, we kept the packs covered with our slickers. I cooked pancakes for our first breakfast and, but for the fact that they were burned on the outside and doughy inside, they were good. We began immediately the practice of using sand and grass to wash our dishes, for they are about the only things that will take grease out of a frying pan. We had stomach aches and no appetites for a week, which seemed strange, because always before we had eaten ravenously when in the woods. This was due, of course, to the intense heat and to our own bad cooking.

We were aiming for Hudson Bay, which is straight north of Minneapolis, but the first six days we paddled directly south to Mankato, twenty-five miles from the Iowa border. At this point the Minnesota River bends to the west and north.

Near the little town of Carver, we met our first little stretch of fast water.

It was a tiny rapid compared to those we later encountered, but we were very excited and paddled and poled furiously to get up through it.

At Shakopee we bought a copy of the *Star* and there, right on the front page, were our pictures and a long story about the trip. They said it was "daring." I guess it made us both think the same thing — "We've got to do it now."

Paul Gallico on Golfing with Bobby Jones, Catching Herb Pennock's Curveball, Auto Racing with Cliff Bergere at Indy and More (1937)

Paul Gallico's career as a participatory journalist was launched, ironically, when he was knocked cold sparring with Jack Dempsey. A New York City native, Gallico assumed the post of sports editor at the New York Daily News *in 1923, writing daily columns while gradually segueing into a career as a fiction writer after placing short stories in such leading magazines as* Vanity Fair *and* Saturday Evening Post, *the latter of which published his O. Henry Award-winning story "The Snow Goose." After selling the rights of his stories to Hollywood, Gallico quit his desk-bound newsroom gig and moved to Europe where he wrote his seminal book of essays* Farewell to Sport, *from which the chapter below appears. His essay "The Feel" is considered a manifesto for participatory journalism and a defining influence on George Plimpton. A World War II correspondent and popular novelist and screenwriter, Gallico was also a formidable athlete. Prodigiously versatile as well as prolific, he helped organize the Golden Gloves amateur boxing competition and pursued fencing and deep-sea fishing with gusto while authoring more than forty books and twenty movies, including* The Poseidon Adventure, *which was made into a feature film in 1972 and again in 2006. Though the 1937 copyright date of* Farewell to Sport *places Gallico's memoir after the period typically classified as the Golden Age, the events Gallico recollects fall firmly within the chosen time period.*

"The Feel"

A child wandering through a department store with its mother, is admonished over and over again not to touch things. Mother is convinced that the child only does it to annoy or because it is a child, and usually hasn't the vaguest inkling of the fact that Junior is "touching" because he is a little blotter soaking up information and knowledge and "feel" is an important adjunct to seeing. Adults are exactly the same, in a measure, as you may ascertain when some new gadget or article is produced for inspection. The average person says: "Here, let me see that," and holds out his hand. He doesn't mean "see," because he is already seeing it. What he means is that he wants to get it into his hands and feel it so as to become better acquainted.

As suggested in the foregoing chapter, I do not insist that a curiosity and capacity for feeling sports is necessary to be a successful writer, but it is fairly obvious that a man who has been tapped on the chin with five fingers wrapped up in a leather boxing glove and propelled by the arm of an expert knows more about that particular sensation than one who has not, always provided he has the gift of expressing himself. I once inquired of a heavyweight prizefighter by the name of King Levinsky, in a radio interview, what it felt like to be hit on the chin by Joe Louis, the King having just acquired that experience with rather disastrous results. Levinsky considered the matter for a moment and then reported: "It don't feel like nuttin,'" but added that for a long while afterwards he felt as though he were "in a transom."

I was always a child who touched things and I have always had a tremendous curiosity with regard to sensation. If I knew what playing a game felt like, particularly against or in the company of experts, I was better equipped to write about the playing of it and the problems of the men and women who took part in it. And so, at one time or another, I have tried them all, football, baseball, boxing, riding, shooting, swimming, squash, handball, fencing, diving, flying, both land and sea planes, rowing, canoeing, skiing, riding a bicycle, ice-skating, roller-skating, tennis, golf, archery, basketball, running, both the hundred-yard dash and the mile, the high jump and shot put, badminton, angling, deep-sea, stream-, and surf-casting, billiards and bowling, motorboating and wrestling, besides riding as a passenger with the fastest men on land and water and in the air, to see what it felt like. Most of them I dabbled in as a youngster going through school and college, and others, like piloting a plane, squash, fencing, and skiing, I took up after I was old enough to know better, purely to get the feeling of what they were like.

None of these things can I do well, but I never cared about becoming an expert, and besides, there wasn't time. But there is only to find out accurately human sensations in a ship two to three-thousand feet up when the motor quits, and that is actually to experience that gone feeling at the pit of the stomach and the sharp tingling of the skin from head to foot, followed by a sudden amazing sharpness of vision, clear-sightedness, and coolness that you never knew you possessed as you find the question of life or death completely in your own hands. It is not the "you" that you know, but somebody else, a stranger, who noses the ship down, circles, fastens upon the one best spot to sit down, pushes or pulls buttons to try to get her started again, and finally drops her in, safe and sound. And it is only by such experience that you learn likewise of the sudden weakness that hits you right at the back of the knees after you have climbed out and started to walk around her and that comes close to knocking you flat as for the first time since the engine quit its soothing drone you think of destruction and sudden death.

Often my courage has failed me and I have flunked completely, such as the time I went up to the top of the thirty-foot Olympic diving-tower at Jones Beach, Long Island, during the competitions, to see what it was like to dive from that height, and wound up crawling away from the edge on hands and knees, dizzy, scared, and a little sick, but with a wholesome respect for the boys and girls who hurled themselves through the air and down through the tough skin of the water from that awful height. At other times sheer ignorance of what I was getting into has led me into tight spots such as the time I came down the Olympic ski run from the top of the Kreuzeck, 6000 feet above Garmisch-Partenkirchen, after having been on skis but once before in snow and for the rest had no more than a dozen lessons on an indoor artificial slide in a New York department store. At one point my legs, untrained, got so tired I couldn't stem (brake) any more, and I lost control and went full tilt and all out, down a three-foot twisting patch cut out of the side of the mountain, with a two-thousand-foot abyss on the left and the mountain itself on the right. That was probably the most scared I have ever been, and I scare fast and often. I remember giving myself up for lost and wondering how long it would take them to retrieve my body and whether I should still be alive. In the meantime the speed of the descent was increasing. Somehow I was keeping my feet and negotiating turns, how I will never know, until suddenly the narrow patch opened out into a wide, steep stretch of slope with a rise at the other end, and *that* part of the journey was over.

By some miracle I got to the bottom of the run uninjured, having made most of the trip down the icy, perpendicular slopes on the flat of my back. It was the thrill and scare of a lifetime, and to date no one has been able to persuade me to try a jump. I know when to stop. After all, I am entitled to rely upon my imagination for something. But when it was all over and I found myself still whole, it was also distinctly worthwhile to have learned what is required of a ski runner in the breakneck *Abfahrt* or downhill race, or the difficult slalom. Five days later, when I climbed laboriously (still on skis) halfway up that Alp and watched the Olympic downhill racers hurtling down the perilous, ice-covered, and nearly perpendicular *Steilhan*g, I knew that I was looking at a great group of athletes who, for one thing, did not know the meaning of the word "fear." The slope was studded with small pine trees and rocks, but half of the field gained precious seconds by hitting that slope all out, with complete contempt for disaster rushing up at them at a speed often better than 60 miles an hour. And when an unfortunate Czech skidded off the course at the bottom of the slope and into a pile of rope and got himself snarled up as helpless as a fly in a spider's web, it was a story that I could write from the heart. I had spent ten minutes getting myself untangled after a fall, without any rope to add to the difficulties. It seems that I couldn't find where my left leg ended and one more ski than I had originally donned seemed to be involved somehow. Only a person who has been on those fiendish runners knows the sensation.

It all began back in 1922 when I was a cub sportswriter and consumed with more curiosity than was good for my health. I had seen my first professional prizefights and wondered at the curious behavior of men under the stress of blows, the sudden checking and the beginning of a little fall forward after a hard punch, the glazing of the eyes and the loss of locomotor control, the strange actions of men on the canvas after a knockdown as they struggled to regain their senses and arise on legs that seemed to have turned to rubber. I had never been in any bad fist fights as a youngster, though I had taken a little physical punishment in football, but it was not enough to complete the picture. Could one think under those conditions?

I had been assigned to my first training camp coverage, Dempsey's at Saratoga Springs, where he was preparing for his famous fight with Luis Firpo. For days I watched him sag a spar boy with what seemed to be no more than a light cuff on the neck, or pat his face with what looked like no more than a caressing stroke of his arm, and the fellow would come all apart at the seams and collapse in a useless heap, grinning vacuously or twitching strangely. My burning curiosity got the better of prudence and a certain reluctance to expose myself to physical pain. I asked Dempsey to permit me to box a round with him. I had never boxed before but I was in good physical shape, having just completed a four-year stretch as a galley slave in the Columbia eight-oared shell.

When it was over and I escaped through the ropes, shaking, bleeding a little from the mouth, with rosin dust on my pants and a vicious throbbing in my head, I knew all that there was to know about being hit in the prizering. It seems that I had gone to an expert for tuition. I knew the sensation of being stalked and pursued by a relentless, truculent professional destroyer whose trade and business it was to injure men. I saw the quick flash of the brown forearm that precedes the stunning shock as a bony, leather-bound fist lands on cheek or mouth. I learned more (partly from photographs of the lesson, viewed afterwards, one of which shows me ducked under a vicious left hook, an act of which I never had the slightest recollection) about instinctive ducking and blocking than I could have in ten years of looking at prizefights, and I learned, too, that as the soldier never hears the bullet that kills him, so does the fighter rarely, if ever, see the punch that tumbles blackness over him like a mantle, with a tearing rip as though the roof of his skull were exploding, and robs him of his senses.

There was just that — a ripping in my head and then sudden blackness, and the next thing I knew, I was sitting on the canvas covering of the ring floor with my legs collapsed under me, grinning idiotically. How often since have I seen that same silly, goofy look on the faces of dropped fighters — and understood it. I held onto the floor with both hands, because the ring and the audience outside were making a complete clockwise revolution, came to stop, and then went back again counterclockwise. When I struggled to my feet, Jack Kearns, Dempsey's manager, was counting over me, but I neither saw nor heard him and was only conscious that I was in a ridiculous position and that the thing to do was to get up and try to fight back. The floor swayed and rocked beneath me like a fishing dory in an offshore swell, and it was a welcome respite when Dempsey rushed into a clinch, held me up and whispered into my ear: "Wrestle around a bit, son, until your head clears." And then it was that I learned what those little love-taps to the back of the neck and the short digs to the ribs can mean to the groggy pugilist more than half knocked out. It is a murderous game, and the fighter who can escape after having been felled by a lethal blow has my admiration. And there, too, I learned that there can be no sweeter sound than the bell that calls a halt to hostilities.

From that afternoon on, also, dated my antipathy for the spectator at prizefights who yells: "Come on, you bum, get up and fight! Oh, you big quitter! Yah yellow, yah yellow!" Yellow, eh? It is all a man can do to get up after being stunned by a blow, much less fight back. But they do it. And how a man is able to muster any further interest in a combat after being floored with a blow to the pit of the stomach will always remain to me a miracle of what the human animal is capable of under stress.

Further experiments were less painful, but equally illuminating. A couple of sets of tennis with Vinnie Richards taught me more about what is required of a topflight tournament tennis player than I could have got out of a dozen books or year of reporting tennis matches. It is one thing to sit in a press box and write caustically that Brown played uninspired tennis, or Black's court covering was faulty and that his frequent errors cost him the set. It is quite another to stand across the net at the back of a service court and try to get your racket on a service that is so fast that the ear can hardly detect the interval between the sound of the server's bat hitting the ball and the ball striking the court. Tournament tennis is a different game from weekend tennis. For one thing, in average tennis, after the first hard service has gone into the net or out, you breathe a sigh of relief, move up closer and wait for the cripple to come floating over. In big-time tennis second service is practically as hard as the first, with an additional twist on the ball.

It is impossible to judge or know anything about the speed of a forehand drive hit by a champion until you have had one fired at you or, rather, away from you, and you have made an attempt to return it. It is then that you first realize that tennis is played more with the head than with the arms and the legs. The fastest player in the world cannot get to a drive to return it if he hasn't thought correctly, guessed its direction, and anticipated it by a fraction of a second.

There was golf with Bob Jones and Gene Sarazen and Tommy Armour, little Cruickshank, and Johnny Farrell, and Diegel and other professionals; and experiments at trying to keep up in the water with Johnny Weissmuller, Helene Madison, and Eleanor Holm, attempts to catch football passes thrown by Benny Friedman. Nobody actually plays golf until he has acquired the technical perfection to be able to hit the ball accurately, high, low, hooked or faded and placed. And nobody knows what real golf is like until he has played around with a professional and seen him play, not the ball, but the course, the roll of the land, the hazards, the wind, and the texture of the greens and the fairways. It looks like showmanship when a topflight golfer plucks a handful of grass and lets it flutter in the air, or abandons his drive to march two hundred yards down to the green and look over the situation. It isn't. It's golf. The average player never knows or cares whether he is putting with or across the grain of the green. The professional *always* knows. The same average player standing on the tee is concentrated on getting the ball somewhere on the fairway, two hundred yards out. The professional when preparing to drive is actually to all intents and purposes playing his *second* shot. He means to place his drive so as to open up the green for his approach. But you don't find that out until you have played around with them when they are relaxed and not competing, and listen to them talk and plan attacks on holes.

Major League Baseball is one of the most difficult and precise of all games, but you would never know it unless you went down on the field and got close to it and tried it yourself. For instance, the distance between the pitcher and catcher is a matter of twenty paces, but it doesn't seem like enough when you don a catcher's mitt and try to hold a pitcher with the speed of Dizzy Dean or Dazzy Vance. Not even the sponge that catchers wear in the palm of the hand when working with fastball pitchers, and the bulky mitt are sufficient to rob the ball of shock and sting that lames your hand unless you know how to ride with the throw and kill some of its speed. The pitcher, standing on his little elevated mound, looms up enormously over you at that short distance, and when he ties himself into a coiled spring preparatory to letting fly, it requires all your self-control not to break and run for safety. And as for the things they can do with a baseball, those Major League pitchers...! One way of finding out is to wander down on the field an hour or so before game time when there is no pressure on them, pull on the catcher's glove, and try to hold them.

I still remember my complete surprise the first time I tried catching for a real curveball pitcher. He was a slim, spidery left-hander for the New York Yankees, many years ago, by the name of Herb Pennock. He called that he was going to throw a fast breaking curve and warned me to expect the ball at least 2 feet outside the plate. Then he wound up and let it go, and that ball came whistling right down the groove for the center of the plate. A novice, I chose to believe what I saw and not what I heard, and prepared to catch it where it was headed for a spot which of course it never reached, because just in front of the rubber, it swerved sharply to the right and passed nearly a yard from my glove. I never had a chance to catch it. That way, you learn about the mysterious drop, the ball that sails down the alley chest high but which you must be prepared to catch around your ankles because of the sudden dip it takes at the end of its passage as though someone were pulling it down with a string. Also you find out about the queer fadeaway, the slow curve, the fast in- and out-shoots that seem to be timed almost as delicately as shrapnel, to burst, or rather break, just when they will do the most harm — namely, at the moment when the batter is swinging.

Facing a big-league pitcher with a bat on your shoulder and trying to hit his delivery is another vital experience in gaining an understanding of the game about which you are trying to write vividly. It is one thing to sit in the stands and scream at a batsman: "Oh, you bum!" for striking out in a pinch, and another to stand twenty yards from that big pitcher and try to make up your mind in a hundredth of a second whether to hit at the offering or not, where to swing and when, not to mention worrying about protecting yourself from the consequences of being struck by the ball that seems to be heading straight for your skull at an appalling rate of speed. Because, if you are a big-league player, you cannot very well afford to be gun-shy and duck away in panic from a ball that swerves in the last moment and breaks perfectly over the plate, while the umpire calls "Strike!" and the fans jeer. Nor can you afford to take a crack on the temple from the ball. Men have died from that. It calls for undreamed-of niceties of nerve and judgment, but you don't find that out until you have stepped to the plate cold a few times during batting practice or in training quarters, with nothing at stake but the acquisition of experience, and see what a fine case of the jumping jitters you get. Later on, when you are writing your story, your imagination, backed by the experience, will be able to supply a picture of what the batter is going through as he stands at the plate in the closing innings of an important game, with two or three men on base, two out, and his team behind in the scoring, and fifty thousand people screaming at him.

The catching and the holding of a forward pass for a winning touchdown on a cold, wet day always makes a good yarn, but you might get an even better one out of it if you happen to know from experience about the elusive qualities of a hard, soggy, mud-slimed football rifled through the air, as well as something about the exquisite timing, speed and courage it takes to catch it on a dead run, with two or three 190-pound men reaching for it at the same time or waiting to crash you as soon as your fingers touch it.

Any football coach during a light practice will let you go down the field and try to catch punts, the long, fifty-yard spirals and the tricky, tumbling end-over-enders. Unless you have had some previous experience, you won't hang on to one out of ten, besides knocking your fingers out of joint. But if you have any imagination, thereafter you will know that it calls for more than negligible never to judge and hold that ball and even plan to run with it, when there are two husky ends bearing down at full speed, preparing for a head-on tackle.

In 1932 I covered my first set of National Air Races, in Cleveland, and immediately decided that I had to learn how to fly to find out what it felt like. Riding as a passenger isn't flying. Being up there all alone at the controls of a ship is. And at the same time began a series of investigations into the "feel" of the mechanized sports to see what they were all about and the qualities of mentality, nerve, and physique they called for from their participants. These included a ride with Gar Wood in his latest and fastest speedboat, *Miss America X*, in which for the first time he pulled the throttle wide open on the Detroit River straightaway; a trip with the Indianapolis Speedway driver Cliff Bergere, around the famous brick raceway; and a flip with Lieutenant Al Williams, one time U.S. Schneider Cup race pilot.

I was scared with Wood, who drove me at 127 miles an hour, jounced, shaken, vibrated, choked with fumes from the exhausts, behind which I sat hanging on desperately to the throttle bar, which after a while got too hot to hold. I was on plank between Wood and his mechanic, Johnson, and thought that my last moment had come. I was still more scared when Cliff Bergere hit 126 on the Indianapolis straightaways in the tiny racing car in which I was hopelessly wedged, and after the first couple of rounds quite resigned to die and convinced that I should. But I think the most scared I have ever been while moving fast was during a ride I took in the cab of a locomotive on the straight, level stretch between Fort Wayne, Indiana, and Chicago, where for the first time we hit 90 miles per hour, which of course is no speed at all. But nobody who rides in the comfortable Pullman coaches has any idea of the didoes cut up by a locomotive in a hurry, or the thrill of pelting through a small town, all out and wide open, including the crossing of some thirty or forty frogs and switches, all of which must be set right. But that wasn't sport. That was just plain excitement.

I have never regretted these researches. Now that they are over, there isn't enough money to make me do them again. But they paid me dividends, I figured. During the great Thompson Speed Trophy race for land planes at Cleveland in 1935, Captain Roscoe Turner was some eight or nine miles in the lead in his big golden, low-wing, speed monoplane. Suddenly, coming into the straightaway in front of the grandstands, buzzing along at 280 miles per hour like an angry hornet, a streamer of thick, black smoke burst from the engine cowling and trailed back behind the ship. Turner pulled up immediately, using his forward speed to gain all the altitude possible, turned and got back to the edge of the field, still pouring out that evil black smoke. Then he cut his switch dipped her nose down, landed with a bounce and a bump, and rolled up to the line in a perfect stop. The crowd gave him a great cheer as he climbed out of the oil-spattered machine, but it was a cheer of sympathy because he had lost the race after having been so far in the lead that had he continued he could not possibly have been overtaken.

There was that story, but there was a better one too. Only the pilots on the field, all of them white around the lips and wiping from their faces a sweat not due to the oppressive summer heat, knew that they were looking at a man who from that time on, to use their own expression, was living on borrowed time. It isn't often when a Thompson Trophy racer with a landing speed of around 80 to 90 miles an hour goes haywire in the air, that the pilot is able to climb out of the cockpit and walk away from his machine. From the time of that first burst of smoke until the wheels touched the ground and stayed there, he was a hundred-to-one shot to live. To the initiated, those dreadful moments were laden with suspense and horror. Inside that contraption was a human being who any moment might be burned to horrible, twisted cinder, or smashed into the ground beyond all recognition, a human being who was cool, gallant, and fighting desperately. Every man and woman on the field who had ever been in trouble in the air was living those awful seconds with him in terror and suspense. I, too, was able to experience it. That is what makes getting the "feel" of things distinctly worthwhile.

BIBLIOGRAPHY

Adams, George H. "Foreword." In *Canoeing with the Cree* by Arnold E. Sevareid. New York: Macmillan, 1935.
Aflalo, Frederick G. *Sunshine and Sport in Florida*. Philadelphia: G.W. Jacobs & Co., 1907: 158–163.
Anderson-Gilman, Wilma. "The Woman's Weapon." *Outing* (February 1914): 590.
Burroughs, John. 1870. "Speckled Trout." *Atlantic Monthly* (October 1870): 437–40.
Camp, Walter. "Making a Football Team." *Outing* (November 1912): 131–32.
Clark, Lawrence S. "Six Weeks in a Ford." *Outing* (July 1922): 162–63
Connibear, Hiram. "Coaching a Varsity Crew." *Outing* (June 1914): 315–16.
Danzig, Allison and Peter Brandwein, eds. *Sport's Golden Age*. New York: Harper, 1948.
Darwin, George B. "Confessions of a Practicer." *Country Life* (1919). In *Bernard Darwin on Golf*, edited by Jeff Silverman. Guilford, CT: Lyons Press, 2003: 33–36.
Dickens, Charles. *The Letters of Charles Dickens*. Vol. 1. Edited by Mamie Dickens and Georgina Hogarth. New York: Scribner's, 1880: 160–64.
Eagan, Eddie. *Fighting for Fun*. New York: Macmillan, 1932: 65–73.
Earhart, Amelia. *20 Hrs. 40 Min*. New York: G. P. Putnam's, 1928: 178–97.
Ederle, Gertrude. "Gertrude Tells Own Story of How She Conquered Channel." *Chicago Tribune*, Aug. 7, 1926.
Edwards, William H. *Football Days: Memories of the Game and the Men Behind the Ball*. New York: Moffat, Yard, 1916: 391–95
Ford, Henry. *My Life and Work*. In collaboration with Samuel Crowther. Garden City, NY: Doubleday, Page, 1922: 36–37; 50–51; 57.
Fountain, Charles. *Sportswriter: The Life and Times of Grantland Rice*. New York: Oxford University Press, 1993.
Fox, Edward L. "Learning to Sail an Ice-boat." *Outing* (January 1912): 451–53.
Freeman, Lewis R. *Down the Yellowstone*. New York: Dodd, Mead, 1922: 90–94.
———. "A Fijian Field Day." *Outing* (March 1914): 703–07.
Gallico, Paul. *Farewell to Sport*. Reprinted from 1937, 1938 edition by arrangement with Alfred A. Knopf, Inc. Freeport, NY: Books for Libraries Press, 1970: 287–298. Page references are to the 1970 edition.
Grey, Zane. *Tales of Fishes*. New York: Harper, 1919: 107–15.
Harris, Eddy L. *Down the Mississippi*. New York: Reader's Digest Association, 1995.
Harris, Fred H. "How I Learned to Ski" *Outing* (January 1922): 159–60; 188–89.
Hemingway, Ernest. "The Best Rainbow Trout Fishing." *The Toronto Star-Weekly*, Aug. 28, 1920.

_____. "The Swiss Luge." *The Toronto Star Weekly*, March 18, 1922.
Hosfield, May H. "Sum Fishin'" *Outing* (Aug. 1919): 295–96; 320.
Huggins, Mike. *The Victorians and Sport*. London: Hambledon and London, 2004.
Jones, Robert T., Jr., and O. B. Keeler. *Down the Fairway; The Golf Life and Play of Robert T. Jones, Jr.* New York: Blue Ribbon Books, 1927: 148–52.
Keeler, O. B. *The Autobiography of an Average Golfer*. New York: Greenberg Publishers, 1925.
Kenney, Karen. "The Realm of Sports And the Athletic Woman, 1850–1900." In *Her Story in Sport: A Historical Anthology of Women in Sports*, edited by Reet Howell. West Point, NY: Leisure Press, 1982.
Kephart, Horace. "Adventures in a Cavern." *Outing* (Oct. 1914): 85–89.
King, John Lyle. *Trout Fishing on the Brulé River, or Lawyers' Summer-Wayfaring in the Northern Wilderness*. Chicago: Chicago Legal News Company, 1879: iii–v; 82–87.
Knowles, Joseph. *Alone in the Wilderness*. Boston: Small, Maynard & Company, 1913: 1–8; 65–78.
Kovach, Bill, and Tom Rosenstiel. *The Elements of Journalism: What Newspeople Should Know and the Public Should Expect*. New York: Three Rivers, 2001.
Kretchmar, R. Scott. "Distancing: An Essay on the Abstract Thinking in Sports Performances." In: *Sport Inside Out: Readings in Literature and Philosophy*, edited by David L. Vanderwerken and Spencer K. Wertz. Forth Worth: Texas Christian University Press, 1985.
Lardner, Ring. "Sport and Play." In *Civilization in the United States: An Inquiry by Thirty Americans*, edited by Harold E. Stearns. New York: Harcourt, Brace, 1922: 457–61.
Leale, Winifred L. "Rifle Shooting." In *Ladies in the Field*, edited by Violet Greville, 159–172. New York: D. Appleton, 1894.
London, Jack. *The Cruise of the Snark: A Pacific Voyage*. New York: Macmillan, 1908: 75–90.
Martelli, Kate. "Tigers I Have Shot." In *Ladies in the Field*, edited by Violet Greville, 145–156. New York: D. Appleton, 1894.
Muir, John. *Stickeen: The Story of a Dog*. Boston: Houghton Mifflin, 1909: 3–73.
Naismith, James. *Basketball: Its Origin and Development*. New York: Association Press, 1941: 42–60.
Nash, Roderick. *Wilderness and the American Mind*. 4th ed. New Haven: Yale University Press, 1967.
Neihardt, John G. *The River and I*. New York: G.P. Putnam's, 1910: 172–74; 192–206.
Nevill, Ralph Henry. *Sporting Days and Sporting Ways*. New York: Brentano, 1910.
Phillips, Gertrude B. "My First Salmon." *Outing* (October 1913): 305–08.
Pinkerton, Kathrene G. "Paddling Her Own Canoe" *Outing* (May 1914): 220–21.
Plimpton, George. *The Best of Plimpton*. New York: Atlantic Monthly Press, 1990.
Powel, Harford, "Introduction." In *The Omnibus of Sport*, edited by Grantland Rice. New York: Harper, 1932.
Rice, Grantland. "The Golden Panorama." In *Sport's Golden Age*, edited by Allison Danzig and Peter Brandwein. New York: Harper, 1948.
Roosevelt, Theodore. *Hunting Trips on the Prairie and in the Mountains*. New York: G.P. Putnam's, 1885: 33–51.

Ross, Malcolm. *A Climber in New Zealand*. London: E. Arnold, 1914: 287–296
Savory, Isabel. *A Sportswoman in India: Personal Adventures and Experiences of Travel in Known and Unknown India*. London: Hutchinson, 1900: 171–77.
Sevareid, Arnold E. *Canoeing with the Cree*. New York: Macmillan, 1935: 1–14.
Slocum, Joshua. *Sailing Alone Around the World*. New York: Century, 1899: 9–12; 23–33.
Soiland, Albert. *The Viking Goes To Sea: Being an Account of the Honolulu Race of 1923*. Los Angeles: Times Mirror Press, 1924: 13–27.
Stevenson, Robert Louis. *An Inland Voyage*. New York: Scribner's, 1895: 1–3; 10–13
Tilden, William T. *The Art of Lawn Tennis*, revised and enlarged edition. New York: G.H. Doran, 1922: 77–78; 92–95.
Twain, Mark. *Roughing It*. Hartford: American Publishing Company, 1871: 524–526.
Whitman, Walt. *Prose Works*. Philadelphia: David McKay, 1892: 98; 104–05; 116–17.
Whymper, Edward. *Scrambles Amongst the Alps in the Years 1860–1869*. London: John Murray, 1871: 389–400.
Willard, Frances E.. *A Wheel Within a Wheel: How I Learned to Ride the Bicycle*. London: Hutchinson, 1895: 18–27; 72–75.
Wills, Tennis. *Tennis*. New York: Scribner's, 1928: 198–214.
Xenophon. *The Sportsman*. Translated by H. G. Daykns. http://www.gutenberg.org/dirs/1/1/8/1180/1180.txt

INDEX

Adams, George H. 5, 224
Aflalo, Frederick G. 7, 76–80
"ah nuts" sportswriting 7
airplanes 14, 121, 208, 211, 224, 227, 230, 236–37; derby 14, 206
Alaska 71, 88, 101, 183
All England Club 213–14, 216–17
Allen, Phog 47
alpining 23, 143–48; *see also* mountain climbing
Alps 23, 25, 231
amateur (amateurism) 1, 3–4, 12–15, 34, 128, 135, 143, 151, 184, 194, 202–5, 212, 219, 220–21, 229
angling (angler) 17, 76, 155, 157, 160–63, 168, 230
archery 193, 230
Armour, Tommy 203–4, 234
Associated Press (AP) 170, 201
Atlantic Ocean 5, 15, 68–70, 205–6, 225
Augusta National Golf Club 203
auto racing 14, 173, 178–81, 229

Badlands 40, 174, 176
badminton 50, 230
bait 17, 36, 58, 116, 155–57, 159–63, 165–66, 169
barracudas 154–62, 164
baseball 8, 14, 48, 127, 131, 149, 162, 181–83, 191–92, 226, 230, 232, 234–36
basketball 8, 14, 46–55, 230
Bergere, Cliff 229, 236
bicycling 62–67, 134–35, 180, 230
billiards (pool) 193, 230
bobsledding 219
Bonds, Barry 3
bonefish 162–67
Boston 5, 10, 36, 67–68, 112, 114–15, 206
Boston Globe 201
Boston Post 7, 10
bowling 131, 193, 230
boxing 12, 80, 128, 131, 167, 192–93, 219–23, 229–32
Brennan, Bill 219
bridge 193
British Amateur 152, 203–5
British Open 203–5
Brulé River 34–36

Burroughs, John 14–15, 17–21, 34
bush leagues 181

California 76, 102, 127, 154, 158, 195–96, 206, 215
Camp, Walter 47, 110–12, 134, 149
Canada 5, 76, 184, 188, 224–25
canoeing 1, 3–5, 14, 20–21, 27–30, 34–36, 88–91, 102–7, 123, 126–29, 131–33, 167–68, 188, 223–29
Carrel, Jean Antoine 24
Catalina 155–56, 168
Chicago Tribune v, 34, 190, 200
Chicago White Sox 9, 134, 190
Clark, Lawrence S. 7, 173–78
Cleveland 179, 206, 236
coaching 15, 46–55, 110–12, 128, 134–36, 149–50, 186, 236
Cochet, Henri Jean 217
Coleridge, Samuel Taylor 138
Colorado 175, 177, 221
Columbia University 232
Connibear, Hiram 47, 134–36
cricket 48, 127–28, 131, 201, 216
Croz, Michael 23–24, 26
Cruickshank, Bobby 234

Dartmouth College 183–84, 187
Darwin, Bernard
Davis Cup 171
de Alvarez, Lili 214, 218
Dean, Dizzy 234
deep-sea fishing 154–62, 229–30
Delaware River 15, 17
Dempsey, Jack 10, 12–13, 170, 194, 203, 219–23, 229, 232–33
Denver 174–75, 177, 219–20
Detroit 178–79, 236
Dickens, Charles 14–15, 30–33
Diegel, Leo 234
diving 230–31
Douglas, Lord Francis 23, 26

Earhart, Amelia 5, 11, 14–15, 67, 205–11
Ederle, Gertrude 8, 14, 200–2
England 31, 55, 62, 73, 128, 101, 201, 204, 216
English Channel 8, 200

243

Farrell, James T. 9
Farrell, Johnny 234
fencing 80, 229–30
Fiji 127–32
Firpo, Louis 232
first-person accounts 1, 8–11, 13, 15, 30, 58, 80, 107, 110, 178, 188, 190
Fisher, Carl 173
fishing 1, 3, 8, 14, 15, 17–21, 34–37, 67–68, 76–77, 79, 89, 121–25, 155–69, 229
Fitzgerald, F. Scott 190
Fliverist 7, 173
Florida 7, 76–77, 203
Floto, Otto 220–23
fly-fishing 19, 35, 122–24, 167–69
football 8, 14, 47, 49–53, 110–11, 127, 131, 134, 149–51, 192–93, 226, 230, 232, 234–36
Ford, Henry 7, 14, 17, 173, 178–81
Forest Hills 215
Fountain, Charles 6, 9
France 3, 28, 200
Freeman, Lewis R. 121–31, 143, 181–83
Friedman, Benny 234
Fulton, Fred 219

gaff 77–78, 124–25, 159–60, 198
Gallico, Paul 1, 4–7, 9–12, 14, 190, 229–37
"Gee Whiz" sportswriting 6
Gilded Age 1–10, 13–14, 16–17, 31
glaciering 25, 75, 88–102, 147
Golden Age 1–11, 13–17, 47, 102, 131, 134, 136, 151, 173, 190, 194, 202, 211–12, 219, 229
Golden Gloves 229
golf 8, 11–12, 14, 143, 151–54, 191–93, 202–5, 216, 229–31, 234
Gordon, "Slim" Louis 206, 208
Graf, Steffi 212
grand slam 3, 203
Grey, Zane 11, 14, 162–67
Grosse Point 179–80

Hagen, Walter 203
handball 230
Harris, Eddy L. 4
Harvard University 149–51, 202, 223
Hawaii 67, 80, 85, 87, 207
Hemingway, Ernest 1, 11, 14, 121, 162, 167–69, 188–90
hero worship 6–7, 190, 193–94
high jumping 127–29, 230
Hintermeister, John Henry 1
hockey 48, 50, 193
Holm, Eleanor
Honolulu 87, 194–97
hook 19–20, 36, 67, 124–25, 155, 157, 159–61, 165, 169
horse racing 192–93
horseback riding 7, 14, 42, 60, 62–63, 66, 230
Hudson, Charles 23, 26
Hudson Bay 5, 223–26, 228

Huggins, Mike 12, 14
hunting 3, 7–8, 14, 16–17, 34, 37, 40–46, 57–62, 73, 77–80, 90–91, 101, 112, 119, 163

ice-boating 14, 107–10
ice-skating 230
Illinois 62, 175, 177
India 8, 57–58, 62, 73, 162
Indiana 173, 236
Indianapolis 500 173, 178, 229
Indianapolis Speedway 236
Iowa 102, 177, 228
Ireland 206, 210–11

Jackson, Shoeless Joe 3
Jones, Bobby v, 1, 3, 6, 12–15, 151–52, 202–5, 219, 229, 234
journalism 6, 9, 10–11, 21, 30, 67, 80, 152, 167, 190, 224, 229

Kanaka 3, 11, 21–22, 81, 83, 85
Kansas 47, 175, 177
Kansas City 174–75, 177
Kashmir 8, 73, 76
Kearns, Jack 220–21, 233
Keeler, O.B. v, 12, 151, 203
Kennard, Vic 149, 151
Kephart, Horace 6, 13, 136–43
Kipling, Rudyard 224–25
Knowles, Joseph 5, 7, 9–10, 23, 112–21, 224
Kretchmar, R. Scott 13

lacrosse 47–50, 193
Lake Winnipeg 225, 227
Landis, Kenesaw Mountain 149
Lardner, Ring 1, 5, 7, 9, 14, 190–94
Lenglen, Suzanne 212, 214
Lewis and Clark 226
Lindbergh, Charles 206
London 30, 55, 144, 207, 210, 216
London, Jack 1, 3, 9, 10–11, 14, 77, 80–87, 162
Long Island 107, 191, 231
Los Angeles 194
Los Angeles Times 127
lugeing 188–90

Madison, Helene 234
Maine 5, 7, 10, 112, 115
Major League Baseball 234
Manhattan 38–40
marathons 127, 128, 130
Martelli, Kate 8, 57–62
Massachusetts 47, 68, 112
match play 170, 214–15
Matterhorn 23–26
Michigan 34, 37
Minneapolis 174–75, 177, 225–28
The Minneapolis Star 5, 224–26, 229
Minnesota 132, 177, 223, 225
Minnesota River 5, 224–25, 227–28

Mississippi River 4, 138–39, 227
Missouri 102, 106, 136, 175, 177
Missouri River 102–7, 177
Model B 7, 178, 181
Montana 102, 177, 181–82
Montreal 185
Morris, Carl 219
motorboating 230
Mount Cook 143, 148
Mount Vesuvius 30–31
mountain climbing 8, 17, 23–27, 30–33, 73–76, 96, 99, 143–48
moutaineering 23, 73–76, 90, 96, 99, 147; *see also* mountain climbing
Muir, John 1, 4, 14, 88–102
Murrow, Edward R. 224

Native Americans 35–36, 88–90, 92, 101, 112, 116, 120, 226
naturalist 11, 17, 151, 163
Navratilova, Martina 212
New York City 9, 39, 77, 110, 121, 123, 149, 201, 215, 229, 231
New York Daily News 9, 200, 229
New York Times 121
New York Yankees 235
New Zealand 143–48, 162
Newfoundland 121–22, 205
Niagara Falls 140, 180, 222
North Dakota 174, 224

The Odyssey 12, 210
Oldfield, Barney 173, 178, 180
Olympic Games 47, 184, 201, 219, 231
one-hundred yard dash 135, 230
Outing magazine 125, 127, 131, 136, 184

participatory sportswriting vi, 1–4, 6–7, 9, 10–13, 17, 21, 23, 27–28, 31, 62, 67, 102, 113, 136, 152, 162, 194, 211, 223, 229
Pebble Beach 156, 162
Pennock, Herb 229, 235
Philadelphia 71, 172
piloting 14, 72, 121, 206, 230, 236–37
pistols 125–27
pitching 182, 191, 234–35
Plimpton, George 10–11, 229
poker 193
polo 51, 193
Polo Grounds 194
Port, Walter 5, 223, 227–28
Powel, Harford 5
Professional Football League 149
professionalism 6, 12–15, 134, 149, 170, 180, 203–4, 212, 220, 223, 232, 234
Putnam, George 206

Red River 225
refereeing 11, 15, 53, 149, 220
Rice, Grantland 3–6, 9, 13, 15, 203, 212
Richards, Vinnie 233

rifles 37, 41, 43, 55–57, 59, 61, 77–79, 106, 126, 133
Rocky Mountain National Park 174
rods 1, 34, 37, 122–24, 155, 157, 161, 163, 165, 167–68
roller-skating 230
Roosevelt, Theodore 1, 7, 14, 17, 40–46
Roosevelt National Park 174
rugby 47, 49, 51, 118
Ruth, Babe 3, 13, 169, 203

sailing 5, 14, 28–29, 37, 39–40, 67–72, 80, 88–91, 108–10, 194–200
St. Louis 136
salmon 67, 89, 121–25, 164
San Francisco 9, 67, 121, 191
Saratoga Springs 232
Sarazen, Gene 234
Savory, Isabel 8, 73–76
Schneider Cup 236
Scott, Blanche Stuart 121
Sevareid, Eric 5, 223–29
shot put 127, 128, 130, 230
ski jumping 183–88, 231
skiing 3, 183–88, 230–32
sledding 21, 131, 188–90
Slocum, Joshua 5, 14, 67–72, 199
soccer 49–52, 131, 143, 193
spectators 13, 150, 185, 191, 193, 212–14, 217, 221, 233
squash 48, 230
Stanford University 127, 182
Stevenson, Robert Louis 1, 3, 14, 27–30, 191, 225
Stultz, Wilmer 206–11
surfing 10–11, 21–22, 80–87
swimming 8, 36, 65, 80, 83, 8586, 127–30, 200–2, 230

tackle 123, 125, 160–61, 163–64, 168
tennis 8–9, 15, 48, 50, 127, 143, 169–73, 193–94, 211–18, 230, 233–34
tents 24, 35, 37, 76, 92, 132, 143–44, 168, 175–76, 228
Tilden, Bill 1, 14–15, 169–73, 217
Time magazine 134, 149
trapshooting 193
trout 15, 34–35, 37, 119, 122–23, 167–69
Turner, Roscoe 236–37
Twain, Mark 15, 21–22

umpiring 51–53, 149–51, 172, 235
United States Golf Association (USGA) 204
University of Kansas 47
University of Missouri 102
University of Pennsylvania 149–50, 162
U.S. Open 3, 203

Vance, Dazzy 234
Vardon, Harry 14, 152
Vermont 113, 184, 186

Waikiki 11, 80, 82, 83–85
Wales 205–6
Walker Cup 152, 204
Walton, Izaak 168
war correspondents 127, 143, 224, 229
Weissmuller, Johnny 234
Whitman, Walt 1, 14–15, 17, 37–40, 105
Willard, Frances Elizabeth 1, 8, 13–15, 62–67
Willard, Jess 220
Wills, Helen (Moody) 9, 14–15, 170, 211–18
Wimbledon 15, 211–18
Wisconsin 35, 175, 177
Wood, Gar 236

Woods, Tiger 3
wrestling 15, 37–39, 193, 230, 233
Wyoming 175–77

Xenophon 4, 16

yachting 14, 40, 107, 129, 194–200
Yale University 110, 149–51, 223
Yellowstone 174–75, 177, 181, 183
YMCA 46–47, 52
Yosemite National Park 91

Zbyzsko, Stanislaus 191